METHOD ACTING RECONSIDERED

Theory, Practice, Future

Edited by David Krasner

St. Martin's Press
New York

ISBN 0-312-22305-6 (cl.)
ISBN 0-312-22309-9 (pbk.)

Library of Congress Cataloging-in-Publication Data
Method acting reconsidered: theory, practice, future / edited by David Krasner
    p. cm.
    Includes index.
    ISBN 0–312–22305–6—ISBN 0–312–22309–9 (pbk.)
    1. Method (Acting)   2. Acting.   I. Krasner, David, 1952-
PN2062.M48 2000
792'.028—dc21   00–035269

Design by Letra Libre, Inc.

First edition: September, 2000
10 9 8 7 6 5 4 3 2 1

For Lynda

CONTENTS

III.
FUTURE

IV.
METHOD SCHOOLS

ACKNOWLEDGMENTS

It was Phillip Zarrilli who suggested that I write an article on Method acting for Alison Hodge's *Twentieth-Century Actor Training*. This collection would not have come about without his thoughtful encouragement. This book was published with the assistance of the Frederick W. Hilles Publication Fund of Yale University. My assistant, Jan E. Foery, and her assistants, Maria-Christina Oliveras and Abigail Sendrow, came to my aid whenever I faced computer problems or office crises. My colleagues and students at Yale have consistently inspired and challenged me. Steven Bayne is, as always, a great critic and friend. Polina Klimovitskaya has been a great resource on Stanislavsky. I want to thank all of the contributors; they have given this work a depth that could not have been achieved by one voice. I deeply appreciate all the support from St. Martin's Senior Editor, Michael Flamini, and his staff, particularly Alan Bradshaw, Amy McDermott, Amanda Johnson, and the anonymous copy editor. My greatest support comes from Lynda. I also want to thank my parents, who taught me to appreciate passion for ideas, and my teachers throughout my life, especially Paul Mann, Barbara Loden, and Kim Stanley.

ABBREVIATIONS

AP   Constantin Stanislavski, *An Actor Prepares*. Elizabeth Reynolds Hapgood, tr. New York: Theatre Arts, 1984.

BC   Constantin Stanislavski, *Building a Character*. Elizabeth Reynolds Hapgood, tr. New York: Theatre Arts, 1949.

DP   Lee Strasberg, *A Dream of Passion: The Development of the Method*. New York: Plume, 1987.

ISC   Stella Adler, *On Ibsen, Strindberg, and Chekhov*. New York: Alfred A. Knopf, 1999.

MA   Sanford Meisner and Dennis Longwell, *Sanford Meisner on Acting*. New York: Vintage, 1987.

MLA   Constantin Stanislavski, *My Life in Art*. J. J. Robbins, tr. New York: Theatre Arts, 1924.

SB   Jean Benedetti, *Stanislavski: A Biography*. London: Routledge, 1988.

SS   *Strasberg at the Actors Studio*, Robert Hethmon, ed. New York: Viking, 1965; TCG, 1991.

TA   Stella Adler, *A Technique of Acting*. Toronto: Bantam, 1988.

INTRODUCTION

CHAPTER ONE

I HATE STRASBERG

Method Bashing in the Academy

David Krasner

TOBY: *You never play anything outwards. I've noticed you keep it all in. So you draw in the audience. So it's up to them. And somehow they make the effort. [. . .] How do you do that?*
ESME: *It comes with the passage of time.*
TOBY: *You go deeper.*
ESME: *Exactly.*
TOBY: *You go on down to the core.*

—*David Hare*, Amy's View[1]

I was a tomato! A tomato doesn't sit!

—*Dustin Hoffman*, Tootsie

What follows is an examination of Method acting based on analysis of its theories, practice, and potential for future development. This work probes the accomplishments of the Method and assesses its relationship to other theories of performance. After writing an essay that summarized what Method acting is,[2] I concluded that a book would be required to explain in full what Method acting means. Because much has been said in criticism about the Method, this work seeks to set the record straight. It is an attempt to tie down the variety of meanings of the term "Method acting" and to illuminate its purposes in part by clearing up prevailing misrepresentations. By exploring a balanced view of the Method as well as other theories of performance, we will bring actor training into clearer perspective. The chapters in this book, I believe, will make this possible.

This book largely proceeds along four modes of inquiry: first, the theoretical; second, that of the practitioner; third, from the standpoint of the actor training across several techniques; and fourth, contemporary training. Part I, "Theory," is designed for the academic. Its chapters consider the Method's relationship to theory and culture. Part II, "Practice," brings into view practical application. Here the chapters explore Method practices involved in acting technique. In Part III, "Future," the authors grapple with actor training from a wider perspective, incorporating other contemporary approaches to performance. Finally, Part IV, "Method Schools," concludes with an update from the three major schools of Method acting. By bringing together in one volume theory and practice, the contributors and I hope to bridge the gap between those who think about acting and those who teach it in practice. Let us begin by clarifying what "Method acting" is.

According to Group Theatre founder and director Harold Clurman, Method acting is both a "means of training actors as well as a technique for the use of actors in their work on parts."[3] This technique combines work on the role, with an emphasis on researching and experiencing the character's life, and work on the self, which stresses the actor's personal investment and commitment to memory, experience, and worldview. Lee Strasberg (also a founder of the Group) maintains that all great actors "work in two spheres—the actor's work on himself and the actor's work on the role." In the process of this work, "one aspect of the actor's art may be emphasized temporarily at the expense of the other, but before a complete and convincing image can be created on the stage both must be mastered."[4] Stella Adler (leading actor of the Group) adds to this, noting that the actor must put herself in the circumstances of the play and must work from the self: "Define the difference between your behavior and the character's, find all the justification of the character's actions, and then go on from there to act *from yourself*, without thinking where your personal action ends and the character's begins" (*ISC* 103, Adler's emphasis).

The Method is an acting technique that stresses truthful behavior in imaginary circumstances. It trains the actor to make demands on the body through the use of stimuli and imagination, so that the body responds creatively. It builds from Stanislavsky's observation that in good acting, the actor's "bodies were at the call and beck of the inner demands of their will" (*MLA* 463). The Method actor creates an organic and imaginative performance by "experiencing" or "living through" the role (what Stanislavsky termed *perezhivanie*).[5] For example, if an actor is required to play a cook, then the actor must at least observe and experience what cooking means. If an actor plays a farmer, then she must experience farming to a significant degree. As Strasberg explains, the actor's task "is to create that level of belief on stage, so that the actor is capable of experiencing the imaginary events and objects of the play" spontaneously, inventively, and honestly. Using the notion of *as if* (If I am living through the character's circumstances, how would I behave?), the actor, Strasberg asserts, is able to express "the full complement of those automatic physiological responses which accompany a real experience" (*DP* 132).

While the Method actor creates a believable performance in numerous ways, the technique relies principally on the following ideas: justifying every word of the text, where justification comes from motivation, which in turn leads to actions, intentions, and objectives. The actor's actions and objectives acquire a sense of urgency; they are supported by subtext and sense memory; they are based on a belief in the given circumstances of the play; and they become particularized within a broad range of emotions. The actor emphasizes actions and emotions through real behavior. Method acting teacher and director Robert Lewis explains that real behavior on stage must be "really experienced, but artistically controlled, and correctly used for the particular character portrayed, the complete circumstances of the scene, and the chosen style of the author and play being performed."[6] Method actors reject indicating, what director Elia Kazan calls the "external imitation." The Method actor, Kazan explains, "must be going through what the character he's playing is going through; the emotion must be real, not pretended, it must be happening, not indicated."[7] Indicating, in acting terms, means pretending, or anticipating the next moment, *tipping your hand* to events rather than dealing with them spontaneously. Rather than indicating, the Method actor re-acts on impulse to other actors and events on stage within the play's cir-cumstances. Reacting means relying on the impression of impulse and activity in realization of what Method teacher Sanford Meisner calls "the reality of doing" (*MA* 16). Real behavior means *real doing*, not indicating or pretending.

In addition, the actor brings the role to life by *physicalizing the perfor-mance*, by incorporating actions and behavior as a means of embodying the role. Strasberg describes one method of physicalization as animal ex-ercises. He explains that the exercise (imitating animals) "trains the actor by forcing him to deal with the character's behavior rather than relying on his own feelings," and "leads toward physical characterization" (*DP* 147). Method acting scholar and critic Steve Vineberg enumerates several ad-ditional principles of the Method: verisimilitude, super-objectives, gen-uine emotion, encouraging improvisation in rehearsals, promoting communication between actors, using objects for their symbolic value, and demanding the actor's religious devotion.[8]

From its inception in the Group Theatre in the 1930s and extending into the late twentieth century, Method acting has been the most popu-lar yet controversial form of actor training in America.[9] Its principal teachers were Lee Strasberg (1901–1982), Stella Adler (1901–1992), and Sanford Meisner (1905–1997), but Uta Hagen, Robert Lewis, Paul Mann, and Sonia Moore have also influenced it. It is widely understood to have evolved from Stanislavsky's System and the training programs de-vised by Group Theatre actors. Later it would branch out, yielding new variations. Along the way Method acting has been praised and damned, defended and denounced, and certainly argued about by many.

Method acting has enjoyed its greatest success outside of academia. Within universities, Method acting has fallen into disfavor. Despite its popularity among actors, in university theatre departments "Method bashing" is vogue. Method acting practices, including *motivation, justifi-cation, personalization, affective memory, believability, authenticity, subtext, organic behavior,* and *subjectivity,* have come under considerable criticism. Recent works, in particular Richard Hornby's *The End of Acting* (1992), John Harrop's *Acting* (1992), Colin Counsell's *Signs of Performance* (1996), David Mamet's *True and False* (1997), and Charles Marowitz's

The Other Way (1999), as well as essays by Robert Brustein,[10] have criticized the Method as narrow and dogmatic. Critics have labored mightily to purge performance of Method acting's emphasis on the actor's truthful behavior. Disdain for Strasberg in particular has become so intense that understanding it requires less reliance on objective reason and more on psychopathology. Professor Richard Hornby exemplifies the extreme, saying that Strasberg's Method "shackles American acting" and that one of Strasberg's exercises, emotional memory, "can be seen partly as a cause, but even more as a result, of the decline of the American theatre."[11] Critic Robert Brustein admits having never met Strasberg; yet this fact has not restrained him from writing a play, *Nobody Dies on Friday*, in which Strasberg is portrayed as a neurotic autocrat. This depiction has not escaped *New York Times* reviewer Peter Marks, who in his comments on the play notes that the "Lee Strasberg of Robert Brustein's 'Nobody Dies on Friday' is one seriously unappetizing fellow."[12] Many critics and teachers who have never come in contact with Strasberg would concur with Brustein's characterization.

Assailing Strasberg has become a favorite pastime, particularly for many with a rhetorical ax to grind and few facts upon which to grind it. Having never studied with Strasberg, or interviewed him, or attended his classes, or read his publications, appears to be sufficient qualification for his more "enlightened" critics. It matters little that Strasberg has been dead since 1982. In the 1990s and beyond, it appears that the stronger the condemnation the greater the accolades, and the weaker the case against him the greater likelihood of an audience, both in print and at conferences. Conditioned by guaranteed approval, Strasberg's programmatic attackers set upon him indiscriminately; he is red meat tossed to the salivating Pavlovian dogs. A case in point is the denigration by contemporary critics of Strasberg's 1964 production of Chekhov's *The Three Sisters*. Despite the fact that the production received favorable New York reviews (although they were less than favorable London reviews), "knowledgeable" historians dismiss the work without attempting a balanced judgment. Howard Traubman's opening night review in the *New York Times* reported that the "Actors Studio Theater is doing the best work of its youthful career," with "an admirable sense of unity in the production." In his Sunday review in the *Times,* he noted that Strasberg's "admirable luminous revival" of *The Three Sisters* conveys "fine performances."[13] Despite this and other complimentary reviews, this production is frequently offered as the best evidence yet of the Method's shortcomings. By contrast, while Antonin Artaud's experiential productions were poorly received, Artaud is draped in saintly praise; and while several of Jerzy Grotowski's productions were anything but successful, academics shrink from criticism, which attests to their failure of nerve in the face of potential collegial disapproval. Strasberg, however, is condemned on the basis of a single, highly experimental production, even by those who have never so much as seen his *Three Sisters* performed. It comes, then, as no surprise that director and critic Charles Marowitz derides Strasberg's production of *The Three Sisters* for having "never come alive."[14] Marowitz fails to cite a single review or offer any opinion of the production other than his own. He omits telling us when and where he saw the production (in workshop? New York? London? on video?), which cast, or whether he even saw it at all. But teachers and scholars summarily dismiss these details: Why provide documentation when the evidence counts for nothing and critics are likely to be assured an audience at a public hanging?

Despite the attacks, a glance at acting schools in New York and in other urban centers suggests that Method acting refuses to go away. In fact, notwithstanding the academic trend, it flourishes among real-world performers. This situation has, however, produced some benefits. It has compelled both sides of this dispute to clarify their positions, and here is where this study fits in. Contributors to this collection assess the Method, defining its intent, and reveal its values that have somehow been lost amid the confusion. In what follows I present four criticisms of the Method in an attempt to clear away misconceptions.

CRITICISM #1: FIXED CHARACTERIZATION

First, Method acting, it has been argued, is rooted in fixed characterization. This criticism is given expression in a number of ways. It is said that Method actors find a characterization from the text and then fix their performances accordingly. Flexibility and spontaneity are eschewed, while "mere" character acting is preferred. Ideas of "self" are tied to the character, not the actor, and are unchanging. Theatre historian Michael Quinn tells us that, in Method acting, "the actor is the central subject, and the Other is the character—not the audience, the acting partner, or the director." In respect to its emphasis on character, he further maintains, "the problem addressed in his [Meisner's] class is teaching actors to project themselves into an Other that is already there, written in terms which are fixed into the fiction."[15] The character, already "fixed into the fiction," becomes moribund and devoid of personal investment. Critic Denis Salter condemns the Method for related reasons, noting: "To a far greater extent than any other contemporary Western acting style, Method acting has a vested interest in being an art of sublimated pretense—in which actors disappear as autonomous identities, effaced within the transcendent, psychology reality of their characters."[16] The actor's "personality" thus disappears into the character. Elsewhere Salter remarks that by "effacing cultural differences in what is often an insidious way, the Method tends to make actors subservient: you become a character by seeming to disappear inside in an act of personal sacrifice; you don't stand outside the character, as it were, in order to explore yourself and your attitudes (emotional, psychological, physical, and ideological) towards it at every deliberately exposed moment of your 'performance.'"[17] In this way, actors turn their backs on self-evaluation, cultural values, and politics. Feminist scholar Elaine Aston makes much of such characterization, but goes further in stating that "the objectification of women" is apparent in the "character-based, Method-acting, derived from the teachings of Constantin Stanislavski."[18] David Mamet describes the Method as unyielding: "The Method school would teach the actor to prepare a moment, a memory, an emotion for each interchange in the play and to stick to that preparation."[19] Thus, character-based Method actors are said to lack spontaneity, to objectify women, and to commit acts of personal sacrifice as a result of uncompromising preparation. Richard Hornby, who criticizes the Method's reliance on self and praises character acting, condemns Strasberg's performance in *The Godfather II* as similar to that of "thousands of other Hollywood character actors."[20]

Careful observation of Method practices reveals these criticisms to be one-dimensional. Method actors create art from real-life experiences, struggling to find the underlying meaning of a role from their personal viewpoint. Strasberg has said repeatedly: "The essential thing for the actor is to use himself" (*SS* 84). The self is a dynamic, not static, conception. The Method views the self as being in a state of continual rediscovery. Method actors believe they can configure their own nature and character through an act of choice. Adler was adamant about making choices outside the script; "in your *choice*," she said, "*is your talent*. Acting is in everything but the cold words" (*TA* 26, Adler's emphasis). For Adler, performance is an achievement that is accomplished through the difficult struggle of making choices, choices that come from the actor's view of the world and not necessarily from the text. She maintains that inner "justification" of the role "is the thing that belongs to the actor." The actor must justify the words by way of the acting, rather than the other way around, because, as Adler says, "the words stink" (*ISC* 301). There are limitations to what can be absorbed from the language of a play. Character, then, is what the actor makes of it by her actions and responses to the living conditions she encounters. Meisner's trademark repetition exercise is based on observing other actors, the audience, or the surroundings. According to Meisner, the actor responds to real-world circumstances that lie beyond the periphery of the text, residing instead in real-life interactions. Method acting historian Foster Hirsch observes that for Method actors, impulses that come up "may not be right for the character or the scene, but that doesn't matter as much as the actor being free and loose and discovering what it feels like not to censor himself." Method acting, he says, "endows the performer with a keen self-awareness."[21]

Rather than "sticking to the preparation" and being "subservient" to the role as it is "fixed into the fiction," Method actors create a performance by living spontaneously in the role. The Method insists on the actor's creative commitment to the life of the character and to imaginatively improvising to find the most dynamic way to convey that life. Hence, in Method terms, a fixed performance is rigid, insensitive, unimaginative, and ipso facto dull. In typical instances of conventional theatre the script is primary, and actors conform to the demands of the role; in the Method, actors consider themselves creative artists whose life and inspiration are part of the fabric of the role. (This approach differs from Stanislavsky to the degree that he placed greater emphasis on the actor's "transformation" into the role.) Method acting, says Charles

Marowitz, "encourages the actor to approach a role as if it were an invitation to reveal himself."[22] The self is not lodged in some intractable, Platonic form; it is rather the changing subject that gives reality to whatever forms it takes, and this change in choices is an act of freedom on the part of the artist. Actors' personal makeup changes with each role, but one thing remains: *their personal investment in the performance.*

Method actors are known for improvisation (gibberish for Strasberg, paraphrasing for Adler, and repetition for Meisner). They react spontaneously to events on stage. Strasberg is absolutely clear on this: "[T]he actor has to know what he is going to do when he goes on the stage, and yet he has to permit himself to do it so that it seems to be happening for the first time. This means that the body, the voice, every facet of expression, must follow the natural changes in impulse; even though the actor repeats, the strength of the impulses may well change from day to day" (*SS* 167).[23] Method buzzwords like *moment to moment, playing off the partner, reacting to immediate stimuli, private moment, justification, impulse,* and *personalization* describe a technique that is improvisatory and self-exploratory.

The Method is driven by a teleological dynamic. The aim of the Method actor is to develop a purpose (goal, objective, action, task, intention, spine) that may change, being open to all the imagined possibilities, but primarily the essence of Method acting is the actor as agent who invests purposeful, creative action. Purposeful action is action guided by thought, and thought is the power to create. The Method insists that the actor is a thinking contributor to the production, rather than being a puppet subservient to the play and the director. It assumes that the actor actively contributes thoughtfully and creatively to the stage experience. According to Strasberg, the "Method considers the actor as a creative artist who must translate the ideas, intentions, and words of the author into living presentation" (*DP* 198). The Method, says actress Geraldine Page, "allows you to discover less obvious connections between yourself and your character." It opens up, she contends, "a whole field of connections you can *consciously* bring from yourself." She adds that it widens your perceptions, resulting in the actors' ability to "add more of [their] own color to the tapestry of [their] character."[24] Marowitz put it best when he said that Method acting "encourages the expression of emotional color which can come from nowhere else but the spectrum of that actor's personal make-up. It is a theory based on the conviction that people are more interesting than types, and truth more compelling than fraud—no matter how spectacular that fraud may be."[25]

Method's adherence to the self over the role (i.e., the actor's personal choice over the way the role is written) can be related to certain facets of feminist performance theory. Certain performance art takes the critical step of bringing private life into the public sphere. Performance artists can be said to make the Strasbergian private moment a public confession. In Strasberg's private moment/affective memory work, actors attempt to recall specific events of the past. He first asks actors to recall physical sensations through the inducement of personal objects. Actors touch, smell, taste, and observe objects that possess for them emotional content. The more sophisticated actors develop personal recall, evoking images that stimulate subsequent emotions and actions. However, by focusing on past sensory images rather than emotions per se, actors call into existence inspiration, an inspiration that evokes creativity. It is possible, then, for actors to channel these experiences, actions, and feelings into political or social statements. Memories are personal, but they also can be political. For example, an actor may recall memories of abuse and use the ensuing anger to inform her work. Recalling personal experiences can help her identify with others fighting abuse. She extends her experience into performance as a way of understanding others who experience similar misfortunes.

Playwright and performance artist Robbie McCauley's performance of *Sally's Rape* serves as a good example. According to McCauley, the "acting roles and what they were connected to begin to open up voices inside me, especially the roles of rebel, intellectual, [and] angry black woman," and her work "comes out of mournings I have within me."[26] Personalizing experiences means first associating memories to the role and then molding the emotions and actions that emerge from these memories into artistic shape. Acting, McCauley says, "has to do with rage." McCauley adds: "I personalize the moment. It is about the rage that I have embraced, that is necessary, that is healing, and I release it out of a personal need to do so."[27] Director John Harrop rejects this, claiming that the "basis of acting isn't personal feelings. Anyone can feel."[28] McCauley, however, defends her way of working: "[T]he actor," she says, "has to be connected to the subtext."[29] This is precisely what the Method encourages: the emotional experience that is connected by way of the actor's subtext.

Elaine Aston describes an exercise for feminist theatre that is indiscernible from Strasberg's own prescription relating to sense memory and emotional recall. Aston asks the performer to set "aside some time to improvise regularly with an object to which you have a strong emotional attachment." This exercise, she says, "aims to develop the control (physical memory) of the performer with the personal (emotional memory). Working privately on objects in your group (each woman finds her own space to work in, concentrating solely on her own object, her own improvisational play), is a way of encouraging the emotional memory to surface."[30] This is precisely the technique of a Method actor. The benefit of this exercise, says Strasberg, is that the performer "will then be accomplishing the primary task of the actor: to act—that is to do something, whether it be psychological or physiological" (*DP* 165).

Feminist critic Sue-Ellen Case claims that Freudian psychology, with its "gender-specific" notions of women, provides "the basis of Method acting." Method techniques, Case argues, rely "on Freudian principles, leading the female actor into that misogynistic view of female sexuality."[31] While the Method may borrow from Freudian psychology, it is fundamentally not Freudian but Pavlovian.[32] Moreover, the Method approach would appear to be ideal in accommodating Feminist practices. If, as Case and others maintain, "the personal is the political,"[33] no technique of actor training will more successfully promote the personal than the Method. To be sure, Feminism and the Method are complex ideologies and techniques that differ in ways and means. Still, both emphasize the personal to a significant degree, and to the extent that the personal is the political, both share this agenda. Feminist scholar Jeanie Forte has argued that the "intensely autobiographical nature of women's performance has evidence the insistence on a woman's ability to 'speak' her subjectivity."[34] Method acting consistently demands an "intensely autobiographical" approach, requiring actors to speak from their subjective experiences.

In Method acting, the self is central. This does not mean that the actor fails to create a character. Method actors such as Rod Steiger, Ossie

Davis, Ruby Dee, Estelle Parsons, Karl Malden, Burgess Meredith, Eli Wallach, Anne Jackson, Julie Harris, Lee J. Cobb, Joanne Woodward, Dustin Hoffman, and many others are *character actors*. Method actors will *experience*, or *live through*, the life of their character significantly more than other actors (Robert De Niro's taxi driving and prize-fighting, for examples). But at its root, Method actors find a theme, or interpretation, that allows them to build a role from conviction. The Method induces an authenticity rooted in that conviction. Authenticity in Method acting is an ontological grounding in faith, conviction, and inspiration. This authenticity need not be illusionary. The Method actor can address the audience, break the theatrical convention of a fourth wall (pretending that there is no audience), and comment on the character. Standing outside "character" as Bertolt Brecht would have it is not antithetical to the Method. The actor may speak to the audience, provided that the actor is motivated by faith in her purpose. The clichéd joke of the Method actor crying "What's my motivation?" makes this fact clear: The actor is committed to motivation, which is the source of her creativity.

In the film *Tootsie*, Dustin Hoffman tells his agent that he refuses to sit when playing a tomato. ("I'm a tomato! A tomato doesn't sit!") Hoffman roots his faith and conviction in his belief that tomatoes *cannot* sit; he is motivated by his conviction and sense of purpose. If he is to be an *authentic* tomato and true to his conviction, sitting contradicts the source of his interpretation. As a tomato (a highly unrealistic character), his faith in tomato-ness is a circumscription of the nature of his actions. Hoffman's insistence on remaining still is not "fixity of self" but rather an adherence to a conviction based on what Adler and Strasberg call choice, belief, and faith in the actor's interpretation. Hoffman's character presents a stubborn position, and the film satirizes his recalcitrance. Yet it also points out why Method actors are good performers; their conviction and creativity are compelling to watch. Their sense of purpose gives rise to creative behavior that produces unorthodox and dynamic performances. This is what Strasberg means when he says that dynamic acting demands "belief, faith, and imagination. To believe, one must have something to believe in; to have faith, one must have something that encourages faith; to have imagination, one must be able to imagine something specific" (*DP* 123). Acting for the Method is in the details.

Rather than paying homage to technical skills of voice and movement (Laurence Olivier's acting, for example), the Method actor creates from conviction. Hoffman's arrogance in *Tootsie* typifies that of the Method actor; they are often difficult to work with because they struggle to maintain their interpretative "belief" system. Some Method actors deserve criticism: They can be irascible at times, stubbornly defending their motivation at the expense of director and playwright. But Method actors do not play a role reflective of their personality. Rather, they find in each role an original inspiration that provokes engaging and sometimes electrifying performances.

Method acting is not so much a merging of character and self as it is *an act of faith the actor imposes on the role.* The actor builds on interpretation and inspiration; inspiration, or faith, is what gives the performance its definition. This act of faith is not a parlor trick evoking mere emotion; it must reverberate deeply, cutting poignantly close to the bone. Certainly Method actors play different characters. Method actor Dustin Hoffman, playing the *role* of Method actor Michael Dorsey, takes this to a desirable extreme, going so far as to cross gender lines in *Tootsie* to demonstrate the quality of his characterization. However, Method actors share common idioms: faith, conviction, and inspiration. Hoffman (Dorsey) crosses gender lines in order *to prove that he is a great actor.* This choice (conviction) stimulates his will to create, to act, and to live through the role. Ultimately it is what compels audiences to observe him, watching with eager anticipation his unpredictable and persuasive behavior.

Strasberg defines inspiration as "the appeal to and function of the actor's imagination" and says that the problem of creation for the actor "is the problem of starting the inspiration." His goal as a teacher was based on the question: How does the actor trigger the creative process? He claims that Stanislavsky's "entire search, the entire purpose of the 'Method' or our technique or whatever you want to call it, is to find a way to start in each of us this creative process" (*SS* 85, 87). Strasberg would have it that creative processes are matters of psychology and past experience; the actor draws stimuli from memory in order to ground conviction. Adler would have inspiration emerge from the actor's faith in the power of imagination, the play's circumstances, and the actor's political-social viewpoint. Meisner takes a different view, arguing that the actor's faith is shown in the give-and-take of interaction. For him, the moment on stage is the point of reference, and the presence of another is the source of inspiration. But all three believed acting involves an essential act of *inspiration* and *free will*. (More on free will shortly.)

Great acting, British director Deborah Warner says, "is about using all of oneself. It's not about pretending to be someone else." To be a great actor, she adds, "you have to be a very remarkable person. You have to have the size of personality to be able to embrace the size of the extraordinary personalities that have been created by writers."[35] What surfaces in performances of remarkable acting is a broad range of emotions, intellectual depth, vulnerability, naïveté, inspiration, conviction, passion, and organic behavior, all of which emanate from the self, from one's beliefs. This emphasis on self has drawn criticism of a different sort.

CRITICISM #2: RELIANCE ON THE SELF

The second criticism is the opposite of the first, claiming that Method actors devote attention to the self at the expense of the text. Here critics take the Method to task for promoting the self over the role. Scholar and director Colin Counsell argues that improvisation "occupies a central and distinct position" in Method acting, in that improvisation "enables the actor to build for the character a detailed inner life, but does so in disregard of the play from which that character is taken." Counsell believes that Stanislavsky and the Method divide along the following lines. For Stanislavsky, he says, "characters are created to satisfy the play's requirements: in the Method they are constructed *despite* those requirements, for the Strasbergian actor's notion of the character's internal reality takes precedence over the play."[36] According to Richard Hornby, the Method actor draws "on his personal experiences, but, more important," the actor is "reliving his emotional traumas." In his attempt to characterize the Method as psychobabble, Hornby says that the Method actor "plays himself, not somebody else; acting is basically a form of emotional release."[37] Robert Brustein complains that what he calls the "subjective, autobiographical approach" is reflective of Method acting, "where the current jargon includes phrases like 'personalization' and 'private moment,' signifying techniques with which to investigate one's own psychic history."[38] Even though the self is ever changing, Counsell, Brustein, and Hornby consider Method acting anathema to character acting and neglectful of the material. They believe that Method actors graft their personality onto the role while ignoring its context.

Accusations of self-centeredness have some basis of fact; too many actors rely on simpleminded views of their selves in determining what constitutes "truthful" behavior. Harold Clurman said it best: "With the immature and more credulous actor [Method acting] may even develop into an emotional self-indulgence, or in other cases into a sort of therapy. The actor being the ordinary neurotic man suffering all sorts of repressions and anxieties seizes upon the revelation of himself—supplied by the recollection of his past—as a purifying agent." However, this "was not Stanislavsky's aim nor does it represent the purpose of the Method teachers in America."[39] Shallow choices, banal self-revelations, and unimaginative behavior amount to simple laziness. Strasberg, Adler, and Meisner have condemned this, and neither should the Method itself be faulted for the shoddy work of others.

The difference between the first and second criticism is remarkable, revealing the depth of misunderstanding of the Method and its goals. In order to clear up some of the misconceptions, it is important to clarify the distinction between role and self. Notions of character and actor and how they are related depend on certain philosophical conceptions of free will and determinism. In Method acting, actors are recognized as being guided by their own intentions; in contrast, non–Method acting frequently views actors as subject to the imposition of external events. Philosopher Robert Kane defines free will as *the power of agents to be the ultimate creators (or originators) and sustainers of their own ends and purposes*" (emphasis in original). To will freely, he adds, is "to be the ultimate creator (prime mover, so to speak) of your own purposes."[40] Philosopher Morton White more or less agrees, noting that free will means human beings are "free to perform actions."[41] The Method maintains that actors are free to perform and control actions and to determine their goals and objectives. This control, says Strasberg, "is the foundation for the actor's creativity" (*DP* 105).

Free will asserts that the actor is a conscious human being capable of reflecting on both her own situation and that of the play. Strasberg makes this clear: "*The actor to appear alive and real must really think on the stage;* he must not only make believe he thinks, he must really think" (emphasis in original).[42] The actor forms intentions and objectives as an act of choice, thinking through situations that enable her to determine the direction of her creativity. For example, if an actor is portraying a character about to be guillotined, she need not think about the guillotine, the blade, or death (especially if these images fail to strike a chord in her). Instead, she may be thinking about a cold shower. If a cold shower is personally terrifying, she has created a choice that evokes physical expressivity and believability. The point is that actors *choose to think of something from their imagination and personal experience that evokes truthful and provocative behavior.* Actress and teacher Uta Hagen distinguishes this idea of free choice when she says: "All life has a subliminal cause that sends you to a destination. Nothing is, in that sense, random. The actor has to know why that character is doing that. There has to be a cause."[43] The actor must select a motive that provokes action and behavior.

Method acting, particularly Strasberg's version of it, is rooted in ideas of free will. Strasberg says that everything "that the actor does demands some effort of will, thought, muscle, and emotion."[44] Robert Hethmon, editor of Strasberg's tapes, contends that for Method actors, volition "functions as the master control station that starts the engine and directs its power in the proper channels." As a result, the will "enters every phase of training from the beginning. Nothing is allowed to happen without the actor's will being thereby strengthened" (*SS* 153). Strasbergian free will is a performance of the self. The self is vulnerable, protean, and flexible in emotional content. Still, subject-actors are "free" to interpret the role, a freedom that empowers them. They may conform to traditional views of the role or cut against the grain. Either way, Method actors must impose their "stamp" upon the role. Dustin Hoffman's "tomato" will not sit; this is his interpretation, and he will not relent. His is an assertion of the will.

The Method actor's expression of free will combines sensations and thoughts. Strasberg's sense memory bridges the gap between the two. In sense memory, sensations of touching, tasting, smelling, hearing, and seeing objects stimulate the imagination, which in turn heighten sense awareness. For Strasberg, the interaction between the physical and the mental is dialogic. Senses communicate from the private and subjective (mind, imagination) to the physical and sensual (touch, taste, smell, etc.), or the other way around. The mental and the physical are not free floating but instead are systematically related by acts of will. The fluid movement from mind to body, possible only through relaxation and concentration, gives rise to truthful behavior, which in turn brings more sensation, evoking new desires, images, and movement. At the core of Strasberg's sense memory, the location of stimuli moves from the imagination to the visceral and back to the mind again. Strasberg asserts that this stimulates emotion and imagination "through the memory of thought and sensation" (*DP* 113).

Sense memory and Strasberg's controversial affective memory exercises are meant to evoke physical action. Affective memory is designed not merely to provoke emotion but to motivate the actor *to act, to produce active, physical behavior.* Strasberg structures the affective memory as a way of recovering creative action rather than preordained, eidetic images. His use of memory proceeds from the actor's associative chain of events that inspire creative action rather than simply recalling events for the sake of emotion. Affective memory is grounded in creativity rather than in stable identity and emotional excess. Despite its misuse by many teachers, affective memory is intended to help actors repeat motives and make actions sustainable in long-running rehearsals and performances. (It is therefore a technique meant for theatre, not film.) Along these lines, Adler adds that every "physical action has an inner action, and every inner action has a physical action that expresses its psychological nature. The unity between the two must be organic action on the stage" (*ISC* 103). When operating correctly, thought and sensation (mental and physical action) work simultaneously, inducing convincing performances repeatedly.

For Method actors, objects, images, and experiences exist in consciousness. Subconscious events merely *trigger physical behavior* elicited by images, the senses, or memories. The Method actor sees the physical world as a logical construct of human sense-experience. This position stands in contrast to certain facets of determinism, which sees the physical world as independent of the human mind. Determinism sees objects not in consciousness but in space. It challenges free will by positing the doctrine that all of our goals and actions are either socially determined or necessitated by factors beyond the agent/actor's control (e.g., fate). While there are various forms of determinism, the view is generally taken to be that free will is an illusion; humans ultimately cannot be the creators of their own destinies since cultural conditions and fate fix action. Actors and their roles are dominated by the material world of cause-and-effect that exercises considerable and necessitating pressures.

Colin Counsell claims that most American acting lacks "a substantial social-determinist component, a thoroughgoing conception of the subject as constructed—not merely repressed—by social environment." The Method, Counsell adds, far "from being informed by a Marxist, social-determinist perspective," seeks a "state of Rousseau-like freedom."[45] For Counsell and other determinists, actors are incapable of controlling events; they are, rather, subject to events as they occur. Materialistic determinists undercut claims of purposiveness in our actions; materialistic determinism aims to reduce the world to what can be seen and tested. Determinists subordinate any seeming higher, transcendent reality to the status of illusion. Actors' inquiry into things spiritual is futile. Once they accept their own material presence, they are given over to what David Mamet calls "the actual courage of the actor," a courage that when "coupled with the lines of the playwright [creates] the illusion of character." Actors cease to graft their individuality onto the role and accept their position as *Übermarrionettes*. Now, according to Mamet, "open the mouth, stand straight, and say the words bravely—adding nothing, denying nothing, and without the intent to manipulate anyone: himself, his fellows, and the audience."[46] For Mamet and Counsell, acting well is merely to be conditioned by factors entering into the script.

Determinism is not without some plausibility. Directors Anne Bogart and Robert Wilson have demonstrated the influence of formalistic determinism on the theatre to an impressive degree. (Although Uta Hagen sees it otherwise, lamenting that "the gaping hole" in the theatre is directors who "have made themselves stars by manipulation of actors like puppets.")[47] The deconstruction of meaning posited by postmodern directors amounts to the cancellation of any pretensions to truth and denies any metaphysically based control by actors. The materialistic determinist challenges actors who, in their act of creative signification, seek to impose some transcendental significance onto the role.

The active will of Method actors imposes a motivated presence through felt objectives and inwardly determined actions. Steve Vineberg opines that Strasberg "was primarily concerned with the soul of a performance, not with its form."[48] Method actor Morris Carnovsky concurs, saying that the Method actor must ask: "What is the movement of his soul in the midst of the body? What is the nature of the body that accompanies the movements of the soul?"[49] In contrast to soul searching, determinist actors are constrained to negotiate only in the realm of material laws, acting somewhat like falling rocks. Rather than spirituality, determinist actors look to material form—the body—for inspiration. They no longer create inwardly but simply express their causal relation to space. Movements, gestures, and appearances, what actor Tadashi Suzuki calls "the physically perceptive sensibility" that heightens the actor's "innate expressive abilities,"[50] become modes in a matrix of overt behavior.

Whereas Method actors follow the path of their creative will, determinist actors obey phenomenal laws of motion and gravity. Therefore, that determinism should draw its inspiration from choreography and puppetry comes as little surprise. Literary deconstructionist Paul de Man claims that "puppets have no motion by themselves but only in relation to the motions of the puppeteer, to whom they are connected by a system of lines and threads." By itself, de Man says, the motion of the puppet "is devoid of any aesthetic interest or effect. The aesthetic power is located neither in the puppet nor in the puppeteer but in the text that spins itself between them." Unlike Method acting, where living performers allow their interpretative expressions to flow and are not on loan from the script, the puppet dance, de Man maintains, "is truly aesthetic because it is not expressive: the laws of its motion are not determined by desire [the Method's emphasis on motivation] but by numerical and geometric laws or topoi that never threaten the balance of grace." For the dancing puppet, de Man says, "there is no risk of affectation, of letting the aesthetic effect be determined by the dynamics of the represented passion or emotion rather than by the formal laws of tropes."[51] The puppet is a pure "sign" independent of actors' feelings. Puppetry deflects attention from actors' psychology and shifts it to the realm of overt cause-and-effect. The puppet brings nothing more than an inorganic purity devoid of personality.

The Method maintains that interiority and inwardness, as tools of creativity, are part of actors' spiritual quests for clarity and meaning in the performance. For postmodernists, performance is not a manifestation of a "higher" form of consciousness but rather a body in motion. Method actors seek ways of aligning subject (the performers) and object (the characters) through their interpretive viewpoint. Postmodernists reject the notion that actors have control of the will and can pour meaning into a role. Postmodernism bleeds human subjects of meaning, removing all traces of agency. It regards human subjects as lacking a privileged point of view; the great merit of puppets and marionettes is that they can be made to show how meaning is constructed onto a performance from without, not within. Puppets cannot layer a role with personal baggage; rather, they manage to provoke experiences in the audience merely by dint of their movement. This view supplies the substance of Counsell's objection to the Method actor's intrusion. For him, Method actors "employ numerous breaks in speech and hesitant pauses, inferring a self that lies beyond its linguistic inscription." This groping for words "proffers an image of the human subject as possessing a deep psychology, one more profound than they can express." Thus the Method actor "produces a rich mist of generalized signs of the psyche, a cascade with vast but unspecific potential for meaning, whose parts are then turned into semic units in the spectator's interpretative gaze."[52]

Counsell is wrong, however, in suggesting that Method actors produce generalized signs. For Method actors, precision and specificity are essential. These actors are known for their scrupulous attention to details; they will devote hours to discussing motives, actions, and behavior. Counsell condemns the Method actor's "behavioral minutiae" that "swamp all else so that practically the only reading possible is one contained within a discourse of psychic disturbance," yet he praises postmodern artists when they "exceed the frame" of reference, evoking a contradictory theatre experience. He draws upon an example from the Wooster Group's *Brace Up*, where actors "drank and joked but their words were inaudible, and their actions played no discernible part in the fiction being created in the main stage area."[53] Both Method actors and the Wooster Group "exceed the frame." But for the Method, the actor becomes a messenger of meaningful intention; in the case of the Wooster Group, meaning creation either is simply avoided or is given over to the director's conceptualization.

The Method's emphasis on free will reaches its apogee with Strasberg; without nullifying the playwrights' and directors' importance, for him the actor is the ultimate creator. One of Strasberg's great contributions as a teacher was his ability to view a performance and articulate problems that blocked the progress of the actor's work. He was skilled at perceiving the depth of an actor's conviction and was able to explain what was important and how to attain it. In their effort to break free of Strasberg's influence, Adler and Meisner sought ways of incorporating determinism to stimulate motivation. For Adler, the given circumstance of the play and the actor's imagination would join with free will and inspire creativity. Here the actor devotes less to past psychology and more to imagination as it applies to the play's circumstances. Like Brecht, to whom she should be compared, Adler introduced social conditions as motivating factors. The actor secures the performance by giving over to events in the play's social background. For Adler, a play's circumstances and the actor's imagination inspire understanding of physical actions; these circumstances would replace Strasberg's emphasis on psychology as the motivational trigger. She quotes Stanislavsky to the effect that the "truth in art is the truth of your circumstances" (*TA* 31). Adler acknowledges the significance of drawing on oneself, but the source of inspiration is not merely past experience (as in the case of Strasberg); it is rather, at least in part, the actor's imagination and the social world that inspires. For Adler, the "playwright gives you the play, the idea, the style, the conflict, the character, etc. The background life of the character will be made up of the social, cultural, political, historical, and geographical situation in which the author places him." She insists that characterization must be understood "within the framework of the character's own time and situation."[54] In order for actors to comprehend a character, they must read, observe paintings, study architecture, and listen to music. Then and only then will they become what Method acting teacher Paul Mann calls "actor-anthropologist[s]."[55] One of Adler's great contributions as a teacher was her ability to coach actors in those roles Adler understood completely, explaining in detail the social and political background that stimulate the imagination.

Adler did not abandon her belief in the actor's inner faith; she merely shifted the emphasis from the psychological to the imaginative. She never entirely freed herself from the idea that the actor's creative will was paramount and said "[the] most important thing I look for in young actors is the will."[56] The conflict between Adler and Strasberg had to do as much with personality as ideology. Stanislavsky scholar Sharon Carnicke is scrupulous in her observation that Strasberg and Adler emphasized elements of acting "which suited their own needs best." Strasberg, she says, "was a distant, unemotional person," and thus "personal emotions and private moment exercises were clearly necessary to Strasberg in his own work on himself. Adler, in contrast, exhibited an extravagant personality, entering rooms with her entourage in tow."[57] Indeed, action and imagination suited Adler's taste. Despite their quarrels, they shared a belief in the actor's role as interpreter.

While Meisner, too, believed in the actor as interpreter, he presented an alternative that sought compatibility with both the notion of free will and determinism. He required a way of incorporating determinism into the actor's craft by stressing relationships. The way actors communicate with their fellow performers became a central feature of Meisner's technique. The material presence of another person is a real presence for Meisner; the text's circumstances, while important, are mere artifice. The contours of acting are determined by the interaction of communication rather than by a single will. Meisner's ability to formulate exercises that assisted actors during performance was one of his great contributions. Relationships, for him, inspire action. He did not oppose preparation but diminished its relevance as compared to Strasberg and Adler.

According to Meisner, actors acquire an understanding of who they are in the role and in themselves through communion. Identity is negotiated through the repetition of phrases with another being. We acquire an identity and motivate our actions both by observing and by being observed, and through this exchange (combined with the acquired ideal of active "doing"), self-formation (character) is realized. His repetition exercise developed a sense of self through communication: We become the role and the self in the actual moment of performance. The other actor is granted intrinsic integrity, so that in seeing the face and hearing the voice of the other, the performer responds to the exterior gaze and sound rather than carrying on an internal conversation. The actor does not merely create self/character from memory, imaginary circumstances, or the author's story, but rather encounters the words and actions of the other actor and responds to them. In the process of reacting, character is formulated as a dynamic of being-with-another. Like director Jerzy Grotowski, to whom he should be compared, Meisner believed the self to be based on impulse. We are not who we are by virtue of our free will alone but by a product of dialogic exchanges. Self and role emerge together at the very moment of performance, when our active engagement with others and the environment stimulate our reactions. Our sense of self/role then becomes open to new perspectives transcending the will. In this way Meisner offers a somewhat more accessible technique to approaching nonrealistic texts than does Strasberg.[58]

CRITICISM #3: USEFUL ONLY FOR REALISM

A third criticism of Method acting maintains that outside of kitchen-sink realism, Method actors are simply adrift. The Method actor's supposed inability to use language has drawn complaints. According to Richard Hornby, "I speak, therefore I am, and how I speak is what I am. How a character speaks is what he is, and finding the way the character speaks is fundamental to acting."[59] Method actors are, in fact, well known for incorporating accents and dialects in explicit detail. Nevertheless, it is also true that some Method actors have difficulty with Shakespeare and verse plays. This problem arises not only for Method actors but also for twentieth- and twenty-first century American actors more generally. While nineteenth-century American theatre saw a plethora of Shakespearean performances, mid- to late-twentieth-century American actors have had, with notable exceptions, less success with Shakespeare. This is due, in part, to an emphasis on what in America counts as authenticity.

During the early part of the twentieth century, a struggle to define the American identity and correlatively, the emergence of "authenticity," took place. Authenticity presupposes honesty and sincerity rather than deception. It holds that one can exhibit a true self based on self-conscious awareness of identity. This identity may evolve, but it must remain open

and available for scrutiny at any given time. A diversity of cultures during
the early twentieth century made national unity difficult to attain; the notion of authenticity helped mediate the individual's claim to a national
sense of self. Social critic Miles Orvell contends that the deemphasis of
imitation and the rise of authenticity as a mark of national identity "has
been a key constituent in American culture since the Industrial Revolution and assumes crucial importance in the shift from nineteenth to the
twentieth centuries."[60] While nineteenth-century America was comfortable with imitation, a cultural shift during the early twentieth cen-
tury/modern age led to the rejection of imitation in favor of authenticity.
According to social historian Daniel Joseph Singal, the modern, industrial age has "demanded nothing less than 'authenticity,' which requires a
blending of the conscious and unconscious strata of the mind so that the
self presented to the world is the 'true' self in every respect."[61] Such emphasis on the *true self* over imitation took root in America. By the time of
Stanislavsky's tour of the United States in 1923, the nation was responsive to his ideas of *authentic* behavior.

It is only a slight oversimplification to say that the inner emotional
realm seems authentic to Americans. This view has powerfully shaped
American life. With its rampant individualistic excesses and absence of
effective central control over hurly-burly capitalism, America has encouraged individual prosperity and personal inventiveness over social
responsibility. By the early twentieth century, the United States had
revolutionized its capitalist economy and ushered in a long period of
what social critic Thomas Harrison dubs the "metaphysics of egoism,"
where "self-assertion motivates all individuals and groups."[62] In a society based on mass consumption and self-assertion, the United States
showed considerable antipathy toward collectivism. Acting in the
United States thus encouraged the star system, a reflection of the power
of individual self-assertion over ensemble, as opposed to other nations
and continents where ensemble acting is strongly emphasized. There
are no doubt exceptions to this, but the popularity of the Academy
Awards, Emmys, and Tony Awards testifies to the aggrandizement of
stars. Actors have, in general, been influenced by this situation, which
has developed not as a result of the Method but of a culture rooted in
individualism and celebrity.[63]

Authenticity has been associated with a *Gatsbyesque* individualized image of the self, an *inside* that is not only defended against external forces but is also believed to be the source of identity. The inner self is allegedly the true self; the outer self is the mere trapping of civilization. "Get real," "be for real," "the real thing," and "genuine article" are popular phrases in American culture that stress authenticity and originality as opposed to phoniness and pretense. Holden Caulfield, novelist J. D. Salinger's protagonist in *The Catcher in the Rye*, gained popularity as an American icon by admonishing pretentiousness. His folk status owes to his preference for the authentic over the fraudulent (what Caulfield calls "phony"), a preference many Americans share.

Authenticity appeals to the inner life construed as an expression or state of the self, offering physical and psychological understanding of identity. The social world may compel self-awareness of our class, gender, race, and/or ethnicity, but the alleged true self is thought of as independent of the social world. Psychologist Jill Morawski, for example, believes that there existed in the cultural discourse of America during the early twentieth century a picture of the individual "becoming caught up in the magnification and glorification of the self—via self-interest, self-realization, self-control, self-presentation—and placing less significance on nineteenth-century ideals of self-sacrifice, strenuousness, and the control if not repression of desire."[64] In the twentieth century, Emersonian self-reliance replaced Calvinist self-sacrifice in the national consciousness. The rising interest in psychoanalysis added weight to the idea that there exists a deeper, perhaps subconscious self, one more real than the social self. The individualistic view brings with it the idea of being *true* to one's originality. Proponents of authenticity hold that we are being true and original when we exclude social pressures that impose standards appropriate merely to our external identity leading us toward imitation (thus the popularity of the lone individual over the mob).[65]

American actors in general resist Shakespeare because they desire a *gritty reality* expressive of freewheeling "cowboy" individuality rather than the *stagy unreality* associated with verse. So it goes: The grittier you are, the more real you are. The more actors dig into primal urges and cull out the id, the more likely they are apt to emit guttural sounds. Elevated prose, Shakespearean verse, and exquisite articulation seem too "British" and antithetical to "gutsy" authenticity and originality. However, the notion that the commonplace inadequacies of American actors follow upon slavish adherence to Method acting needs to be corrected. (John Wayne was not a Method actor.) Notwithstanding large enclaves of poverty and the increasing income gap between rich and poor in America, the rising standard of living in capitalism has reduced for many the need for social support systems, encouraging more Americans to embrace what sociologist Andrew Cherlin calls a self-reliance that relishes "the levels of personal achievement and emotional gratification that they have attained as a result."[66] The emphasis on self-reliance and personal gratification over ensemble is not the result of Method acting but of America's cultural attitudes.

The goal of the Method is to combine inner depth and eloquence of expression. Imagination, script analysis, articulation, and a passionate belief in the character's desires as they relate to the actor's life are the basic principles of Method acting. The task of the actor is to work out (and work with) the tension between raw authenticity and fluid expressivity. This task takes hard work and years of training. Few actors are willing to submit to the rigors, both physical and mental, of technique, training, and rehearsal. Instead, actors and directors take shortcut approaches, such as: "I need you to cry now," says a superficial director, "so think of your dying mother lying at the edge of the stage!" Encouraged by unimaginative directors and teachers, actors often seek the easy path, using little more than superficialities to achieve treacle feelings. This problem will not be resolved by harping about the Method.

CRITICISM #4: BETRAYING STANISLAVSKY

A fourth criticism holds that the Method, and Strasberg in particular, betrayed Stanislavsky. Richard Hornby, for example, complains that Strasberg never knew Stanislavsky and was therefore ill equipped to make himself Stanislavsky's spokesperson. Hornby adds that unlike "Stanislavsky, one of the great actors of history with a wide range of roles, Strasberg did little acting himself."[67] It is worth noting that Hornby himself, who was born the year Stanislavsky died, could not have seen the latter perform.[68] Nevertheless, he grinds his ax against the stone of religion. For him, Stanislavsky is "Jesus Christ" while Strasberg is "St. Paul, who never met Jesus in the flesh but who felt he knew him better than anyone because of a mystical communion, and who felt the need to spread the Gospel in Jesus's name rather than his own."[69] This criticism, however, is flawed.

Strasberg knew a great deal about Stanislavsky's work and saw Stanislavsky perform on stage but never made claim to a mystical communion.[70] He never felt this to be necessary; he had his own ideas about acting. These ideas may be criticized, but he did not play sycophant to Stanislavsky. Strasberg, Adler, Meisner, and other teachers are not to be regarded as mere shadows of Stanislavsky. Grotowski and Meyerhold parted company with Stanislavsky, but few if any would criticize them for "betraying" him. While Strasberg is targeted, criticism of Grotowski and Meyerhold has been muted because they carry certain intellectual cachet. There is a double standard here, one that fails to take the facts into account. The Method, Strasberg says, "is based not only on the procedures of Stanislavsky's work, but also on the further clarification and stimulus by [Euvgeny] Vakhtangov." He continues: "I have also added my own interpretation and procedures" (DP 84). The genealogy of Method procedures took root from three sources besides Stanislavsky: the emphasis on authenticity (already discussed); Vakhtangov's idea that it is the actor's life, and not necessarily the role, that inspires; and the influence of the Yiddish theatre.

Vakhtangov had argued that feelings of the actor "must not be ready-made beforehand somewhere on the shelf of his soul." Rather, they must "arise spontaneously on the stage, depending upon the situations in which the actor finds himself." This is what Vakhtangov called "agitation from the essence."[71] Strasberg, Adler, and Meisner developed their techniques in the way they found to *agitate,* or inspire, the actor. Vakhtangov departed from Stanislavsky, believing that the actor's justification, motivation, and inspiration are not necessarily related to the circumstances of the character. Justification for Vakhtangov is the actor's secret; he believed it has the power to lead the actor to a more convincing sense of reality then merely mining the character's beliefs. In order to agitate from the essence, Vakhtangov says, "it is necessary to live your own temperament on the stage and not the supposed temperament of the character."[72] This departure from Stanislavsky, who maintained that motivation should surface primarily from the role, allowed actors to look outside the script for inspiration. More than Strasberg, Adler borrowed from Vakhtangov. Thus she remarked that justification "is not in the lines; it is in you. What you should choose as your justification should agitate you. As a result of the agitation you will experience the action and emotion" (*TA* 48). Seeking images outside the text derives primarily from Vakhtangov, and Strasberg, Adler, and Meisner draw heavily from it.

An important part of the history of the Method is rooted in Yiddish theatre. In their effort to articulate a method for the actor, Strasberg, Adler, Meisner, and Clurman shared a similar social milieu. All four (as well as Robert Lewis, Paul Mann, and Morris Carnovsky) were born into the world of *Yiddishkeit* ("Yiddish-ness," or Yiddish life) both on stage and off. Yiddish was their *Mame-loshn* ("mother tongue"), and most of them spoke Yiddish fluently throughout their lives. Their first exposure to theatre was the Yiddish stage, and they were sons and daughters of immigrant Jews. Strasberg began his theatrical career on the Yiddish stage; Adler in particular belonged to a famous Yiddish theatre family and had frequently performed in the Yiddish theatre as a child actress. According to Foster Hirsch, Strasberg and Adler's teachings were spiced with "earthy Yiddish folk wisdom."[73] Jewish historian Stephen Whitfield claims that the formation of the Group Theatre by Adler, Clurman, and Strasberg was "not exactly a clean break" with the Yiddish stage.[74] This is made evident by cultural observer Hutchins Hapgood's 1902 description of Yiddish acting, which bears remarkable similarities to the Method. The acting on the Yiddish stage, he tells us, supplies "even to the plays having no intrinsic relation to reality a frequent quality of naturalness." Yiddish players, he observes, "act with remarkable sincerity. Entirely lacking in self-consciousness, they attain almost from the outset to a direct and forcible expressiveness. They, like the audience, rejoice in what they deem the truth."[75] In addition to stage "naturalness," the Yiddish world influenced Method teachers in several other ways.

In Method acting, the actor experiences an inner, personal conflict. While the idea of inner conflict derives from Stanislavsky, it also builds on an immigrant worldview. Method teachers, saturated in Yiddish life, saw themselves amid the conflicting passions between Old World values and New World experiences. This conflict played out in what Hapgood calls the three concentric influences of the Yiddish artist-intellectual: Orthodox Judaism, American assimilationism, and Socialism. In America, Hapgood observed, Jewish children found themselves in a social world that stood "in violent contrast with the orthodox environment" of their past.[76] Jewish immigrants reflected a life strenuously assimilating (but not yet fully assimilated) into an environment that provided deceptive appearances of tolerance and security but was in fact a false picture of social integration that did not exist. The psychological conflict among American Jews in clinging to Old World traditions, adapting American modernism, and embracing socialism as a way of circumventing intolerance was passed down to the psyche of the Method actor's soul. In Yiddish culture, there existed conflicts between parent and child, tradition and New World values, Yiddish and Hebrew, capitalism's potential for wealth and socialism's belief in justice, and the desire to enjoy American prosperity and the reality of anti-Semitism, all of which carried over, in some way or another, into the teaching of the Method to future generations.

Hornby claims that Strasberg and Adler's immigrant background and fear of prejudice makes it "understandable that they would have embraced a theory of acting that stressed a rigid, unchanging self."[77] This is misleading. Strasberg and Adler's teachings created the very *opposite* of a rigid self. They lived in a world of identity in crisis and no doubt found comfort in acting where change offers no surprise. Influenced by the Yiddish theatre and Yiddish life, Method actors are in fact mixtures of several consciousnesses at once.

Method actors experience a double consciousness that pulls them in opposing directions. The idea of double consciousness has had a significant influence in social areas as well. For instance, social historian W. E. B. Du Bois's 1903 thesis states that there exists a black double consciousness, where one "ever feels his two-ness—an American, a Negro; two souls, two thoughts, two unreconciled strivings; two warring ideals in one dark body, whose dogged strength keeps it from being torn asunder."[78] Du Bois's descriptive condition of African American life influenced the acting of Sidney Poitier, Ossie Davis, and Ruby Dee, and the directing of Lloyd Richards, particularly during their work together on the groundbreaking 1959 production of Lorraine Hansberry's *A Raisin in the Sun.* Here the inner conflicts between the characters' desires for as-similation on the one hand, and resistance to the residual prejudice they have endured on the other, clash in their dramatically powerful perfor-mances. This dual consciousness also has roots in the Method, where ac-tors are in conflict between two sets of opposing values. It is not an insignificant fact that Poitier, Davis, Dee, and Richards developed their techniques of acting under the tutelage of Method teacher Paul Mann. (Richards was even Mann's assistant for a time.) Method acting's influ-ences and the spiritual conflict of Du Bois's "two warring souls" become evident in their acting and directing. Method actors are torn between an attachment to the past and the search for a new (and better) life. This condition transfers in large measure from the Yiddish experience as learned by Method acting teachers to the inner conflict of Method actors' performances. Conflict and self-investigation nurture Method actors, and this resultant soul-searching is what Hornby rejects.

It is not uncommon for Method actors to be torn apart emotionally. For example, James Dean's performance in *Rebel Without a Cause* is para-digmatic of the conflict between parent and child, old and new, and the experience of finding a place in the American landscape that had ap-peared in early-twentieth-century American Jewish life. Although seem-ingly far removed from the turn-of-the-century Yiddish experience, Dean's introspection is much like that of Strasberg and Adler within Yid-dish culture. Dean's portrayal of a youth unable to conform to the mid-dle-class world of his parents or to fit into the social world of his high school peers is played out as a conflict within his soul. His acting assim-ilated the struggle that results from the efforts to be a good Jew as well as a good American, and the struggle involved in turning one's back on the past and conforming to a modern and frequently anti-Semitic world (al-beit reconfigured into a mid-American setting). In that film, Dean's de-sire to belong with his peers is pitted against the ridicule he encounters for being "different." The conflict between belonging and being different also surfaces in the *Godfather* movies, where once again Method acting's internalized struggle takes root in the Italian American immigrant expe-rience. The ethical imperatives that inspire Method actors are related in the struggle for self-understanding and the burden of choice that follows upon it. Method actors face emotional dilemmas, and their performances achieve their power from the inner conflict that surfaces in the actor's be-havior. The conflict inherent in such choices becomes part of actors' arse-nals; it enables impulsive responses and allows for the exhibition of vulnerability and conviction.

Furthermore, the notion of acting as a religious experience is rooted in the Method's relationship to Jewish traditions. Strasberg, Adler, Meisner, Lewis, Carnovsky, Mann, and Clurman's veritable Talmudic devotion to the art of acting was grounded in their spirituality and faith. This affected their teaching in several ways. First, Jewish traditions of a "people of the book" encouraged medicine, teaching, and law as respected professional endeavors; acting was considered a mere hobby, linked to an itinerant lifestyle and frequently discouraged. Method acting teachers wanted to infuse acting with its own form of legitimacy, giving it cultural value rather than being considered "child's play." Second, they wanted to re-spond to anti-Semitism constructively by bringing dignity to their work. In a world where "nonethnic good looks" frequently provided an entrée into the casting of leading roles, Method teachers sought actorial depth beyond surface appearances. Third, the emphasis on individuation in Ju-daism finds a correlative in the Method. By living distinctively and sepa-rately, Jewish survival is made manifest. It is up to the individual to sustain traditions. Only through particular and specific lifestyle patterns can Judaism endure. Social critic Waldo Frank asserts that in Jewish cul-ture, the "universal expresses itself ever and only through the particular."[79] Similarly for the Method actor, the universal is found in the particular, where attention to the details of task-related activities and specificity of behavior is heavily stressed. Fourth, Method teachers, particularly Adler and Meisner, have much in common with Jewish philosopher Martin Buber, who stressed "I-Thou" relationships in which identity is formu-lated through interaction, dialogue, and being-in-the-world.[80] Adler be-lieved actors must be socially responsible, and Meisner used Buber's notion of being-with-another as grist for the actor's mill. Finally, the an-alytical impulse inspired by Jewish philosophical tradition of conceptual thought and psychology helped steer Method teachers toward probative analyses of plays, characters, and psychological interpretations. Jewish in-fluences on modern intellectual life, brutally interrupted by Nazism, deeply influenced Strasberg, Adler, and Meisner. They wanted to give acting the intellectual heft found in music, art, philosophy, psychology, and literature. Their heritage enriched the soul-searching that eventuated in the Method.

Method acting is not simple. Affective memory, physical actions, motivation, experiencing the role, and relationships must work simultaneously. The Method also breaks down barriers. Barriers come in many forms, but Method training maintains that if actors cannot satisfy their desires, they will teach themselves not to desire at all. If actors cannot achieve goals, they will learn to desire only what they can reasonably obtain. This is a form of emotional retreat into an inner citadel. Student actors repress desire, fearful of failure. A defensive wall gradually wedges them in, minimizing exposure; they want to be as little wounded as possible. Reducing desires to the minimum diminishes the chances of exposing vulnerability and taking risks. The Method seeks ways to reverse defensive postures. Strasberg raises the important point that while every human being wants to avoid the pain and frustration involved in creativity, "when artists like Dostoevsky create, they write about their diseases, and they write about their fits. They use it in their work." But in acting, Strasberg contends, "it's a much more difficult process because it has to be used physically."[81] Sharing one's pain, joy, sorrow, happiness, and love is part of the actor's job. The following chapters subject the Method to a rigorous analysis, revealing its complexity, depth, and energy.

NOTES

1.   David Hare, *Amy's View* (London: Faber and Faber, 1997), 113–14.
2.   David Krasner, "Method Acting: Strasberg, Adler, Meisner," *Twentieth-Century Actor Training,* Alison Hodge, ed. (London: Routledge, 2000), 129–50.
3.   Harold Clurman, *The Collected Works of Harold Clurman,* Marjorie Loggia and Glenn Young, eds. (New York: Applause, 1994), 369.
4.   Lee Strasberg, "Introduction," *The Paradox of Acting & Masks or Faces?* (New York: Hill and Wang, 1957), xiii.
5.   See Sharon M. Carnicke's discussion of the way the American Method changed Stanislavsky's ideas in her book, *Stanislavsky in Focus* (Australia: Harwood Academic Publishers, 1998), 65 *passim.*
6.   Robert Lewis, *Method or Madness?* (New York: Samuel French, 1958), 99.

7. Elia Kazan, *A Life* (New York: Alfred A. Knopf, 1988), 143.

8. Steve Vineberg, *Method Actors: Three Generations of American Acting Style* (New York: Schirmer Books, 1991), 6–7.

9. For history of the Group Theatre, see Harold Clurman, *The Fervent Years: The Story of the Group Theatre and the Thirties* (New York: Harcourt Brace Jovanovich, 1945, 1975); Cheryl Crawford, *One Naked Individual: My Fifty Years in the Theatre* (Indianapolis: Bobbs-Merrill, 1959); and Wendy Smith, *Real Life Drama: The Group Theatre and America, 1931–1940* (New York: Alfred A. Knopf, 1990).

10. See, for instance, Robert Brustein, "America's New Cultural Hero: Feelings Without Words," *Commentary* 25 (January 1958): 123–29; "The Keynes of Times Square," *The New Republic* (December 1, 1962): 28–30; and "Are British Actors Better Than Ours?" *New York Times*, April 15, 1973, sec. 2, pp., 1, 30.

11. Richard Hornby, *The End of Acting: A Radical View* (New York: Applause, 1992), 5, 184. Hornby fails to make clear what he means by "decline." Given the rise of theatre's popularity in the 1980s and 1990s, this is an unsubstantiated assertion.

12. Peter Marks, "Tantrums of a Teacher of Stars," *New York Times*, April 30, 1998, E5. *Nobody Dies on Friday* opened at the American Repertory Theatre, Cambridge, MA, on April 16, 1998, and reopened for the Fall season on September 30. Brustein admits to having "never met Strasberg" in *The Lively Art*, Arthur Holmburg, ed. (Chicago: Ivan Dee, 1999), 230. Certainly writers need not have met the living character they portray in order to depict them in fiction. However, Robert Brustein has maligned Strasberg and the Method for several decades (see note 10); his play is thus part of a history of antipathy toward someone he admittedly never met.

13. Howard Taubman, *New York Times*, June 23, 1964, p. 24, and *New York Times*, July 5, 1964, sec. 2, p. 1. Douglas Watt of the *Daily News* called Strasberg's *Three Sisters* "a stunning achievement," adding that the play has "first rate players" here "in abundance" and that for his direction, Lee Strasberg "is the true hero of the occasion" (June 23, 1964, 43). Jerry Tallmer of the *New York Post* said the play was produced "with all the creative truth and strength a human being can command" and that it is "difficult to believe that there has ever been a more organic and total production of 'The Three Sisters' anywhere at anytime" (June 23, 1964, 16). John Gassner called it "a highly successful production" and noted that Kim Stanley "was superb as Masha," though he criticized a lack of ensemble playing and a "certain lassitude in the production" ("Broadway in Review," *Educational Theatre Journal* 16.3 [October 1964]: 286–87). Michael Smith of the *Village Voice* also noted reservations, saying that "there is a droning flatness of rhythm throughout the play," yet he called Kim Stanley and Geraldine Page "two of the best naturalistic actresses at work" (July 2, 1964, 11, 12). John McCarten of

the *New Yorker* called the production an uneven but nevertheless enterprising interpretation that "develops the mood that Chekhov was aiming at" (July 4, 1964, 56).

14. Charles Marowitz, *The Other Way: An Alternative Approach to Acting and Directing* (New York: Applause, 1999), 119.

15. Michael Quinn, "Self-Reliance and Ritual Renewal: Anti-theatrical Ideology in American Method Acting," *Journal of Dramatic Theory and Criticism* 10.1 (Fall 1995): 14.

16. Denis Salter, "Acting Shakespeare in Postcolonial Space," *Shakespeare, Theory, and Performance*, James C. Bulman, ed. (London: Routledge, 1996), 128.

17. Denis Salter, "Body Politics: English-Canadian Acting at National Theatre School," *Canadian Theatre Review* 71 (Summer 1992): 13.

18. Elaine Aston, *Feminist Theatre Practice: A Handbook* (London: Routledge, 1999), 7.

19. David Mamet, *True and False: Heresy and Common Sense for the Actor* (New York: Pantheon Books, 1997), 20.

20. Hornby, *End of Acting*, chides the Method for avoiding character and script analysis, saying that character acting "needs to be valued much more highly than it is in the United States" (23).

21. Foster Hirsch, *A Method to Their Madness: A History of the Actors Studio* (New York: Norton, 1984), 207, 211.

22. Charles Marowitz, *Stanislavsky & the Method* (New York: Citadel, 1964), 43.

23. Hirsch, *Method to Their Madness*, notes that at The Actors Studio, the actor was considered a "*creator* more than an *interpreter*" (227).

24. Geraldine Page, "Interview" *Actors on Acting*, Joanmarie Kalter, ed. (New York: Sterling, 1979), 21.

25. Marowitz, *Stanislavsky & the Method*, 43.

26. Robbie McCauley, Interview, "Obsessing in Public" (1993), *A Sourcebook of African-American Performance*, Annemarie Bean, ed. (London: Routledge, 1999), 236, 239.

27. Ibid., 241.

28. John Harrop, *Acting* (London: Routledge, 1992), 42.

29. McCauley, "Obsessing in Public," 236.

30. Aston, *Feminist Theatre Practice*, 177–78.

31. Sue-Ellen Case, *Feminism and Theatre* (New York: Routledge, 1988), 122.

32. Strasberg makes this point clear when he says "Emotional response is conditioned response" and that the emotional basis of his work with the actor is based on the control of emotions through the conditioned reflex actions that Pavlov developed (*SS* 113).

33. Case, *Feminism and Theatre*, 50. Not all feminists support the notion of "the personal is the political." Some feminist theories reject the personal, favoring instead the idea of socially constructed gender formation.

34. Jeanie Forte, "Women's Performance Art: Feminism and Postmodernism," *Performing Feminisms: Feminist Critical Theory and Practice,* Sue-Ellen Case, ed. (Baltimore: John Hopkins University Press, 1990), 258.
35. Deborah Warner, interviewed by Helen Manfull, *In Other Words: Women Directors Speak* (Lyme, NH: Smith & Kraus, 1997), 107–8.
36. Collin Counsell, *Signs of Performance: An Introduction to Twentieth-Century Theatre* (London: Routledge, 1996), 65.
37. Hornby, *The End of Acting,* 6.
38. Brustein, "Are British Actors Better Than Ours?," 1. Brustein's criticism of the Method's "subjective, autobiographical approach" is nearly identical to Jean Forte's praise of women's performance quoted earlier.
39. Clurman, "The Famous Method" (1958), *Collected Works,* 373.
40. Robert Kane, *The Significance of Free Will* (New York: Oxford University Press, 1998), 4.
41. Morton White, *The Question of Free Will: A Holistic View* (Princeton, NJ: Princeton University Press, 1993), 8.
42. Lee Strasberg, "Acting and Actor Training," *Producing the Play,* John Gassner, ed. (New York: Dryden, 1941), 142.
43. Uta Hagen, in an interview by Mark Steyn, "An Elegant Toughie in Defense of Her Art," *New York Times,* Arts Section, October 22, 1995, 4.
44. Strasberg, interviewed by Richard Schechner, *TDR* 9.1 (Fall 1964): 119. Strasberg warns that energy can lead to tension. As a consequence, he stressed relaxation as a way of avoiding excessive pushing and strain.
45. Counsell, *Signs of Performance,* 62, 63.
46. Mamet, *True and False,* 21, 22.
47. Uta Hagen, quoted in Marilyn Stasio, "Uta Hagen: In Praise of Common Sense," *American Theatre* 15.7 (September 1998): 75.
48. Vineberg, *Method Actors,* 112.
49. Morris Carnovsky, qtd. in Peter Sander, "The Actor's Eye," *The Soul of the American Actor* 1.2 (Summer 1998): 6. My thanks to Dorothy Chansky for alerting me to this publication.
50. Tadashi Suzuki, "Culture Is the Body," *Acting (Re)considered: Theories and Practices,* Phillip Zarrilli, ed., Kazuko Matsuoka, tr. (London: Routledge, 1995), 155.
51. Paul de Man, "Aesthetic Formalization in Kleist," *The Rhetoric of Romanticism* (New York: Columbia University Press, 1984), 285, 286.
52. Counsell, *Signs of Performance,* 68–9, 69–70, 71.
53. Ibid., 71, 228.
54. Stella Adler, "The Reality of Doing," *TDR* 9.1 (Fall 1964): 149, interviewed by P. Gray.
55. Paul Mann, "Theory and Practice," *TDR* 9.2 (Winter 1964): 87, interviewed by R. Schechner.
56. Stella Adler, "Interview," *Educational Theatre Journal* 28.4 (December 1976): 512.
57. Carnicke, *Stanislavsky in Focus,* 60.

58. According to Joanne Woodward, Strasberg's technique is "more intellectual" than Meisner's. Meisner's whole concept, she says, "was about play" (*Eight Women of the American Stage*, Roy Harris, ed. [Portsmouth, NH: Heinemann, 1997], 122, 23).

59. Hornby, *End of Acting*, 45.

60. Miles Orvell, *The Real Thing: Imitation and Authenticity in American Culture, 1880–1940* (Chapel Hill: University of North Carolina Press, 1989), xvi.

61. Daniel Joseph Singal, "Towards a Definition of American Modernism," *American Quarterly* 30.1 (Spring 1987): 14.

62. Thomas Harrison, *1910: The Emancipation of Dissonance* (Berkeley: University of California Press, 1996), 147.

63. Or, as Joshua Gamson put it, "celebrity is a primary contemporary means to power, privilege, and mobility." See, Gamson, *Claims to Fame: Celebrity in Contemporary America* (Berkeley: University of California Press, 1994), 186.

64. Jill G. Morawski, "Educating the Emotions: Psychology, Textbooks, and the Psychology Industry, 1890–1940," *Inventing the Psychological: Toward a Cultural History of Emotional Life in America*, Joel Pfister and Nancy Schnog, eds. (New Haven: Yale University Press, 1997), 219.

65. For an interesting discussion on American individualism as it relates to the loner and the pastoral Western, see Conal Furay, *The Grass-Roots Mind in America* (New York: New Viewpoints, 1977), 32–36.

66. Andrew J. Cherlin, "I'm O.K., You're Selfish," *New York Times Magazine*, October 17, 1999: 50.

67. Hornby, *End of Acting*, 173.

68. Hornby frequently defines "great" actors as ones from past generations. He cites, for example, the Barrymores, Minnie Madden Fisk, Katherine Cornell, Eva LaGallienne, and the Lunts as "world-class stage actors" (Hornby, "Against Performance Theory," *Theater Week* [October 17, 1994], 31). It is unlikely that he saw these performers on stage at a mature age. Strasberg, however, did see Stanislavsky perform in Chekhov's *The Three Sisters* in 1923.

69. Hornby, *End of Acting*, 176.

70. Strasberg had a great deal of contact with the Moscow Art Theatre, Meyerhold, and other Russia theatre artists.

71. [Euvgeny] Vakhtangov, "Preparing for the Role," from Vakhtangov's diary, in *Acting: A Handbook of the Stanislavski Method*, Toby Cole, ed., B. E. Zakhara, tr. (New York: Crown Trade, 1955), 145.

72. Ibid., 146.

73. Hirsch, *Method to Their Madness*, 217. Hirsch adds that if "Strasberg was the remote Jewish father, withholding approval behind a stolid mask, Adler is the domineering Jewish mother, forever tisking and scolding" (218). Michael Wager says "being at the Studio was like participating in

a terrible Jewish family romance, with all the goy actors wondering what was going on" (qtd. in Ibid., 166).

74. Stephen J. Whitfield, *In Search of American Jewish Culture* (Hanover, NH: University Press of New England, 1999), 44.

75. Hutchins Hapgood, *The Spirit of the Ghetto* (1902) (Cambridge, MA: Harvard University Press, 1967), 137.

76. Ibid., 18, 23.

77. Hornby, *End of Acting,* 32.

78. W. E. B. Du Bois, *The Souls of Black Folk* (1903), *Three Negro Classics,* John Hope Franklin, ed. (New York: Avon, 1965), 215.

79. Waldo Frank, *The Jew in Our Day* (New York: Duell, Sloan and Pearce, 1944), 149.

80. Martin Buber, *I and Thou* (1923), Walter Kaufmann, tr. (New York: Touchstone, 1996).

81. Lee Strasberg, "Reunion: A Self-Portrait of the Group Theatre," *Educational Theatre Journal* 28.4 (December 1976): 546.

PART I

THEORY

CHAPTER TWO

SALVAGING STRASBERG
AT THE FIN DE SIÈCLE

Marc Gordon

In June 1997, the Moscow Art Theatre organized an international conference to celebrate its centennial. Robert Brustein, on his first visit to Russia, described the atmosphere as more like a peace conference than a theatre conference. Brustein writes: "[T]he whole complicated affair had been carefully engineered by the theatre's brilliant and personable literary director, Anatoly Smeliansky—an expert ironically enough, on Mikhail Bulgakov, one of Stanislavsky's most unforgiving critics." Recognizing that many of the old rivalries were represented at the conference— including Yuri Lyubimov, former director of the Taganka Theatre and a follower of Meyerhold—Brustein concludes: "The chorus of praise for Stanislavsky and the ecumenical atmosphere of the proceedings were somewhat surprising—considering how many present had broken off into radically different theatrical directions."[1] In short, the conference became a forum for unity between Stanislavsky and those who diverged from his Russian System.

Brustein, uncomfortable in this harmonious setting, represented the lone dissenting voice. He has found little to appreciate in Lee Strasberg's legacy to American acting, and the Russian conference seemed the appropriate place to display his dissatisfaction. Referring to a conference procedure in which participants turned to pose a question to two empty chairs representing both Stanislavsky and Nemirovich-Danchenko, Brustein directed his question to the former's chair: "I asked him how much responsibility he was willing to take for Lee Strasberg. The question would have been rhetorical even had Stanislavsky been alive to answer it." Brustein went on to disengage Strasberg from Stanislavsky's legacy with the now-familiar story that goes as follows: After visiting Stanislavsky in Paris in 1934 "Stella Adler had already reported on the master's disapproval of Strasberg's use of 'private moments' and 'emotional memories' as unwarranted intrusions into the actor's psyche," stressing instead the method of physical actions. Then, in order to punctuate his disapproval of Strasberg, Brustein concluded his evidence: "[O]ne of Lee Strasberg's leading examples of a great American actress was Marilyn Monroe."[2]

This vilification of Strasberg alongside Stanislavsky's deification exemplifies an important by-product of the controversy surrounding the American Method and the Russian System: Strasberg's interpretation of Stanislavsky's ideas. Brustein assumes that Stanislavsky disapproved of emotional memories and private moments because Stella Adler said that he did, and because Stanislavsky's research had apparently gone in another direction toward the end of his life. Underscoring the alleged weaknesses of the American Method, Brustein reminds us that troubled sex symbol Marilyn Monroe, a pupil of Strasberg, is emblematic of Method acting. He fails to include the abundance of noteworthy actors who also studied with Strasberg. In this way, Brustein sought to degrade Strasberg's work, ignoring the facts by disassociating Strasberg from the Stanislavsky System. Consequently the Method is to blame for the "poor" quality of American acting during the middle and later parts of the twentieth century. Richard Hornby asserts of the Method: "it shackles American acting," and that nothing "less than a radical attack on Strasbergian ideology, going right to its assumptions, will break its shackles."[3]

The Method is not a carbon copy of the System. The same can be said for the techniques administered by Adler and Sanford Meisner, both of whom, like Strasberg, worked with the Group Theatre and became prominent acting teachers. Collectively, the ideas formulated by Strasberg, Adler, and Meisner have influenced American actors for nearly seventy years. Individually, each owes a certain debt to Stanislavsky yet each moved separately and independently in the development of training techniques. Why, then, has Strasberg's Method become the victim of vitriolic attacks by many in the American acting establishment while the teaching of both Meisner and Adler has largely escaped criticism? According to theatre scholar Christine Edwards, the Method as taught by Strasberg "is equivalent to early Stanislavsky."[4] Is early Stanislavsky of little value to his later work? Does the method of physical actions replace affective memory, or does it work in conjunction with it?

Lee Strasberg's affective memory, private moment, and substitution, the hallmarks of the Method, are labeled a distortion of Stanislavsky's teachings—emotion memory, public solitude, and the "magic if," respectively. Of emotional memory John Harrop writes: "This is not what Stanislavski had in mind when calling for a greater concern with inner process;"[5] yet today, what Stanislavsky "had in mind" is being called into question.

We can say for certain that when the Moscow Art Theatre came to the United States in 1923 and 1924, it changed the way acting was both taught and performed in America. In a way the pump was primed for a systematic approach to actor training; Americans were eager to embrace the steady stream of Russian ideas. The questions implicit in this discussion are whether Strasberg helped facilitate the process or simply obstructed its flow; whether "pure" Stanislavsky is actually taught in America; and, in the end, whether historians should have to defend Strasberg against those who blame him for nearly all of the ills of American acting.

When the productions of the Moscow Art Theatre (MAT) were presented to American audiences, the effect on American actors was nothing short of remarkable. A young Lee Strasberg witnessed how individual performances demonstrated the work of a true repertory company (*SS* 13). Each role, no matter how small, was a carefully crafted character study that, rather than promote individual virtuosity, contributed to the overall work of the ensemble. After the MAT left, members Richard Boleslavsky (already in America for several years) and Maria Ouspenskaya remained behind to train American actors in the System. Here, the dissemination of ideas would begin to undergo a filtering process. As

Stanislavsky's missionary, Boleslavsky was experienced in the exercises and techniques of the early System, those focusing on emotional memory, improvisation, and non-verbal exercises. Stanislavsky returned to Russia and his work, it is generally agreed, would later take him in alternative directions.

The training at the New York American Laboratory Theatre (Lab) was to last two years. The first year, mostly spent with Ouspenskaya, covered given circumstances, characterization, and affective memory. In the second year, according to theatre historian Ronald A. Willis: "Boleslavsky analyzed a play according to its spine, mood, and beats. Actors were taught to analyze their roles according to their characters' desires and intentions."[6] In essence, the first year was spent in great part on the actor's self, and the second on character work, technique, and action. Lee Strasberg attended the Lab, taking away much of what would later become the foundation of his actor training method.

Strasberg became the first major *American* teacher of Stanislavsky's theories. When he, along with Cheryl Crawford and Harold Clurman, founded the Group Theatre, their roles were clearly defined. According to Foster Hirsh: "Strasberg, intensely interested in acting problems and interpreting Stanislavsky's system, was placed in charge of actor training and directing."[7] As both director and acting teacher for the Group, Strasberg continued to be involved in every production until he left in 1937. When he was not directing, he served as acting coach on the most important productions. Of the contribution of the Group to American theatre, Group Theatre historian Wendy Smith writes: "The sincerity, realism, and emotional depth of their performances were a revelation to audiences and fellow actors alike." For Smith, the "idea of a systematic approach to the craft of acting was firmly implanted in the vast majority of American actors, with emotional truth as its 'foundation.'"[8]

After Strasberg left the Group Theatre in 1937, he found employment in the late 1940s with the Actors Studio, where, under his guidance, some of the most prominent actors in America received their training.[9] Of American popular culture of the 1950s, after the Method really caught on, social historian Marianne Conroy writes, "Method actors appeared as Rebel heroes and hipster intellectuals."[10] They were outsiders American culture identified with. However, popularity does not ensure critical success, and Strasberg and the Method have withstood a nearly endless barrage of criticism since the early 1930s.

The earliest objections to Strasberg's version of the System during the Group Theatre days stemmed from the disagreements among members over the attention that Strasberg paid to emotions in his teaching. Indeed, affective memory, just one part of the Stanislavsky puzzle, became the subject of contention. Curiously, little was said publicly prior to the 1950s, when Robert Lewis spoke out about the Method in an effort to "clear the air." Formerly in charge of acting with the Actors Studio, Lewis outlined the differences between the System and Method. Although he did not identify the Actors Studio by name, he implied that its students were taught to focus on emotion almost to the exclusion of the external factors of characterization, which Stanislavsky articulated in his second book, *Building a Character.* His criticism also included a perceived stress on the actors' personal emotional preoccupation over the characters'.[11] The controversy had gone public as discussions over what was truly Stanislavskian became frequent after the 1949 publication of *Building a Character;* at the same time, Strasberg took over direction of classes at the Actors Studio. The Studio also adopted the formal term "Method acting" in place of the Stanislavsky System. This change, according to Edwards, "was an unfortunate choice, for disparagers of the Actors Studio began calling it *The* Method, and the talk was about 'Method' and 'non-Method' actors."[12] As the popularity of the Studio grew, so did the criticism, and when *Creating a Role* was published in 1961, validating Adler's advocacy of physical actions, she and her then husband Clurman must have felt vindicated. From then on, their criticism of Strasberg and the Method would be vocal and virtually nonstop. When former Group members spoke out against the Method, Stanislavsky's name was regularly invoked as the standard from which Strasberg deviated. Of the Method, Clurman wrote: "[I]t becomes a distortion of art in general and of Stanislavsky's teaching in particular."[13] Common complaints centered on the cult like nature of the Studio and training, which, to some, resembled psychotherapy.

Stories circulated that aspiring Method actors were suffering nervous breakdowns at the hands of the demon Strasberg, who perversely exorcised them of their deepest fears with private moment and emotion memory exercises. Such was the mystique, not the truth, surrounding the Method. Of affective memory, criticism also focused on the amount of attention given to one technique that Stanislavsky recommended to be used in conjunction with the given circumstances of the text. This, along with what many in actor training schools perceived to be the exclusion of the actor's basics—physical work and vocal development—set Strasberg at odds with his contemporaries, especially Adler and Meisner. Even after Strasberg's death, Adler could not resist a final parting shot. According to Elia Kazan, the morning after Strasberg died, Adler came to class and announced: "It will take a hundred years before the harm that man [Strasberg] has done to the art of acting can be corrected."[14] During his lifetime, Strasberg chose to fight back only occasionally, opting instead to continue to train actors.

Much of the anger from former Group members during the mid-1960s emerged from professional and personality conflicts. Meisner, for instance, believed Strasberg played the role of guru and received credit for training actors he did not, in fact, train. Interviewer Stephen Harvey determined that "Meisner has never wanted to play anybody's daddy but it still galls him that Strasberg got so much credit for the achievements of so many of his own theatrical progeny." For Meisner, Strasberg was "both wrong headed and prone to seducing Meisner's own prize pupils to change allegiances."[15]

Recent scholarship focuses on perceived problems with the Method without being motivated by the personal rivalries associated with the Group Theatre. Brustein, complaining that the Method created many more movie stars than theatre artists, has forgotten the thousands of actors who have simply made a living on both the stage and screen, thanks to their training at the Actors Studio. The Method also tends to be associated primarily with realism, but few modern directors would argue against the importance of a psychological approach to character or the value of emotional memories as preparation for the performance of classical tragedies of the Greeks or Shakespeare.

Harrop and Hornby lobby very hard in their respective books for physical actions over emotional memory, each trying to sell American actors on the usefulness of Stanislavsky's later work. For Harrop, every acting problem can be approached through physical actions. He states:

"Fundamental to all creativity is the concept that every act of creation starts from some kind of impulse. The impulse may be an idea . . . image . . . or an actor's response to a play text," and adds that it is "here that a focus upon a physical process of response to text helps the actor to accept and go with the initial impulse and be open to all possibilities."[16] Hornby, in particular, is intent on "unshackling" American actors from the so-called vicious imprisonment of Method acting, which he says is "entrenched today at American acting conservatories and university theatre departments with few exceptions."[17] Yet outside of the Actors Studio, not even a handful of universities or conservatories teach Strasberg's Method. Method actors have, for quite some time, been the "exceptions," not the rule, in very diversified American university training programs. More important, however, blaming Lee Strasberg for the ills of American acting ignores his important contributions to the American theatre.

What seems to irritate the Method's opponents is its tenacity. Despite attempts to bury it, the Method is still being taught. In fact, the Actors Studio is experiencing an unprecedented revival outside of the universities as of late.[18] Perhaps that is part of the basis for complaint. Like so many movements in theatre, now come and gone, the Method was marked for extinction long ago. But it has endured, because it achieves results. Strasberg and the Method have become scapegoats for those believing they need to regain what was apparently lost during Strasberg's appropriation of the System. In truth, the Method was and is only one approach in many derived from Stanislavsky.

Where the Method diverges from the System, the shift can be attributed not to Strasberg but Euvgeny Vakhtangov. Theatre historian Marvin Carlson writes that "Strasberg, in charge of actor training for the Group, had several early speeches of Stanislavsky to his students translated, along with Vakhtangov's 'Preparing for the Role,' which became a central document for Strasberg."[19] Genealogy can be traced from Strasberg to Vakhtangov. Vakhtangov said: "It is essential to live your own temperament on the stage and not the supposed temperament of the character. You must proceed from yourself and not from a conceived image."[20] This statement, as we shall see, greatly influenced Strasberg.

When Stanislavsky published *An Actor Prepares* in 1936, Strasberg must have felt that Stanislavsky, especially in light of the differences he had with Adler, had validated his ideas. But on one key point, Strasberg preferred Vakhtangov's approach. Stanislavsky devised the "magic if" as a means for actors to place themselves within the given circumstances of the text. Actors create the "magic if" by asking themselves, "What would I do if I were my character in this situation?" In *An Actor Prepares*, to illustrate this point, Stanislavsky, speaking through the character of the acting teacher Tortsov, describes a situation where a madman is behind a door. The actor, Tortsov recommends, should not attempt to convince himself that a madman actually exists behind the door but instead should ask himself what the character would do if there were.

Strasberg modified Stanislavsky's "magic if" in favor of Vakhtangov's reformulated term, justification. Vakhtangov developed a different set of questions surrounding the "if." He asked: *How do I motivate myself or what would have to motivate me to behave as the character behaves?* Where Stanislavsky incorporated the characters' given circumstances to help actors involve themselves in the life of the play, Vakhtangov's method involved actors' individual thought processes. Based on the premise that actors must *justify* their presence on stage, they can draw on experiences outside of a play's given circumstances. For example: If an actor is portraying Hamlet and the circumstances do not enable him to loathe Claudius in the appropriate way, he may draw on his own personal anger toward the actor playing Claudius, if such anger exists. If the actor must demonstrate great affection for another character but such feelings do not arise out of the playing of the scene, the performer may *substitute* the face of someone he does love onto the other actor. Scholar Mel Gordon writes: "The strength of the actor's fantasy or justification, no matter how ludicrous or unrelated to the given direction, could lead the actor into a more convincing and concrete sense of reality."[21]

Strasberg articulated his understanding of the distinction. The Stanislavsky formulation of the "magic if," when applied to Shakespeare's Juliet, would go like this: "'Here is a girl who falls in love. I have been in love. When I am in love, what do I do?' Vakhtangov rephrased the approach. He didn't say, 'If I were so and so, what would I do?' He said, 'If I am playing Juliet, and I have to fall in love overnight, what would I, the actor, have to do to create for myself belief in this kind of event?" (*SS* 308) Like Vakhtangov, Strasberg stressed going outside of the play into the realm of personal feelings and experience. Coincidentally, both Meisner and Adler also encouraged actors to venture beyond the text, if necessary, in order to justify actions. Yet both Hornby and Harrop attribute the technique solely to Strasberg.[22]

Where affective memory is concerned, only Stanislavsky, Vakhtangov, and Strasberg could be considered advocates. Strasberg said, "Vakhtangov stressed the idea of affective memory as the central expression with which the actor works for high moments on the stage, shock moments. For those, the affective memory is the only thing I know that will work."[23] In Vakhtangov's sixth lecture, he did indeed discuss the use of emotions on-stage, which he referred to as "remembered emotions." Vakhtangov found that these memories, drawn from the performers' emotional past, could be carefully used to accommodate the specific needs for a production. If a character must react to the death of another character, the actor may choose to re-create the memory of a childhood event where the actor's life was threatened; a more recent memory, such as the death of a friend or family member, could also be used. The memory event need not directly parallel the event onstage but should stimulate an analogous feeling, which, in turn, would provide the necessary emotion the role or the situation called for.

Stanislavsky devoted an entire chapter of *An Actor Prepares* to emotion memory. In it he discusses how emotion memory can bring back feelings already experienced. Tortsov asks: "What do you feel either spiritually or physically when you recall the tragic death of an intimate friend?" He answers: "That type of memory which makes you relive the sensations you once felt when seeing Moskvin act or when your friend died is what we call *emotion memory*. Just as your visual memory can reconstruct an inner image of some forgotten thing, place, or person, your emotion memory can bring back feelings you have already experienced" (*AP* 159). Stanislavsky goes on to say that "Time is a splendid filter for our remembered feelings—besides it is a great artist. It not only purifies, it also transmutes even painfully realistic emotions into poetry" (*AP* 163). He realized the importance of emotion memories in his early work and stressed that the actor "should be completely devoted to them [repeated feelings], because they are the only means by which you can, to any degree, influence inspiration" (*AP* 163). Stanislavsky reminds the actor:

An artist does not build his role out of the first thing at hand. He chooses very carefully from among his memories and culls out of his living experiences the ones that are most enticing. He weaves the soul of the person he is to portray out of emotions that were dearer to him than his everyday sensations. Can you imagine a more fertile field for inspiration? An artist takes the best that is in him and carries it over on the stage. [*AP* 166]

The emotion derived from these memories would be very real, and Stanislavsky warned that actors should never lose control: "Never lose yourself on the stage. Always act in your own person, as an artist. You can never get away from yourself. The moment you lose yourself on the stage marks the departure from truly living your part and the beginning of exaggerated false acting" (*AP* 167). In one of several misinterpretations, Hornby argues that Stanislavsky never advocated the actors' use of real feelings or honest emotion in playing a role, citing Stanislavsky's "warnings" as the basis for this theory. Hornby quotes Stanislavsky: "When you are choosing some bit of action, leave feeling and spiritual content alone" (*AP* 38). The chapter that Hornby is quoting from is entitled "Action," not "Emotion Memory," and Stanislavsky is discussing the *abuse* of emotions on stage. Just prior to the words Hornby quotes, Stanislavsky writes: "On the stage there cannot be, under any circumstances, action which is directed immediately at the arousing of a feeling for its own sake" (*AP* 38). Stanislavsky is hardly suggesting that real feelings be avoided; rather, he guards against their misuse. In the chapter "Emotion Memory" he writes: "From the very moment the actor feels that charge take place in him [through an emotional memory] he becomes an active principle in the life of the play—real human beings are born in him" (*AP* 178).

For Stanislavsky, the one-to-one relationship between actor and character means feeling what the character feels: "The actor may feel the situation of the person in the part so keenly and respond to it so actively that he actually puts himself in the place of that person" (*AP* 178). On this point, Stanislavsky and Strasberg part theoretical company. Strasberg made it very clear that when emotion memories are employed, actors should *not* experience "literal" emotions onstage: "Vakhtangov said, 'Remembered emotion not literal emotion.'" For Strasberg, the "basic idea of affective memory is not emotional recall but that the actor's emotion on the stage should never be really real. It always should be only remembered emotion. An emotion that happens right now, spontaneously, is out of control." Instead, "Remembered emotion is something that the actor can create and repeat, [and] without that, the thing is hectic."[24] For Strasberg, actors' emotions are strong and deeply felt but ultimately useless unless achieved consistently and controllably. The process by which real emotion is deemphasized, Strasberg says, is by not focusing on the recalled experience directly but by remembering the sensory conditions that surrounded the event: "You do not start to remember the emotion, you start to remember the place, the taste of something, the touch of something, the sight of something, the sound of something, and you remember that as simply and as clearly as you can. You touch the things in your mind but with your senses alive."[25] Nevertheless, Strasberg and Stanislavsky are in agreement regarding the origin of emotion memories.

For Strasberg, emotions have a conditioning factor; the key is in finding the trigger. Stanislavsky, too, discovered that actors could arouse or evoke certain emotions with the proper inducement. Stanislavsky, biographer Jean Benedetti writes, believed "that all memories of past experiences are recorded by the nervous system" and may be evoked by an appropriate stimulus (*SB* 175). These memories lie hidden in the subconscious and need to be coaxed to the surface. Hornby, however, seeks to separate Stanislavsky from Strasberg regarding the basis of emotion memories. Citing psychologist Théodule Ribot as the source of Stanislavsky's ideas on emotion memory, Hornby attempts to show that the stimulus for affective memories did not "bring back individual emotional responses but a lifetime of them."[26] Benedetti points out that for Ribot, "a touch, a sound, a smell, may enable a patient to relive not just one experience but a grouping of similar experiences which merge to create a single emotional state" (*SB* 175). Hornby concludes that, unlike Strasberg, who advocated the use of individual events, Stanislavsky's approach to emotion memory "relies on the actor's past emotional life *as a whole* rather than the recall of specific instances" (Hornby's emphasis).[27] Conspicuously absent from Hornby's argument is Stanislavsky's corroboration of Ribot's "lifetime" of responses or favoring of collective emotional responses over individual memories. Moreover, every example regarding emotion memory in *An Actor Prepares* quite obviously illustrates the separate individual emotions engendered by the accompanying memory. Hence, emotion memory or affective memory is relatively consistent in the thinking of both Strasberg and Stanislavsky. However, in the case of "private moment," Strasberg's version of Stanislavsky's "public solitude," the techniques are different; the result, nonetheless, is the same.

Stanislavsky believed that it was necessary for actors to feel the privacy of their own world in a public place. As a result, he developed an exercise called public solitude. The concept is an elaboration of the circle of concentration exercise that trains actors to become aware of their surroundings in an imagined, expanding circle of light. Public solitude encourages actors to create an image of an environment inside of the "circle," which actors then react to. Reactions vary depending on the particulars of each imagined environment. The end result is the elimination of the actors' self-consciousness on the stage.

Strasberg found that the self-consciousness actors' feel in performance could not be duplicated in a rehearsal situation. Therefore, actors who are involved in deeply personal aspects of their lives in a classroom exploration exercise are creating a real audience where one did not exist. By "acting out" a private moment, actors lost their self-consciousness by displaying private behavior in front of other acting students and the teacher. It was essential that the exercise not be *performed* for the benefit of those observing. The private nature of the experience meant being one's self—that is, indulging in behavior that typically occurred behind the closed doors of an actor's home.

Private moment can be examined in the following example: An actor who privately plucked strands of hair out of her scalp and chewed on them while alone would be expected to replicate that behavior in a private moment. An actor who was grossly overweight and exceedingly self-conscious about it might decide to remove his shirt in front of the class. These actors must not, however, think of this exercise as one that should require courage. Instead, they must block out all perceptions of the others, act freely and without self-consciousness, as if no one else were present. Strasberg said: "We found that many people who were normally inhibited in expression had wonderfully vivid expressions in private moments [and] with many people we found that this opened up whole new areas of expression."[28] As with affective memory, it was the actual practice with the private moment technique that inflamed the passions of Method detractors. In theory, then, the Method *is* "early Stanislavsky."

Although Strasberg accused Stanislavsky of "going back on himself" after Adler returned from Paris, Strasberg soon realized that the Method was *his* version of the System: "By saying that the Group Theatre used an adaptation of the Stanislavsky Method, we mean that we emphasized elements that he had not emphasized and disregarded elements which he might have considered of greater importance."[29] Meisner, too, seemed certain that his teaching was anything but pure Stanislavsky. Meisner said: "We are Americans. We are not nineteenth century Russians. We create from ourselves and from our world. The creative teacher in America finds his own style, that is, to say his own method as indeed every artist must."[30] Even Adler, who believed that she toed the Stanislavskian line, may not have been teaching what she believed was pure Stanislavsky.

Like Stanislavsky, Adler focused on imagination, circumstances, physical actions, and character. Because she studied with Stanislavsky for several weeks in Paris in 1934 (sources say it was anywhere from four to seven), she believed that she bore the mantle of Stanislavsky's System on American soil. When asked in 1964 if she consciously adhered to what she believed to be the teaching of Stanislavsky or whether she adapted his methods, Adler said: "Although exercises may change in detail and the ideas may vary, the creative key remains the same—to experience the action in the circumstances. It is the foundation of the Stanislavskian System. It is the key that must remain the same to those who are followers and teachers of the system."[31] Adler traveled to meet Stanislavsky in 1934 because she was dissatisfied with the emotion-centered work of Strasberg. At the time, Stanislavsky was in the hospital recovering from an illness. According to Benedetti, Stanislavsky felt Adler was emotionally unstable: "Stanislavski found himself confronted with a woman whom he described as being in a state of panic clutching at him and begging him for help" (*SB* 309). Benedetti then adds that Adler remained for five weeks studying with Stanislavsky and communicating in French. French, of course, was a second language for each of them, so Adler employed a third party—a secretary—to take down Stanislavsky's statements verbatim. One might consider how difficult it would be to communicate in this fashion. It is possible that important meanings were lost in the process. Nevertheless, Adler was very specific in her teaching and writing regarding the content of these meetings.

According to Adler, Stanislavsky told her that he was now (in 1934) building a performance from physical action and given circumstances rather than emotion memory. It has been theorized that Stanislavsky may have downplayed the role of emotion memory because he may have felt that Adler was on the verge of a breakdown; that he, in effect, told her what she wanted to hear. Benedetti attempts to dispel the substance of this theory: "The evidence is against this. What Stanislavski told Stella Adler was exactly what he had been telling his own actors at home [in Russia]" (SB 309). But what if what Stanislavsky was "telling his own actors" was not developed out of his own artistry? What if the method of physical action, influenced by the conditions of Soviet socialism at the time, was devised to conform to the tenets of Stalinist-materialist Marxism?

Theatre scholar Sharon Carnicke advances an argument that suggests that Stanislavsky's creativity in the mid-1930s was sharply curtailed in order to comply with the current Stalinist party line. Carnicke writes: "In 1934, four years before Stanislavsky's death, all writers were united into a single union and were forced to adopt a single style. Socialist Realism was intended to make the arts widely accessible to a largely under educated populace and to depict an idealized reality that viewed the establishment of communism as the logical and teleological goal of history." For Stanislavsky, adds Carnicke, this meant that "more experimental ideas were stifled away; any spiritual and psychological techniques that challenged Marxist materialism were either downplayed or suppressed; his early realism and his Method of Physical Actions were exalted." Carnicke shows how "Russian dialectical materialism rejected all schools of psychology in favor of behaviorism, which seeks physical causes for mental phenomena." [32] More important, Carnicke discusses the censorship of terminology in the letters by Stanislavsky's longtime editor and friend Lyubov Gurevich. Here Gurevich appears to warn Stanislavsky, as early as 1929, that terms such as "affective" memory do not conform to the tenets of behaviorist psychology. Consequently, if Stanislavsky was *forced* to move away from ideas such as affective memory to advocate a method of physical action, then Stella Adler may have received Stalinist propaganda designed to conform with the party line.

The method of physical action, according to theatre scholar Joseph Roach, operates on the principle that all physical action is psychophysical and "rests on the now familiar principle that every thought and feeling is connected to a physical action." Roach concludes, as do many scholars, that "Stanislavski regarded the method of physical actions as the culmination of his life's work."[33] However, nowhere does Stanislavsky recommend that the method of physical actions transcend or replace affective memory. This idea is merely assumed by scholars and practitioners who now advocate an "outside in" approach rather than the reverse that is associated with emotional memory. The System, as exemplified by *An Actor Prepares*, *Building a Character*, and *Creating a Role*, was meant to be a single work; Stanislavsky intended all the books to be read as a whole. Therefore, a better question might inquire whether the exclusion of one of the three books would invalidate a bona fide American version of the System. When asked if she supported the use of emotion memories, Adler responded: "In teaching, I do not require a student ever to go to the emotion itself or ask the student to use emotion as a source" and concluded that the use of emotions as a teaching aid is "unhealthy."[34] If Adler carried the banner for Stanislavsky in America and affective memory is an integral component of the System, then the "creative key" that she calls the "foundation" of the Stanislavsky System is dangerously weak at the corners.

"Selling Stanislavsky" and denigrating Strasberg became the tactics through which many hoped to achieve success in the teaching of acting. Perhaps such criticism is to be expected in America, where Stanislavsky's ideas have taken on new renditions and the competition between acting studios has set former colleagues at odds with each other. But the reaction to Strasberg's teaching cannot be attributed to healthy competition; instead, the attacks resemble a modern day witchhunt.

Today, after the deaths of Stanislavsky's most important American disciples, one might imagine that past differences would be forgotten and an atmosphere of harmony would prevail, much as what transpired at Moscow Art Theatre's centennial conference. The opposite has occurred. Even the Actors Studio, which Strasberg made famous, has sought to distance itself from its most important teacher.[35] Yet attacks on the Method are unfair representations both of the relationship of the Method to Stanislavsky's System and of Strasberg's contribution to the American theatre. Exercises in emotion memories remain useful in culling out performances of great depth, and they often can solve acting problems where other approaches fail. To be sure, many actors, directors, and teachers of acting believe they know much more about psychology than they actually do—certainly enough to be accused of practicing psychotherapy without a license. Today practitioners often fear this tendency in themselves, and so the Method is linked to excesses and self-indulgence. Yet despite the fact that we are emotional creatures, many continue to deny this sensibility and perceive individual investment as a weakness in performance training. What do we have if not our own individual selves and experiences as the source of our artistry and creative spirit? Stanislavsky recognized this when he wrote: "An artist takes the best that is in him and carries it over on the stage. The form will vary according to the necessities of the play, but the human emotions of the artist will remain alive, and they cannot be replaced by anything else" (*AP* 166). For him, "Always and forever, when you are on the stage, you must play yourself" (*AP* 167). The Method can, at the very least, contribute to the actor's overall technique.

NOTES

1. Robert Brustein, "The Heritage of MAT," *The New Republic* 217.6–7 (August 11, 1997): 29.
2. Ibid., 30.
3. Richard Hornby, *The End of Acting: A Radical View* (New York: Applause, 1992), 5, 9. See also, John Harrop, *Acting* (London: Routledge, 1992).
4. Christine Edwards, *The Stanislavski Heritage: Its Contribution to the American and Russian Theatre* (New York: New York University Press, 1965), 271.
5. Harrop, *Acting*, 38.
6. Ronald A. Willis, "American Laboratory Theatre," *TDR* 9.1 (Fall 1964): 115.
7. Foster Hirsch, *A Method to Their Madness: A History of the Actors Studio* (New York: Norton, 1984), 72.

8. Wendy Smith, *Real Life Drama: The Group Theatre and America* (New York: Alfred A. Knopf, 1990), 424–25.

9. See chapter 19 in this volume for a list of Strasberg's students.

10. Marianne Conroy, "Acting Out: Method Acting, The National Culture, and the Middlebrow Disposition in Cold War America," *Criticism: A Quarterly for Literature and the Arts* 35.2 (Spring 1993): 247.

11. Robert Lewis, "Method—or Madness," *New York Times,* June 23, 1957, sec. 2, p. 1.

12. Edwards, *Stanislavsky Heritage,* 261.

13. Harold Clurman, "There's a Method in British Acting," *New York Times Magazine* (January 1964): 62.

14. Elia Kazan, *A Life* (New York: Alfred A. Knopf, 1988), 143.

15. Stephen Harvey, "Another Man's Method," *American Film* 8.7 (1983): 69.

16. Harrop, *Acting,* 55, 56. Harrop's assessment, however, is incorrect. Strasberg discusses the notion of impulse extensively in various books and in his teaching.

17. Hornby, *End of Acting,* 5.

18. See Foster Hirsh, "The Actors Studio at 50," for testimonials by Method actors, *American Theatre* 15.1 (January 1998): 24–29. Studio director Arthur Penn said, "The program has been successful beyond anyone's expectations—we have thousands of applications for each class size of about 90" (28).

19. Marvin Carlson, *Theories of the Theatre* (Ithaca, NY: Cornell University Press, 1984), 377.

20. [Euvgeny] Vakhtangov, "Preparing for the Role," *Acting: A Handbook of the Stanislavski Method,* Toby Cole, ed., B. E. Zakhara, tr. (New York: Crown Trade, 1955), 120.

21. Mel Gordon, *The Stanislavsky Technique* (New York: Applause, 1987), 83.

22. Hornby, *End of Acting,* 176; Harrop, *Acting,* 40–41.

23. Strasberg, interview by Schechner and Hoffman, 132.

24. Ibid.

25. Ibid., 132–33.

26. Hornby, *End of Acting,* 181.

27. Ibid.

28. Strasberg, interview by Schechner and Hoffman, 125.

29. Strasberg's letter to Christine Edwards (April 1, 1960), in *Stanislavski Heritage,* 261.

30. Sanford Meisner, "The Reality of Doing," *TDR* 9.1 (Fall 1964): 140.

31. Stella Adler, "The Reality of Doing," *TDR* 9.1 (Fall 1964): 141.

32. Sharon M. Carnicke, "Stanislavsky: Uncensored and Unabridged," *TDR* 37.1 (Spring 1993): 24, 26.

33. Joseph R. Roach, *The Player's Passion: Studies in the Science of Acting* (Ann Arbor: University of Michigan Press, 1993), 213.

34.   Adler, "The Reality of Doing," 143.

35.   Studio director Arthur Penn advocates a "kinder and gentler approach." Penn adds with characteristic directness and willingness to distance himself from America's most renowned acting teacher: "I am not an undivided devotee to Strasberg." In Hirsch, "The Actors Studio at 50," 28.

CHAPTER THREE

THE REALITY OF DOING

Real Speech Acts in the Theatre

David Z. Saltz

Theatre scholar Bernard Beckerman defines theatre as a show of "illusion" that displays "people pretending to do something. Whatever they do is a representation of some other action."[1] This definition makes explicit a view that many theatre and performance theorists take for granted. In particular, the dichotomy between stage action and "real" action is integral to semiotic theories of theatre, according to which stage action stands to real action as a signifier to a signified. As theatre semiotician Keir Elam writes: "What converts objects, people and action into signs on stage . . . is the removal of the performance from praxis. This may seem self-evident and commonplace, but upon this simple act of severance rests the whole power of theatrical semiosis, indeed its very existence."[2]

Stanislavsky's System constitutes a radical challenge to the commonsense conception of acting as feigning and the clear-cut opposition between acting and reality that underlies it. Toward the beginning of *An Actor Prepares*, Stanislavsky famously rejects the "representational" actor in favor of the "organic" actor who "becomes" the character and "lives" the role. He denounces pretense and imitation on the stage, calling upon actors to perform the character's actions "truly." "To play truly" according to Stanislavsky, "means to be right, logical, coherent, to think, strive, feel and act in unison with your role" (*AP* 14).

The founders of the American Method disagreed on many key points, especially concerning the role of emotion in acting, but all echo Stanislavsky's commitment to truthful action. According to Lee Strasberg, the actor "must somehow be able to convince himself of the rightness of what he is doing in order to do things fully on the stage."[3] Method instructors such as Stella Adler and Sanford Meisner, influenced by the Method of Physical Action developed by Stanislavsky during the final phase of his career, lay even greater stress on the need for actors to perform real actions on stage. Meisner asserts emphatically: "The foundation of acting is the reality of doing" (*MA* 16).

From a semiotic perspective, the Stanislavskian passion for truthfulness in acting seems unscientific and naïve, a Romantic desire to transcend the ineluctably conventional nature of representation. The authenticity that the Method actor seeks can never be more than a mimetic *representation* of authenticity. Indeed, in trying to deny theatre's status as sign system, Method performances are less authentic, less truthful, than performances that emphasize the disjuncture between actor and role, signifier and signified.

Within the postmodern climate of skepticism, even semiotics, with its confidence in scientific objectivity, has come to seem increasingly quaint. How can one begin to take Stanislavsky's ideal of "organic truth" seriously in an age of Baudrillardian simulacra? Ironically, however, by loosening the grip of the semiotic paradigm, postmodernist skepticism may prepare us to accept Stanislavsky's apparently irrational attempt to blur the division between reality and representation.

The question that I will be examining here is this: Is it possible, even in principle, to realize Stanislavsky's goal of real action onstage? This question cuts to the Method's most basic premise. If the semiotic view is correct, and dramatic performance is by definition merely the representation of action, then the Method is founded on a logical fallacy or a delusion. Notice that this question is distinct from that of whether the Method's goals are ideologically or aesthetically desirable. One might share Stanislavsky's commitment to real action onstage while rejecting other elements of his System, such as its humanistic conception of character or its Aristotelian assumptions about dramatic structure and aesthetic unity. Indeed, one might accept that real action is possible onstage yet believe it should be avoided at all costs.

The first challenge is to define the question more precisely. The most rigorous and substantial attempts to frame the question have focused specifically on the status of speech acts onstage, employing the theory of speech acts first set forth by the British philosopher J. L. Austin and further developed by the American philosopher John Searle.[4] The virtually unanimous conclusion of speech act theorists, which has been eagerly endorsed by semioticians, is that actors do not and cannot actually perform their characters' speech acts.[5] Actors, regardless of their training or their artistic objectives, merely *pretend* to do so. This conclusion, if true, would render the Stanislavsky System quixotic at its very core. I will attempt to show, however, that this conclusion is mistaken. It is entirely possible— though far from inevitable—for the speech acts of an actor as a character to fulfill all the requirements set forth by speech act theory. In other words, actors really can perform their characters' speech acts onstage. Perhaps most significantly, defining a precise criterion for "real action" onstage will put us in a position to justify Stanislavsky's repeated insistence that the ideal of real action onstage does not entail the aesthetics of realism. "What does it really mean to be truthful on the stage?," Stanislavsky asks. "Does it mean that you conduct yourself as you do in ordinary life? Not at all. Truthfulness in those terms would be sheer triviality."[6]

ACTING AND PRETENSE

To begin, we must pull into focus the intuition that an actor's actions onstage are not real. After all, at a basic level, actors seem to perform many of their characters' actions in a perfectly straightforward way. When the character raises an arm, the actor really raises an arm. Of course, in certain cases, it seems equally obvious that the actor is not actually doing what the character is depicted as doing. Even Stanislavsky would not demand that an actor playing Juliet kill herself when the character commits suicide.

Theatre critic David Cole properly warns against confusing "the distinction between what is theatre and what is not with the distinction between what is feigned and what is actually done." Between the latter two alternatives, he observes,

> an actor clearly retains some leeway. He may drink the wine the script calls for or drink colored water, feign a slap or deliver it, brush his partner's lips or kiss her passionately on the mouth. But the extent to which the drinking, the slap, or the kiss is *theatre* in no way depends upon the extent to which it is feigned. . . . Two stagehands fooling with prop swords is not theatre, though it is feigning. Hotspur's and Hal's duel is theatre, though the actors were to bare their swords' points. [emphasis in original][7]

If this analysis is correct, what is all the fuss about? What is the difficulty with the controversial project of acting in unison with a character?

ILLOCUTIONARY ACTIONS IN THE THEATRE

When an actor in priest's robes says to a pair of actors in a wedding gown and a tuxedo, "I hereby pronounce you man and wife," the actor really does commit the act of saying the words, just as a real priest would during a real marriage ceremony. But the priest, in saying those words, performs a real marriage. The actor playing the priest does not. If the two actors playing the couple were single when the play began, they would still be single when it ended.

To use the terminology of speech act theory, the actor's act would lack the *illocutionary force* of the priest's act. The illocutionary force of a speech act is the interpersonal action that a person carries out *in the very act of making an utterance.* For example, in the appropriate context, a judge who declares "I sentence you to ten years hard labor" is performing the illocutionary act of *sentencing a prisoner;* a referee who shouts "ready, set, go!" is *starting a race;* and someone who utters the words "please pass the salt" is *making a request.* Austin emphasizes the difference between the illocutionary force of an act and its "perlocutionary effect." For example, the perlocutionary effect of a request for salt might be that the person actually ends up with some salt. But it is also possible that the request will be denied, and a request denied is no less a request than one granted. The request has precisely the same illocutionary force in either case. The utterance "please pass the salt" would lack illocutionary force only if it were not taken seriously as a request at all, in which case the question of granting or denying it would not come up—as, for example, would be the case if I uttered the words "please pass the salt" in the course of reading this paragraph aloud during a lecture.

Speech act theory, which focuses on the performative nature of language, shares many concerns with Method acting. It may not be obvious, however, how the key terms of speech act theory map onto those of the Method. In particular, a Method actor might be tempted to equate Austin's notion of an illocution with Stanislavsky's notion of an objective, but these two concepts are not quite parallel. The illocution is *itself* an action. An *objective* is the point or goal of an action; in speech act terms, it is the speaker's *desired perlocution*. When I ask for salt, I am performing the act of requesting (the illocution), but my objective is not to make a request, it is to get the salt (the desired perlocution). A subtler error is to conflate the illocution with the speaker's *intention*. It is entirely possible for me to intend, for example, to compliment you and to end up inadvertently insulting you. What determines an utterance's illocutionary force is not the speaker's actual intention but the *listener's interpretation* of the speaker's intention—along with a variety of other factors, such as the speaker's authority to issue the speech act in the first place. Ultimately, the illocution is a social fact, not a psychological one. As Austin puts it, we do things *with* words. The action is not something that happens between the lines, or beneath them in a "subtext." The action *is* the utterance. Speech act theory, then, is much closer in spirit to Adler and Meisner's versions of the Method, which follow Stanislavsky's later approach in emphasizing interpersonal action, than it is to Strasberg's version, which emphasizes the actor's internal states.

Part of the reason that the actor playing a priest cannot really perform the illocutionary act of marrying the couple on stage is that he is not really a priest. Unlike an act such as "making a request," the act of "performing a marriage" can be performed successfully (or *felicitously*, to borrow Austin's term) only by someone with authority granted by formalized institutional conventions. If the actor's proclamation of marriage lacked force *only* because the actor was not a priest, marriage would simply be one of those actions, like Juliet's suicide, that actors do not carry out in practice but could in principle. A director might, after all, cast a priest to play a priest. But the problem here runs much deeper. Even if the actor were a real priest, the speech act would not result in a real marriage if it were performed in the course of a play.

This problem extends to all illocutionary acts, such as requesting, ordering, swearing, complimenting, threatening. If an actor makes a promise onstage, we do not hold the actor to the promise once the play ends. If one actor insults another in the course of a play, the second actor would be unlikely to hold it against the first the next morning. As Searle has observed, within a fictional context such as a play, the performance of a speech act invokes "horizontal conventions that . . . suspend the normal illocutionary commitments of the utterance."[8] This suspension of normal illocutionary commitments extends to all theatrical performances, from the most alienated Brechtian performance to the most impassioned Method one. The impact of this suspension of illocutionary commitments is so complete that it prevents an actor from successfully performing even simple assertions onstage. If I say the words "My hair is blond" during a dramatic performance and then during the curtain call remove a blond wig to reveal my jet-black hair, you would not accuse me having lied. The point of a real assertion is to commit the speaker to the truth of a proposition, and we typically do not hold actors responsible for the truth of any assertions they make during a play. This apparent inability to perform real illocutionary actions onstage affects virtually all of the actor's performance, not just special instances such as Juliet's suicide. Hence, in *How to Do Things with Words*, Austin famously excludes the actor's use of language from his analysis of performative utterances, acknowledging that

> a performative utterance will . . . be *in a peculiar way* hollow or void if said by an actor on the stage, or if introduced in a poem, or spoken in soliloquy. This applies in a similar manner to any and every utterance—a sea change in special circumstances. Language in such circumstances is in special ways—intelligibly—used not seriously, but in ways *parasitic* upon its normal use. [emphasis in original][9]

SEARLE'S THEORY OF FICTIONAL DISCOURSE

Austin puts this special case to one side in order to develop an account of
the more standard cases, but Searle, after offering his own account of standard speech acts, has tried to tie up the loose ends. Searle considers the
status of actors' speech acts rather briefly as a special case of fictional discourse, and feels that they function in the same way that speech acts do in
a novel or a poem. The fictional frame in all these cases strips speech acts
of illocutionary force. In other words, in Searle's view speech acts onstage
lack illocutionary force *because they are fictional*, and, conversely, the suspension of illocutionary force is precisely what constitutes the fictionality
of a stage performance. Searle maintains that actors, like novelists, only
pretend to perform illocutionary acts. Specifically, the actors merely *make
the noises* that a person performing the speech act in real life would make.
They pretend to perform the illocutionary act by performing what Searle
calls the "utterance act."[10] Since Searle first published this proposal in
1974, it has enjoyed virtually universal—and uncritical—acceptance
among those who have considered this problem. By 1989, scholar Michael
Issacharoff could simply proclaim, as an established fact, that "the stage,
the area of fictional utterance, is a frame that disengages all speech acts."[11]

WHY SPEECH ACTS FAIL ONSTAGE

Let us consider a specific example of a speech act and see exactly where
it starts to run into trouble onstage. Imagine that one actor, call him
Tommy, asks another, Viola, to "Please give me a backrub." What is necessary for Tommy's words to constitute a real request for a backrub? According to Searle's version of speech act theory, the fundamental
requirement is simply that Tommy *intend* for his utterance to be a request
and that Viola recognize that intention. Thus, Tommy must intend for
Viola to believe that he will consider his utterance successful if she gives
him a backrub and (this part is very important) that she do so *because he
has made an utterance that has this objective.*[12] Of course, sometimes people
act insincerely. For example, Tommy may want an excuse to get angry at
Viola and so may ask for a backrub precisely because he knows she will

refuse. According to Searle, such an action would still have illocutionary force as a request, but, lacking the desire implied by the utterance, would violate the *sincerity condition*.

The actor playing Tommy might have a muscle spasm and crave a backrub, and so satisfy the sincerity condition. But the actor might also detest backrubs. In the vast majority of cases, the things characters ask for in a play are not things of intrinsic interest to the actors playing the parts. More deeply, what if the script dictates that Viola refuse Tommy's request, and this refusal triggers the main events of the play? The actor playing Tommy would then have very good reason for *not* wanting his request granted. Moreover, the actor playing Viola will be fully aware that Tommy would be upset—and surprised—if she were to grant his request and give him a backrub. How can the actor hope to convince her that his request is sincere?

Perhaps it does not matter if the actor satisfies the sincerity condition. Can an actor at least *really* commit insincere actions? Unfortunately, the way out is not so easy. For even insincere requests to have force, speakers must intend to mislead their listeners, suggesting they have a desire they do not. Imagine that the character was making an insincere request to trap Viola into refusing him. The trap would fail utterly if he let Viola know that he was insincere. For the actor playing Tommy to make a real request, even an insincere one, he must make the actor playing Viola believe that he really wants the backrub.

In addition to the sincerity condition, the speech act must meet a second condition before it can truly be said to have illocutionary force. If Viola gives Tommy the backrub, she must do so as a result of his request.[13] However, in a typical play, the script stipulates in advance which requests are granted and which are not. Hence theatrical performances seem to establish a deviant causal chain: The speaker makes a request, the listener grants it, but the first event does not cause the second. The utterance's force as a real act seems to break down at precisely this point.

IMPROVISED PERFORMANCE

The analysis of a request performed onstage has suggested that the act must overcome two obstacles before it can be said to have illocutionary force:

1. It must at least be plausible that the actor is sincerely trying to achieve the action's objective;
2. If the action is successful, it, and not the script, must cause that objective to be met.

The first of these conditions might be described as the Strasberg condition, since it focuses on the actor's internal state, while the second might be called the Meisner condition, focusing as it does on the interpersonal dimension of the speech act. Significantly, both of these obstacles arise because the performance has been scripted and rehearsed, and not, as Searle has suggested, because the events enacted are fictional. The fictional context of a stage performance does not in and of itself strip a performer's utterances of illocutionary force.

Imagine an improvisation in which an actor playing Polly the Police Officer orders another actor playing Barney the Bank Robber to drop his gun, which is actually an empty water pistol. Certainly there is a large dose of pretense here. One actor is pretending to be a police officer, the other a bank robber, and both are pretending that the water pistol is a loaded gun. Nevertheless, if the robber-actor drops the gun, he is not merely pretending to drop the gun but is really dropping it, and he is doing so because the police-actor is not pretending to issue an order but is really issuing the order. And if the robber-actor keeps the gun aimed at Polly, he is disobeying the order, and both actors will need to contend with that fact. The robber-actor's refusal further certifies that the action has illocutionary force; after all, only a real order can be refused.

To suggest that the police-actor is only *pretending* to issue an order would have little meaning here. This order is doing just what orders are supposed to do, according to speech act theory. The pretense is in the context, not in the action itself. One can assert truthfully and literally that the actor who is pretending to be Polly the Police Officer issues an order, making it clear that any commitments implied by the order attach to the actor only in her role as Polly. This assertion describes something done by a flesh-and-blood human being—the actor at a specific place and time in the real world—on the stage on which the actor is improvising during this performance. It is also true, but an entirely different assertion, to say that *the character issued an order.* This latter assertion is about the fiction represented and does not entail the existence of an event of any kind in the real world.

But does the actor playing Polly really have a reason to want the other actor to drop the gun? Why should she? The other actor is not really a threat. The actor must act not on the basis of her own personal needs and desires but on the fictional character's needs.

BORROWED INTENTIONS

It is not only during dramatic performance that one temporarily adopts another person's interests. The actor's situation is, in fact, analogous to that of an employee, or more closely, a player in a game.[14] Game players, like employees, adopt a set of borrowed intentions that govern their behavior only as long as they are in a specific role. The basketball player has no need to ponder deeper motives, and the chess player need bear no particular grudge against the opponent's king. In a game, however, the intentions adopted do not belong to another agent, even an institutional one, such as a company. Chess players do not play on behalf of anyone else or even of the "game of chess." They simply play according to the rules; the motivation is built into the game. Hence, we should distinguish borrowed intentions that derive from another person or an institution from those that derive from the rules of a game, which I will call *game intentions*.

What I am proposing is that actors can perform real and sincere actions onstage simply by accepting, as part of the convention of performance, a rule that they must work to achieve their character's objectives. Stanislavsky's great protégé Euvgeny Vakhtangov maintained that "the fundamental thing which an actor must learn is to wish, to wish by order, to wish whatever is given to the character."[15] The police-actor's reason to issue the order during the improvisation, then, could be just that she believes her character would have reason to do so within what Stanislavsky would call the improvisation's *given circumstances*. By defining the conventions of performance in this way, the actor will always have a reason to commit any action in any play, just as a basketball player has reason to get the ball into the assigned basket, or a chess player has reason to try to capture the other player's king. If the police-actor does not really try to get the robber-actor to drop the gun, she will be *throwing the game*.

Not surprisingly, proponents of improvisational theatre, such as Viola Spolin and Keith Johnstone, often stress the game-like nature of performance. Spolin, for example, insists that the only requisite skill for improvisation is a "willingness to play," and approvingly quotes sociologist Neva L. Boyd's assertion that "[p]laying a game is psychologically different in degree but not in kind from dramatic acting."[16]

BELIEF

Game intentions might provide a way for actors to perform speech acts such as requests or commands. These sorts of speech acts have what Searle calls *world-to-word direction of fit:* The point of the act is to make the world conform to the utterance, to alter the world in some way. For example, Polly's command to drop the gun will be satisfied if, as a result of making this utterance, Barney drops the gun. Actions such as assertions and predictions pose a more difficult problem. The point of these acts is to articulate a true fact about the world. For example, the assertion "I am Hamlet, Prince of Denmark" makes a claim about who I am—a claim that, as it happens, is manifestly false. Such speech acts do not merely imply an *intention* but a *belief.* How can an actor's belief be dictated by the rules of a game?

The mistake here may be to assume that people, onstage or off, can act felicitously and sincerely only on the basis of their own beliefs. A company's public relations officer and a president's press secretary are hired to make the best case they can for the positions held by the institutions or persons they represent. No deceit is involved here, unless the *institution* of the presidency is misleading the public as to *its* beliefs. The listeners are interacting with the representatives in order to ascertain the views of the institutions they represent, and not to discover the spokesperson's personal opinions. People in such roles who do cave in to an irrepressible desire to represent their own beliefs are dropping out of their roles. If they make an assertion that contradicts the official position of the institution and do not make it clear that they have stepped out of their official role, they are misrepresenting their institution.

An actor's personal beliefs might play a similar role in a theatrical performance. An actor, if asked, would unhesitatingly agree that most of the character's assertions are literally false. But this concession is beside the point. Assertions an actor makes refer to the beliefs and desires set forth for the character. Like a press secretary, actors may make real assertions that express the beliefs of the characters they represent, and may be *committed*, while functioning within their roles, to defending those assertions. The audience does not hold actors offstage to the assertions they make onstage precisely because they understand what those assertions refer to. There is no insincerity here; the nature of the game is up front and understood by all.[17]

One way of stating the implications of borrowed belief is to say that actors are committed to acting *as if* they held the implied belief. Hence the centrality of what Stanislavsky called the "magic if." "With this special quality of *if* . . . nobody obliges you to believe or not believe anything. Everything is clear, honest, and above-board" (*AP* 44). As poet and philosopher Paul Valéry once put it: "No skepticism is possible where the rules of a game are concerned, for the principle underlying them is an unshakable *truth*."[18]

SCRIPTED PERFORMANCE

If Polly's order to drop the gun appears in the middle of a script, what would be necessary for it to function as it does in improvisation? First, the actors would need to act from, and be understood to be acting from, borrowed beliefs, desires, and intentions. In other words, they would need sincerely to appropriate the interests and defend the beliefs that they believe their characters would have in the fictional situation. The deeper problem, however, is that contingency between illocutionary act and perlocutionary effect would need to be restored. Indeed, countless hours in basic scene-study classes are spent trying to achieve just this sense of contingency, getting actors to pay close attention to one another and subtly adjust their responses to keep them appropriate to the specific behavior of each other at each moment. Whether it occurs in an improvisation, a rehearsal, or a scripted performance, the ultimate test of whether the command is really functioning as a speech act is if it can be unsuccessful. Suppose the script calls for Barney to obey the command. If it is really the order that gets the actor playing Barney to drop the gun, and not the actor's obedience to the script, then if the actor playing Polly delivers the line in a way that renders it defective—for example, if the line sounds tentative one night because she has something caught in her throat—then Barney will not drop the gun. Such an approach involves an element of risk; it never completely rules out the possibility that Barney will shoot Polly. But the risk is not nearly as great as it may first appear, since the actors are playing with a stacked deck. The definition of the fictional context and the way the actions are performed can be manipulated in rehearsals, so that the speaker can determine just what is necessary to get the listener to drop the gun. If the order falls flat because the actor gets something caught in her throat, she can always clear her throat and try again.

I am positing a game model of dramatic action, wherein actors do not merely *imitate* actions as they would be performed offstage but really do commit illocutionary acts within the theatrical context. These acts function just like illocutionary acts in any other context, with one exception: Their conditions of satisfaction are determined with respect to borrowed intentional states, specifically game intentionality. Because they act from game intentionality, actors remain committed by their stage actions— promises, commands, assertions—only while they are acting within their stage roles, just as a Monopoly player is not committed to buying Boardwalk after the game ends.

REAL ACTION VERSUS REALISM

The conditions of satisfaction of an action onstage may not be the same as they are in life. A dramatic performance can establish constitutive rules that redefine the conditions of satisfaction of certain actions. For example, a rule could establish that touching someone with the point of a dagger counts as stabbing that person. If this rule is in effect, and one actor touches another with a dagger, even accidentally, the second actor would be obligated to acknowledge that action. The lack of any response might well be construed, both by fellow actors and audience, as a kind of cheating. In this example, to touch someone with a dagger is to *pretend* to stab that person in Searle's sense, that is, to perform part of the action of really stabbing someone. But it is also possible to set up more stylized conventions: For example, letting a hand clap count as stabbing. In either case, what are brute actions in real life become conventional actions in theatre.

Toward the beginning of this chapter, I acknowledged that actions like murder could not really be performed onstage. However, I am now in a better position to specify just what kind of actions actors commit in such cases. To say that the actor playing Othello *pretends* to murder the actor playing Desdemona would not be false, exactly, but neither would it tell us much, since it does not help us understand what the actor really *is* doing. I would prefer to say that the actor is (really) committing an action that *counts as* murder within the conventions of the play.

The transformation of physical into conventional causation can be seen clearly in a common situation onstage: When actors flick a light switch onstage, the switch rarely really controls the light; the lighting board operator turns on the light. However, the lighting board operator uses the actor's action as a cue. The actor is in control. The actor's flicking the switch does not physically cause the light to go on, as it would in real life, but *counts as* turning on the light. This action could be even further conventionalized by keeping the lighting on the whole time, obligating the actors onstage to act as if they could not see until the moment one of them flicks the switch. In this way, an action that offstage functions through what Searle calls brute force is redefined onstage as illocutionary action. Far from being *suspended* on stage as Searle suggests, illocutionary force is often *extended*.

Performances also can define purely theatrical illocutionary actions, without any clear real-life reference. For example, during one of the Cirque du Soleil's routines, the band plays a chord every time the clown René Bazinet takes a step. Initially this chord functions as a sound effect, like one that might accompany the walk of an animated cartoon character. Soon, however, Bazinet begins to play with the convention, casting mischievous glances toward the band, taking a series of rhythmic steps and then glancing back to it again. Bazinet's movements assume a uniquely theatrical, but perfectly real, illocutionary force. The game continues as Bazinet brings an audience member into the ring whose movements acquire a similar illocutionary efficacy.[19]

THE GAME MODEL

I began by asking to what extent it is possible for actors to really perform actions onstage. I have suggested that sometimes, as Searle has proposed, actors really commit brute-force actions and only pretend to commit illocutionary actions. But it is *possible* for actors to commit their character's actions at the illocutionary level by treating the conventions of the play like rules in a game. In this case, actors assume the illocutionary commitments of any acts they perform for the duration of the play, as those commitments are defined by the conventions of the play itself. The game model, I believe, describes what happens in free-form role-playing games, such as children often play, and in improvisational theatre. It becomes more problematic as an account of rehearsed and scripted performances.

Actor training in the Stanislavsky tradition is geared toward achieving the spontaneity of improvisation in the performance of scripted plays. The challenge for these techniques is first to find ways for the actors to move beyond the utterance act and find the illocutionary point of the dialogue they perform and then to balance the desire for spontaneity with the demand for control and repeatability. The game model proposed here suggests that the objective is, in fact, possible but also identifies the deep obstacles to obtaining that goal. It provides support for the intuition that performances sometimes, but only sometimes, achieve a kind of theatrical truthfulness—that sometimes something *real* is happening on stage. Furthermore, it provides a nonmimetic criterion for this sense of reality, and so a way of describing how even stylized performances, such as a Molière farce or Jerzy Grotowski's quasi-ritualistic productions, can be performed with conviction and sincerity, and often can be more truthful than a performance that reproduces details of the real world with the most painstaking precision.

The game model provides a philosophical foundation for the Method's most basic premise: that real action onstage is possible. I should stress, however, that the game model, if successful, merely gets us to the point where the Method's real work begins. In *An Actor Prepares*, Stanislavsky affirms the principle of acting "organically" in the first chapter and devotes the vast bulk of the book to helping the actor to make the kind of artistically and psychologically rich choices that make the game worth playing. Even within a purely Method context, acting *truthfully* is a necessary, but not a sufficient, condition for acting *well*.

The game model of acting suggests that the audience's position within the theatre event is sometimes more akin to that of spectators at a sporting event than to that of readers of a printed text. The "story" in this case would not be something communicated but something that happens; or better, it is a summary that the spectator might make of the events on the stage once the play has ended. Efforts to hunt for symbols, or to analyze narrative structure, might not get to the meat of a theatrical event: the real, and often illocutionary, actions that actors commit from moment to moment during the performance. For example, most of Harold Pinter's plays are extremely obscure, if not banal, when reduced to their plots, and yet when performed they yield a remarkable density of illocutionary significance.[20] Effective actors of Pinter's plays must be capable of endowing their actions with a richness of illocutionary implication and an intensity of illocutionary commitment.

In musical comedies, too, the story usually serves almost entirely as a pretext to create a vital theatrical event, though one of a different kind. When Oliver Twist comes to London in *Oliver!* the entire town bursts into an extended song and dance to greet him. The content communicated here probably could be summed up in a single sentence, such as "Oliver feels welcomed and at home for the first time in his life." Clearly, this content could be conveyed far more economically than through this lengthy song and dance. Still, much of the interest in this scene is the extravagant and inventive way that the director, choreographer, and performers expand on the initial premise. The rules of the game here are to use all of the performative resources that this genre of theatre provides to make "Oliver" (i.e., the actor in the Oliver role) feel welcome in "London" (i.e., the theatrical space that counts as London in the context of the performance game).

Theatrical texts written within game conventions such as those described here can be evaluated best in terms of their performative potential. Some plays, like some games, have rules that are more likely to put their players in interesting situations than others, and those are the ones worth playing and watching. Moreover, the rules of tennis will give rise to a very different experience than those of chess or those of *Hamlet*. Still, good actors can be exciting to watch for the same reasons good tennis players are: They push their game to its limits.

One might accuse such actors of indulging in a kind of ludic formalism. The musical comedy example is certainly vulnerable to such a charge. However, once we recognize the possibility of real action within a game structure, we can appreciate more fully the potential power of performance as a transgressive or transformative act. For example, in Split Britches and Bloolips' production of *Belle Reprieve*, the lesbian performer Peggy Shaw sings Muddy Waters's song "I'm a Man," with two gay male performers, Precious Pearl and Bette Bourne, as her backup singers.[21] All three performers are playing the stereotypical role of "a Man," specifically as modeled on Brando's performance of Stanley Kowalski in the film version of *A Streetcar Named Desire*. But Bette Bourne, with his heavy makeup, green windbreaker, and cap, is visibly alienated from the role, while Peggy Shaw, as a "butch" lesbian, embodies it with absolute authority. This is a fact about the performance, and not merely a fact about the fictional world that the performance represents. It is something that the performance *manifests*. Recent critics tend to associate Stanislavsky's conception of "organic" acting with dramatic realism and regard it as a strategy to naturalize hegemonic power structures. As we have seen, however, the notion of acting "truly" is not tied to realism. On the contrary, organic acting—acting that is committed to the real performance of illocutionary actions—transforms whatever social reality the actors choose to portray into a living reality, at least for the duration of the performance event. The notion of organic acting, then, has profoundly anti-essentialist implications. Theoretical models that drive a wedge between performance and reality, such as semiotics and Searle's theory about the status of speech acts in the theatre, suppress the radically transformative potential of theatrical performance. They deny theatre its ability to explore and expose—and not merely to assert or signify—the nature of the games that structure our own lives and to demonstrate ways we might change the rules.[22]

NOTES

1. Bernard Beckerman, *Theatrical Presentation* (New York: Routledge, 1990), 15.
2. Keir Elam, "Language in the Theater," *Sub-Stance* 18/19 (1977): 144.
3. Lee Strasberg, "The Actor and Himself," *Actors on Acting*, T. Cole and H. Chinoy, eds. (New York: Three Rivers Press, 1947, 1970), 625.
4. J. L. Austin, *How to Do Things with Words*, 2nd ed. (Cambridge, MA: Harvard University Press, 1962); and John Searle, *Speech Acts* (New York: Cambridge University Press, 1969), *Expression and Meaning* (New York: Cambridge University Press, 1979), and *Intentionality* (New York: Cambridge University Press, 1983).
5. See Umberto Eco, "Semiotics of Theatrical Performance," *TDR* 21 (1977): 115; Richard M. Gale, "The Fictive Use of Language," *Philosophy* 46 (1971): 324–40; J. O. Urmson, "Dramatic Representation," *Philosophical Quarterly* 22 (1972): 333–43; Nicholas Wolterstorff, *Works and Worlds of Art* (Oxford: Clarendon, 1980), 250–51; Monroe Beardsley, "Fiction and Representation," *Synthese* 46 (1981): 295; and Keir Elam, *The Semiotics of Theatre and Drama* (London: Methuen, 1980), 169–170.
6. Stanislavski, *Stanislavski's Legacy*, Elizabeth Reynolds Hapgood, ed. and tr. (New York: Theatre Arts Books, 1968), 20.
7. David Cole, *The Theatrical Event* (Middletown, CT: Wesleyan University Press, 1975), 77–78.
8. Searle, *Expression and Meaning*, 66.
9. Austin, *How to Do Things*, 22.
10. Searle, *Expression and Meaning*, 68.
11. Michael Issacharoff, *Discourse as Performance* (Stanford, CA: Stanford University Press, 1989), 9.
12. See Searle, *Intentionality*, 170–71.
13. This requirement is built into what Searle calls the "representation intention." See Ibid., 167–68.
14. The great theorists of "play," Johan Huzinga, Roger Caillois, and Jean Piaget, all count dramatic performance as a species of play.
15. [Euvgeny] Vakhtangov, "The School of Intimate Experience," *Actors on Acting*, T. Cole and H. K. Chinoy, eds. (New York: Three Rivers, 1947, 1970), 509.
16. Viola Spolin, *Improvisation for the Theater* (Evanston, IL: Northwestern University Press, 1963), 25, 5.
17. A difference between Method and Brechtian acting is that, while Method performances tend to keep the audience focused on the actions performed *within* the game, Brechtian performances actively direct the audience's attention to the game *itself*. Neither approach, however, actually deceives the audience as to the nature of the game. Brecht's arguments, I believe, are neutral as to the game model; while Brecht does not

explicitly promote "real" action onstage as an ideal, neither does he preclude the possibility.

18. Quoted in Johan Huzinga, *Homo Ludens* (New York: Beacon, 1955), 11.

19. This routine was part of the Cirque du Soleil's 1992 *Saltimbanco.*

20. A number of Pinter scholars have emphasized that the interest of his plays generally lies in the moment-to-moment interplay of speech acts. See, for example, Austin Quigley, *The Pinter Problem* (Princeton, NJ: Princeton University Press, 1975), and my "Radical Mimesis: The 'Pinter Problem' Revisited," *Comparative Drama* 26.3 (1992): 218–36. The point that I am making here is that a performance in Pinter's plays need not merely *represent* a rich illocutionary event but can *constitute* such an event.

21. Bette Bourne, Peggy Shaw, Paul Shaw, and Lois Weaver, *Belle Reprieve,* in *Gay and Lesbian Plays Today,* Terry Helbing, ed. (Portsmouth, NH: Heinemann, 1993), 19.

22. For an earlier version of this argument, see my "How to Do Things on Stage," *Journal of Aesthetics and Art Criticism,* 49.1 (1991): 31–45.

CHAPTER FOUR

ACTING AND ANSWERABILITY

Marla Carlson

In this chapter I want to complicate the picture of Method acting that has accompanied attacks on psychological realism since the mid-1980s. With the help of Bakhtinian concepts, I propose a reexamination of the Method's foundations in Stanislavsky as well as Sanford Meisner's American derivative. I argue that although Method acting can serve to perpetuate the status quo, it also holds the potential to produce change: of emotion, as transformed by memory and by the circumstances of performance; of verbal and nonverbal behaviors, as they are assimilated from others and transformed by reiteration; and finally, of actors and the given dramatic circumstances, as they engage in mutual transformation.

Many otherwise valuable essays on acting proceed from the misleading claim that Stanislavskian actors merely "reincarnate" as the character and that Method actors merely engage in self-revelation. Theatre scholar Timothy Wiles says that Stanislavskian techniques of psychological realism (by which he means all variations of the Method that developed under the influence of Stanislavsky's work and writings) look backward. He argues that the techniques were developed to stage a kind of play where the action is an uncovering and unraveling of a problematic past, in order to explain why things are as they are. Method actors thus develop myriad ways to discover and understand who they are, and why, but not to change their situations *or* to challenge the social forces that brought them about. This critique of Method acting is articulated in contrast to a Brechtian approach, whereby actors' supposedly visible distance from and comment upon their characters encourage spectators to imagine how things could be different. Thus Brechtian-style acting techniques are held to look to the future and have the potential to bring about change.[1]

Wiles's *selective* reading of Stanislavsky has been tremendously influential. For example, performance theorist Philip Auslander's essay "Just be Yourself" relies heavily upon Wiles. Auslander examines acting theory "through the lens of deconstruction" to argue that the "self" supposedly revealed by the actor within a modernist paradigm is *produced*, rather than being revealed, by the performance.[2] Although Auslander is right to assert that the actor's "self" is privileged by Jerzy Grotowski and Bertolt Brecht as well as by Stanislavsky and the Method, I submit that a careful rereading is warranted. I intend to augment Auslander's Derridian lens with a Bakhtinian one and to shift focus away from the actor's self (whether it is produced or revealed) to acting as a process of interrelation (which remains meaningful even if the self is not considered singular, coherent, or stable). In particular, I will use concepts taken from Bakhtin's work on *dialogism* and *answerability* to argue for a reconception of Method acting as a process of *transformational citation* and for the importance of *outsideness* to Method (as well as Brechtian) actors. Before defining and explaining these terms, however, I must address the evidence available in Stanislavsky's writings. Elizabeth Reynolds Hapgood's translations of Stanislavsky may not adequately represent either his practice or his thought, but they remain undeniably important as the theoretical foundation upon which Method acting was built in America.[3]

The American theatre had been deeply influenced by Stanislavsky's practices before any documentation was available. The Moscow Art Theatre first toured the United States in 1923, and émigrés Richard Boleslavski and Maria Ouspenskaya began teaching an early version of the Stanislavsky system in New York shortly thereafter. Among their students were future leaders of the Group Theatre, Harold Clurman and Lee Strasberg. Group member Stella Adler spent approximately six weeks of 1934 working privately with Stanislavsky in Paris. Because Stanislavsky had by this time moved on to the Method of Physical Actions, Adler became convinced that the Method being developed by the Group under Strasberg's guidance was wrong, particularly in its emphasis on affective memory and emotional recall. When Stanislavsky's *An Actor Prepares* appeared in 1936, the appetite for a definitive statement from the author himself was immense, and thus his discussion of emotion was tremendously influential. *Building a Character* was not published until 1949, and neither this second book nor any subsequent publication had a comparable impact because Strasberg's version of the American Method was already in place. The discussion of emotion and memory in *An Actor Prepares* is thus of unparalleled importance as a foundation of Method acting, and this emphasis on emotion lent support to Strasberg's work on affective memory.[4]

In *An Actor Prepares,* Stanislavsky clearly distinguishes the actor from the role and attributes feelings to the former. He writes in two voices, the teacher Tortsov alternating with the student Kostya. As Tortsov, Stanislavsky says:

> You can borrow clothing, a watch, *things* of all sorts, but you cannot take *feelings* away from another person. My feelings are inalienably mine, and yours belong to you in the same way. You can understand a part, sympathize with the person portrayed, and put yourself in his place, so that you will act as he would. That will arouse feelings in the actor that are *analogous* to those required for the part. But those feelings will belong, not to the person created by the author of the play, but to the actor himself. [*AP* 166–67, emphasis in original]

Method actors thus are understood always to remain themselves onstage, with their own feelings. I will argue that one upshot of this identification of feelings with actors is to establish an essential "outsideness" for actors with respect to their roles, enabling them to function as creative coauthors. But first I want to inquire further into Stanislavsky's conception of the actor's feelings.

Auslander maintains that Stanislavsky treats the subconscious as a "database."[5] In raising an objection to this view, he borrows Derrida's argument that thought and emotions are indeterminate: The process by which they are articulated necessarily alters and destabilizes them. To record or articulate a thought is thus not to fish it intact out of storage but to constitute or, in other words, to produce it in material terms. This argument is misplaced as a critique of Stanislavsky, whose discussion of emotion memory in *An Actor Prepares* aptly illustrates the vagaries of mediation. For Stanislavsky, while actors' feelings come from their experiences and their storehouses of emotion memory, they can be combined in myriad ways, in service to *"an infinite variety of objectives, and given circumstances"* (*AP* 167, emphasis in original). The operations of memory as well as the changing circumstances of utterance are shown to transform the emotions, and Stanislavsky places Tortsov's exhortations to "be yourself" shortly after the much-quoted streetcar accident. In this episode, Kostya (Stanislavsky's "student" persona) witnesses a horrible accident on his way home: A man has been run over by a streetcar. Kostya first describes the scene and the immediate impression it makes on him, then the intensification and specification of the mental picture when he wakes in the night, and finally the abstraction of his emotional response into moral valuation. He soon discovers that this accident has been displaced in his memory by his prior observation of a derailed train, and finally that too gives way to another significant memory: the long-past sight of a man weeping over his dead monkey on the sidewalk. Kostya concludes that this last image has more power to stir his imagination than do any of the more recent (and more violent) memories and will ultimately be of more use as an emotion memory to be called upon in service of a play's given circumstances. Stanislavsky then switches to the Tortsov voice to explain that memory transforms experience: *"Time is a splendid filter for our remembered feelings—besides it is a great artist. It not only purifies, it also transmutes even painfully realistic memories into poetry"* (*AP* 163, emphasis in original).

Stanislavsky does recognize that data retrieved from the subconscious are not exactly the same as those which were stored. According to Auslander, Stanislavsky considers experiences that have been distorted by memory to be more useful to actors because they have become more universal.[6] Yet to say that memory aestheticizes and evaluates experience does not necessarily entail making it universal rather than more uniquely individual. I suggest, rather, that memory makes one the author of one's experience by enabling one to view it from the perspective of an "other"—

that is, to occupy imaginatively a location outside of the experiencing self. I turn now to an early essay by Bakhtin to explore the significance of this shift to an outside perspective.

Bakhtin considers *outsideness* a vital component of real dialogue and develops this view using various bodily metaphors. In a 1970 essay, for instance, he says "our real exterior can be seen and understood only by other people, because they are located outside us in space and because they are *others*."[7] In the early 1920s, his very concrete formulation of the same point was that one can see parts of another person's body that are not accessible to that person's gaze, such as the back of her own head. In that essay, "Author and Hero in Aesthetic Activity," Bakhtin discusses at length what is involved in imagining one's own exterior appearance.[8] In order to have an image of my exterior, I have to project myself outside of myself and look back at myself. Even when I do this, I cannot fully see myself the way others see me, because I still possess the inner sense of myself that others do not have. When I dream, for example, I see and experience from "within" myself, from my own perspective. If I then tell my dream to someone, I create a "dream-me" as a character within the narrative. In the telling, I become the author of my dream, and my consciousness both encompasses and *consummates* that of the dream-me.[9] I know more and see more than *any* character within my narrative, including the dream-me, and more than they all know or see collectively. From my position outside the narrative, I can "'fill in' the horizon" by including those elements that are "transgredient" (the opposite of *in*gredient) to the experience of its characters. To bring back an earlier example, I can include a description of the back of any character's head—or a description of all of them together. As author, I objectify the characters—but this term does not carry negative connotations for Bakhtin. From one's own point of view, life is an ongoing process and must remain unfinished. So from her own perspective, a character cannot be objectified or, in Bakhtin's terms, "finalized" or "consummated."[10] As author, I create a "consummating environment" for my character out of my "surplus" or, in other words, the "excess of my own seeing, knowing, desiring, and feeling."[11] Notice that my position as author does not entail neutrality; I have feelings and desires directed toward my characters, and they are part of the "finalized" world of my narrative.

When I tell my dream, then, I consummate the dream-me in order to create a coherent narrative. My listener can in turn see the dream-me as a character among others—from an outside perspective. Or she can project herself into me and see the dream from the dream-me's perspective. Although Bakhtin is arguing for the importance of the outside perspective for aesthetic activity, the moment of projection into the character is a necessary component of authorship as well. I must pause here to mention that the process of creating a character who is not me (or dream-me) is similar but includes the step of first imagining myself to be the "hero" I create (to use Bakhtin's term), before returning to my own perspective as author. "I must empathize or project myself into this other human being, see his world axiologically from within him as *he* sees this world; I must put myself in his place and then, after returning to my own place, 'fill in' his horizon through that excess of seeing which opens out from this, my own, place outside him."[12]

Now, what if the person listening to my dream is an actor, who will play the character I've created? The actor as creative coauthor oscillates between perspectives, and the author's act of "filling in" the horizon of the other can be productively read against Stanislavsky's conception of "living over" a part. In both cases, one does imagine occupying the position of the other, but then necessarily returns to one's own vantage point. This return to a position outside is precisely the *positive* contribution and value of aesthetic activity:

> The life situation of a suffering human being that is really experienced from within may prompt me to perform an ethical action, such as providing assistance, consolation, or cognitive reflection. But in any event my projection of myself into him must be followed by a *return* into myself, a *return* to my own place outside the suffering person, for only from this place can the material derived from my projecting myself into the other be rendered meaningful ethically, cognitively, or aesthetically. If this return into myself did not actually take place, the pathological phenomenon of experiencing another's suffering as one's own would result—an infection with another's suffering, and nothing more.[13]

Without a return to a position outside the other, one cannot be effective either ethically or aesthetically; one can merely be "infected." For actors, the failure to observe and evaluate their performances as characters would result in ineffective performances—providing it was possible to begin with. And as I mentioned earlier, the observation and evaluation is not entirely a matter of rational analysis but includes actors' feelings and desires directed toward the characters.

In "Author and Hero in Aesthetic Activity," Bakhtin shows a sophisticated and complex understanding of what actors do. He begins with the question, When is the actor creative? and answers that he is creative as a simultaneous actor-author-director, stepping back and shaping the character from a position *outside*. As I will show, this function is every bit as vital to Stanislavskian acting as to Brechtian and does *not* mean that the actors are creative only during rehearsal. For the actor as author, Bakhtin distinguishes between creative moments of coauthoring and reincarnation:

> [T]he actor is not creative when he has *"reincarnated"* himself and now, in imagination, experiences the hero's life as his *own* life, whose horizon includes all the other dramatis personae, the scenery, the various objects on stage, etc.; he is not creative when his consciousness includes nothing that would be transgredient to the consciousness of the hero he is playing.
>
> The actor is aesthetically creative only when he produces and shapes *from outside* the image of the hero into whom he will later "reincarnate" himself, that is, when he creates the hero as a distinct whole and creates this whole not in isolation, but as a constituent in the whole of a drama. [emphasis in original][14]

When fully experiencing from *within* the character, the actor is at best a passive tool used by a creative director and/or author, and perceived by a coauthoring spectator. Patricia Suchy, one of the few people to have addressed thus far the implications that Bakhtin's work holds for acting theory, unfortunately relies on Wiles's reading of Stanislavsky as an advocate of "reincarnation." This leads her to dismiss Stanislavskian acting as having less dialogical potential than Brechtian acting.[15] But Stanislavsky, in fact, recommends a complex process by means of which actors imagine themselves in the dramatic circumstances, imagine themselves within a character's life, imagine life from a different perspective, but constantly return to themselves and adjust.

Like Bakhtin, Stanislavsky discusses the way we are positioned in our own fantasies. One can either be a spectator, watching the fantasy from outside without being present in it, or one can imagine oneself as a participant. Being a participant in the fantasy does not, however, necessarily entail adopting the *viewpoint* of a participant: One can still observe passively and picture oneself as a participant along with others—this is what I have earlier described as being the "author" of your fantasy. If you actively enter into the fantasy, however, your perspective must shift and "you will no longer see yourself, but only what surrounds you, and to this you will respond inwardly, because you are a real part of it" (*AP* 60). Stanislavsky says that the actor's perspective must shift in this way. Taken by itself, this recommendation could imply that if you can observe yourself from outside, you will not be able to participate truly in the imagined circumstances and will be incapable of being inwardly moved by them. In this reading, to coauthor in Bakhtin's sense would incapacitate the actor. But a more careful look at the overall structure and through-line of Stanislavsky's acting books shows that the participant position is *always* accompanied by the analyst/observer position.

For example, the second chapter of *Building a Character* is taken up with the student Kostya's experience of authoring a character. The students have been instructed to "prepare an external characterization" and use it to "mask" themselves (*BC* 8). They begin by selecting costumes, and Kostya is irresistibly drawn to a seemingly simple but faded and dusty morning coat. Thinking the coat would make its wearer look like a ghost, he is stirred by "[a]n almost imperceptible squeamishness" along with "a slightly terrifying sense of fatefulness" (*BC* 9). He goes on to narrate the process of completing the costume and makeup without quite finding the identity of "that mildewed man whose clothes [he] had accidentally found" (*BC* 11). Kostya spends three days disturbed by this intruder's presence in his subconscious: "I was not alone but with someone whom I sought in myself and could not find" (*BC* 10). On the day of the masquerade, he observes the other students' more conventional and seemingly more successful personae, then remains alone backstage. He begins to wipe off his inappropriate makeup. As his features take on the same "greenish-grayish-yellowish" hue as his clothing, the character emerges at last: "The fault-finding critic who lives inside of Kostya Nazvanov. I live

in him in order to interfere with his work. That is my great joy. That is
the purpose of my existence" (*BC* 15).

The Critic is a huge success. Kostya is "amazed at the brazen, unpleasant tone and the fixed, cynical, rude stare" he affects while insulting his
teacher, all unpremeditated (*BC* 15). Sounding possessed, he ends up
"happy because [he] had realized how to live another person's life, what it
meant to immerse [him]self in a characterization" (*BC* 18–19). Yet the
character is not exactly another person; he is clearly a part of Kostya, pro-
jected and known from outside. And Kostya never stops observing himself:

> [W]hile I was playing the part of the Critic I still did not lose the sense of
> being myself. The reason, I concluded, was that while I was acting I felt ex-
> ceptionally pleased as I followed my own transformation. Actually I was
> my own observer at the same time that another part of me was being a
> fault-finding, critical creature.
>
> Yet can I really say that the creature is not a part of me? I derived him
> from my own nature. I divided myself, as it were, into two personalities.
> One continued as an actor, the other was an observer.
>
> Strangely enough this duality not only did not impede, it actually pro-
> moted my creative work. It encouraged and lent impetus to it. [*BC* 19]

The actor thus observes the entire process of characterization even as he
participates in it, but he ceases to be *answerable* as himself, within the ordinary circumstances of his life. Tortsov explains that Kostya's "critic" persona allows him to do and say things: "In his own person he would never
dare to speak as he does in the character of this other personality for
whose words he does not feel himself responsible." The character is a
mask that, paradoxically, both hides and reveals. "Protected by it he can
lay bare his soul down to the last intimate detail" (*BC* 28).

Stanislavsky, however, does not recommend that actors engage in un-
relieved soul baring. Rather, he describes throughout his books an oscillation between inside and outside or, to put it another way, between the
character's point of view and the actor's. Even while Stanislavsky takes
pains to identify feelings with actors rather than characters, he distinguishes actors' "everyday thoughts, personal feelings, reflections and realities" from those that properly belong to their roles in a play (*AP* 185).
The actors' real lives and their roles move along separate lines, and while

there is an overlap from one to the other, actors need to be in control of that exchange. Stanislavsky has Tortsov warn his students that when an actor's personal reality intrudes onstage, he is "transported across the footlights into the audience or beyond the walls of the theatre, wherever the object is that maintains a bond of relationship with him," and his acting becomes mechanical (*AP* 185). Although Tortsov says that such lapses disrupt "the continuity of the role," I propose that they more seriously disrupt communion with the other actors, to which Stanislavsky makes reference throughout his writings. In order to understand the nature of this communion, I return to my discussion of memory and emotion and their place within a model of communication in the theatre.

Bakhtin provides tools for this analysis that are every bit as useful as those which Auslander finds in Derrida. Behaviors are, like words, learned through a process of assimilation. Bakhtin describes such a process: "[T]he unique speech experience of each individual is shaped and developed in continuous and constant interaction with others' individual utterances. This experience can be characterized to some degree as the process of *assimilation*—more or less creative—of others' words (and not the words of a language)."[16] In other words, an utterance belongs to three levels of discourse at once. On the *neutral* level, it belongs to a language and could be found in or added to a dictionary. As the word of an *other*, it belongs to and echoes prior utterances. Finally, the word belongs to, or is *owned* by, the particular speaker who utters it in this particular context.[17] Thought, understood to be "inner speech,"[18] is made up of the same building materials—that is, words and their "emotional-volitional" content, to use Bakhtinian terms. Every word and every thought is thus taken from the utterance of another, replete with feelings and desires. These feelings and desires affect intonation, facial expression, gesture, and postural signals—all the paralinguistic signs that accompany both the utterance *and* the unspoken thought. Applying this model to Auslander's title, you can never be *only* yourself, because every utterance (or behavior) is, in fact, an imitation that has already been transformed by iteration. Each reiteration continues the process of transformation. By re-uttering a word or re-performing a behavior, one enters into dialogue not only with its conventional meanings but also with prior nonconventional meanings. And while none of these meanings is necessarily replaced, all may be transformed. In restoring a behavior or reiterating an utterance, or in decoding either, one necessarily transforms both the word/behavior *and* its emotional-volitional content.

Acting, then, can be understood as the transformational citation of behaviors. While the implications of this model could be drawn out for any variety of the American Method, the Meisner repetition exercise provides a most salient example.[19] Two actors begin simply looking at one another, and one makes an observation. The partner then repeats that observation from her own point of view. Students typically begin with concrete physical attributes. The first might say "Your hair is brown," to which the second would reply, "Yes, my hair is brown" or "No, my hair is not brown." They soon begin to comment on one another's behavior and the emotional state that behavior is assumed to indicate: "You're twisting your hair," or "You're a little nervous tonight." In any case, the repetition of this first observation continues back and forth until something happens to make it change. The "something" can be simply that one partner cannot stand to keep repeating the same thing over and over, but ideally it should be the *other* partner who notices and says, "You don't want to do this anymore." When students become more adept, the repetition undergoes a transformation whenever one participant picks up on what the interchange is doing to the partner and comments upon it. In advanced stages of training, actors move more directly into observing and commenting on (assumed) emotional states. The exchange about brown hair might lead quickly to "You'd like to touch my hair," or "You think I'm just ordinary." Or physical observations might be skipped altogether, and an exercise could begin with "You'd like to pull my hair!" The actors are not allowed to create variety by giving line readings or by making conscious decisions; rather, sensitivity to the context of utterance produces transformation (*MA* 21, 27). Meisner's fundamental premise is that "the reality of doing is the foundation of acting" (*MA* 16). The repetition exercise teaches students first to *do* by observing, speaking, listening, and repeating; and, second, to *transform* the repeated utterance into a subtly or radically different utterance by paying close attention to paralinguistic communication (intonation, expression, gestures, etc.) and to their own psychological processes.

Meisner deemphasizes emotion memory, maintaining that emotion does not have to come from one's own lived experience. He stresses the importance of imagination and advocates a kind of "daydreaming" as preparation to activate the emotions called for in a scene. Once actors begin the scene, the circumstances of the daydream are dropped and they work off the exchange with their partner, using the skills developed by the repetition exercise (*MA* chap. 6). Still, emotion memory *does* come into play within scenes. Actors do not *always* work *entirely* off their partners once the scene begins. When the text demands a particular emotion from an actor, and that emotion does not arise spontaneously, Meisner tells his students to act "as if" the "cold" circumstances given within the text were other circumstances with the power to touch them deeply (*MA* chap. 10). Meisner's work on preparation and "particularization" is much the same as Kostya's transformation of the streetcar accident into the sight of a man crying over a dead monkey. In finding analogous emotions for a character, actors cite their own personal emotions—but those emotions can come from various sources. Both memory and aesthetic activity transform and *objectify* experiences and their emotional associations. Kostya's experience with the streetcar accident is constructed to show that memory alters experience (whether it is real or imaginary, one's own or someone else's). Whether an experience is really yours or imaginatively yours is beside the point, because once the experience enters memory, it is necessarily altered. Myself yesterday is an "other" to myself today. I know this other "myself" in a different way from how I know you, but it is still distinct, still constructed, still an object of memory and of language and of imagination. In remembering, I consummate this yesterday-me, just as I consummate the dream-me in telling my dream. As an actor, I make imaginative use of my feelings as the "author" of a character who is both me and not-me.[20] I stand both inside and outside this character, and my performance is an oscillation between these positions.

My performance is also carried out in dialogue with my fellow actors.[21] The actor's feelings are a component of interpersonal relationships, not something contained within the individual. They are communicated by means of both linguistic and paralinguistic signs, including words, intonation, facial expression, gesture, and posture. These signs are, in turn, decoded and responded to by the recipient. A high level of *paralinguistic* communication between actors is understood as a high level of communion. Actors whose attention drifts to personal (offstage) reality may hear their cues and respond with their lines, but they fail to observe the nuances of behavior of their fellow actors within shared dramatic circumstances. Actors, in short, must be fully *answerable* to others. The greatest contribution of Meisner technique is to develop actors' sensitivity to paralinguistic communication. In performance, the emphasis may be on the character's perspective, but the actor continues to shift to a position outside the character, from which she can evaluate her performance *as* the character. The oscillation between these points of view is rapid: The actor occupies the position of the other for a split second and then, as Bakhtin would have it, returns to her own place to fill in the horizon. Moreover, she must do this without causing a breach in communion with her fellow actors.

As I have argued, both feelings and the behaviors by which feelings are communicated are learned through a process of citation and transformation. Actors' feelings are reshaped by memory even before they are reactivated in performance, where they are again transformed by the process of reiteration and by the context within which they are reiterated. In the Stanislavsky System and the American Method, actors own their feelings and use them as analogous to the feelings imagined for their characters; however, the actors let go of the circumstances of their own lives. The imaginary circumstances of the play *and* the spontaneous interchange onstage with acting partners become the dual frameworks within which actors must answer for their actions, reactions, and interactions.

NOTES

1. Timothy J. Wiles, *The Theater Event: Modern Theories of Performance* (Chicago: University of Chicago Press, 1980), esp. 31–32.
2. Philip Auslander, "Just Be Yourself: Logocentrism and Difference in Performance Theory," in *Acting (Re)considered: Theories and Practice*, Phillip Zarrilli, ed. (London: Routledge, 1995), 60.
3. On the production of the books and the role of Elizabeth Hapgood, see Benedetti, *SB*, 289–90, 297–300. On the translation issue, see Sharon Carnicke, "*An Actor Prepares/Rabota aktera nad soboi, Chast'I:* A Comparison of the English with the Russian Stanislavsky," *Theatre Journal* 36.4 (1984): 481–94.
4. See Benedetti, *SB*, 309. *An Actor Prepares* was based on Stanislavsky's work from 1908 to 1914.

5. Auslander, "Just Be Yourself," 61.

6. Ibid., 62.

7. M. M. Bakhtin, "Response to a Question from the *Novy Mir* Editorial Staff," *Speech Genres and Other Late Essays*, Vern W. McGee, tr. (Austin: University of Texas Press, 1986), 7. This essay was written in 1970, in response to a request for Bakhtin's evaluation of the state of literary scholarship at that time.

8. M. M. Bakhtin, "Author and Hero in Aesthetic Activity," *Art and Answerability*, Vadim Liapunov, tr. (Austin: University of Texas Press, 1990), 23, 28–32. This essay was written during the period 1920 to 1923. For an evaluation of Bakhtin's early work, see Caryl Emerson, *The First Hundred Years of Mikhail Bakhtin* (Princeton, NJ: Princeton University Press, 1997), esp. chapter 5, "Outsideness," 207–64.

9. Liapunov uses "consummate" for Bakhtin's *zavershit'*, noting that other translations use the term "finalize." The meaning is "to bring to the utmost degree of completion or fulfillment, to accomplish" (in Bakhtin, "Author and Hero," 233 n. 6).

10. In an essay written between 1919 and 1921, Bakhtin articulated the position that what is real is always subjective because it is fully particularized and includes its particular time of occurrence. Any degree of abstraction or of objectification is a removal from the particular to the universal and as such a removal of/from time, from the flow of events. In that sense, to be concretized (or finalized) is to be no longer alive. See *Toward a Philosophy of the Act*, Vadim Liapunov, tr. (Austin: University of Texas Press, 1993), 2, for an elaboration of this point. Aesthetic activity produces objects, and objects return into relationship with the flow of events through the process of reception. The aesthetic object thus mediates between the events that constitute its creation and those of its reception. This is most easily understood when the object is an artifact such as text, a painting, or even a film. Performance is a different kind of aesthetic object because it is never concrete: The object is itself an event. As a consequence, the aesthetic mediator is itself a process rather than a stable (finalized) object, but it remains an intervention.

11. Bakhtin, "Author and Hero," 12, 25. Liapunov suggests "surplus" and "excess" as alternative translations for *izbytok*.

12. Ibid., 25.

13. Ibid., 26.

14. Ibid., 76.

15. Patricia Suchy, "Co-Authoring Narrative Discourse: The Dialogue of Theatrical Adaptation," Ph.D., Northwestern University, 1995.

16. Bakhtin, *Speech Genres*, 89.

17. Ibid., 88.

18. A thorough argument for the proposition that thought is inner speech is outside the scope of my discussion here. See, for example, Lev Semenovic Vigotsky, *Thought and Language*, Eugenia Hanfmann and Gertrude

Vakar, eds. and trs. (Cambridge, MA: MIT Press, 1962). Inner speech is not to be confused with the Method actor's inner monologue. Although the two concepts are related, the inner monologue is a specific tool used in acting that comes very close in form to the utterance—in fact, students often are instructed to speak their inner monologues in an attempt to produce appropriate affect or to promote mental focus. "Inner speech," on the other hand, is a term meant to encompass *all* thought. The Russian formalists developed a linguistic model of thought, arguing that it is made up of the same materials as speech, although it may be organized differently. In other words, because we do not think without words, thought is not prior to language.

19. The repetition exercise is described at length in *MA*. I studied the technique with Phil Gushee for six months in 1994 and 1995, and my discussion is heavily influenced by his approach.

20. The formulation is Richard Schechner's. For his discussion of the "not-not-me" and "restored behavior," see his *Between Theatre and Anthropology* (Philadelphia: University of Pennsylvania Press, 1985), 35–116.

21. While I believe that the actor's communion with the audience is of at least equal importance, and that it can fit into the model I am developing as well, an adequate discussion of the actor-audience relation is beyond the scope of this chapter.

CHAPTER FIVE

JUST BE YOURSELF

Derrida, Difference, and the Meisner Technique

Louise M. Stinespring

In his essay "Just Be Yourself," performance scholar Philip Auslander calls into question Constantin Stanislavsky's theories of acting and examines them under the lens of Derrida's discourse on "difference."[1] Auslander wants us to observe Stanislavsky's theories in order to take issue with the idea that truthful acting resides in the actor's self. He critiques the Stanislavsky System and, by implication, Method acting, by attaching its ideas to "logocentrism." He defines logocentrism as "the orientation of philosophy toward an order of meaning—thought, truth, reason, logic, the Word—conceived as existing in itself, as foundation."[2] Auslander claims theorists, including Stanislavsky, Bertolt Brecht, and Jerzy Grotowski, "implicitly designate the actor's self as the *logos* of performance" and that for them the self is "an autonomous foundation for acting." He contributes a counterclaim that maintains that the actor's self is not the foundation for acting, but instead "the actorly self" is "produced by the performance it supposedly grounds."[3]

Much of what Auslander describes is based in the acting approaches of Sanford Meisner, an acting teacher who was well known for years in professional theatre circles. Since his death on February 2, 1997, the wider academic community is becoming aware of his contribution to the field of actor training. As one of his former students at the New York Neighborhood Playhouse, I can attest to the values inherent in his methodology. In this chapter, I hope to demonstrate Meisner's approach for the postmodernism Auslander describes. An inquiry into the connection between the theoretical underpinnings of Meisner's technique and Derrida's perspectives will offer a unique view of Method acting.

Derrida's removal of any universal truth, word, and logos in favor of a "free play of signs" provides a theoretical compatibility with the Meisner technique. According to Derrida, the central core of being "is not the center" but is the "determination of Being as presence in all senses of this word." Totalization, for Derrida, "is something defined as useless, and sometimes as impossible," and the center of identity "plays without security."[4] Meisner reconstituted Stanislavsky's System of acting, founded on the principle of "psychological realism," into his own methodology. Meisner's work rests on the premise that any performance that yields "psychological realism" will not result as self-will but emerge through the actor's "reactions" in performance. It will be understood that in order for actors to "be" themselves in their characters' circumstances in performance, they must adhere to the "reality of doing" (*MA* 16). This doing, however, incorporates observable differences in others and using difference as creative grounding.

Meisner's "repetition exercise" functions as a destabilizer of truth in a Derridian sense because the principle that actors behave truthfully is an underlying theoretic subject to interpretation. Rather than pre-planned behavior, actors' instincts or emotional impulses are the driving force behind this truthful behavior. Instinct and impulse are not something preconceived but ephemeral. For Derrida, "there is nothing outside the text,"[5] which means, in acting terms, that there is nothing but that which is present in the moment of discovery, in the moment one discovers the other (be it another actor, the audience, the space, etc.). Therefore, no certain truth or totalization, as Derrida would have it, emerges during the enactment of this exercise. Instead two actors who perform the word repetition game are charged with the responsibility of responding instinctually to each other's behavior. What emerges is a constantly shifting perspective on the truth as each actor attempts to react honestly to his partner from his own point of view. This "ping-pong game" of impulses (*MA* 22) becomes a venue for total freedom of spontaneous self-expression as it simultaneously disallows any one perspective to be privileged.

It will become evident in this chapter that some of the postmodern ideas offered by Philip Auslander are not an argument against Stanislavsky, but rather an argument in favor of Meisner. Auslander's ideas are a rediscovery of what Meisner's acting students over the past fifty years have known all along: that techniques for teaching truthful acting reside in Auslander's premise that the performance does produce the "actorly self," that is, a sense of the self rejecting preconceptions of role, characterization, and essentialized identity.[6] Rather, for Meisner, the actor constructs identity by producing it in performance, what Meisner calls "the doing."

Auslander's primary thesis is that the actor's self is not the logos for the performance. He opposes Stanislavsky's theory that the actor's inner self—past, character analysis, and fixed identity—is the determinant of the actor's portrayal, and he says: "Stanislavski's discourse on acting is inscribed firmly within logocentrism: He insists on the need for logic, coherence, and unity—the 'unbroken line'—in acting." Moreover, he claims that there is "no question but that the presence of the actor's self as the basis of performance is for him [Stanislavsky] the source of truth in acting: he defines good acting as acting based on the performer's own experience and emotions. He privileges the actor's self over his or her role." Finally, he questions Stanislavsky's method by stating: "Stanislavski divides the self into consciousness and the subconscious, identifying the latter as the source of truth, the seat of 'emotions that are dearer to [the actor] than his everyday feelings.'"[7]

Auslander's argument against Stanislavsky centers on his explicit claim against the validity of the actor's subconscious as a useful tool for accessing emotions and feelings. He rejects the actor's personal psychology in the creation of character, favoring instead the presence of performance as the moment of creation. For Stanislavsky, Auslander says, the self "which is supposedly exposed through the medium of acting is in fact produced by the mediation of psychotechnique between the conscious and unconscious levels of the actor's psyche." Auslander defends Derrida's assertion that we cannot trust the accuracy of emotion memory: "[T]he making conscious of unconscious materials is a process of creation, not retrieval." He points to Derrida's phrase, "we are written only as we write," as support for his own claim that the moment of performance, not the moment of past-being, produces the actorly self.[8] We are to understand here that the actor's presence finds no essentialized logos/self in a mutable subconscious. As Auslander sees it, the actor's psyche—the moment of memory—is the source of performance for Stanislavsky.

Meisner asserts something closer to Derrida's rejection of logocentrism and the emphasis on the negative, the "not being" of existence, saying, "What you do doesn't depend on you; it depends on the other fellow" (MA 34). This is, of course, a description of the repetition exercise, but it is also significantly tied to his basic principles of acting. Meisner, unlike Strasberg, downplays emotional or psychological approaches, seeing them as the most delicate and dangerous element in the actor's craft. "Emotion, without which a performance can be effective but yet not affective, is a most elusive element. It works best when it is permitted to come into play spontaneously and has a perverse inclination to slither away when consciously wooed."[9] In this regard Meisner shares with Derrida the principle that identity is produced in the moment of performance, not in the storehouse of memory.

Meisner developed training exercises that were specifically designed to encourage actors to allow their emotions to "come into play spontaneously," at the moment when the self dissolves in the presence of another. Those familiar with the Meisner technique will recognize the term repetition exercise as the catch-phrase that most succinctly distinguishes his unique approach. A brief look at the underlying theory of this "repetition exercise" will help us uncover why Meisner and Derrida share some common ground in their assumptions.

Both Meisner and Derrida by and large agree that the self is not logically constructed via rationalism and logocentrism but is instead a playground for spontaneous behavioral reactions and doings. Meisner's emphasis on spontaneity parallels what literary scholar Rodolphe Gasché calls Derrida's notion of "play." Play, Gasché says, "designates an unrest of sorts that is not yet qualifiable in terms of binary polarization."[10] In other words, characterization is not finalized in the binary structure of identity (I am me but not you) but rather embodies the concept, put forth by Meisner, that the performance (the living exchange of synergy) produces the ephemeral self. If we "write ourselves" in the moment of inscription, we perform ourselves in the moment of performance.

Meisner rejected cold rationalism and the notion that character is fixed into the fiction of the script's narrative, stating: "My approach is based on bringing the actor back to his emotional impulses and to acting that is firmly rooted in the instinctive. It is based on the fact that all good acting comes from the heart, as it were, and there's no mentality in it." (*MA* 37)

From Meisner's perspective, instinct lies at the root of behavior. He developed a technique for training actors that relied solely on instinct as its driving force, a force that resists closure. When asked by a student what he means by instinct, Meisner responds, "You walk into store and see a dress. 'That's for me!' That's instinct" (*MA* 30). He goes on to explain that he eschews the word "automatic" in favor of the word "spontaneous" as a way of describing this concept of instinct (*MA* 30). Seeing a dress is the moment when the character is created in performance. In this moment of seeing, the actor's self is produced by her instinct. Thus, Auslander's claim for the performance producing the self is accurate when viewed from Meisner's unique perspective. The doing (observing) is the moment of creation. Theatre scholar Elinor Fuchs more or less agrees with this assertion, stating: "The actor seeks the actions, not the coherent personality that commits them."[11] Thus, we can understand that the actor's moment of instinctually choosing the red dress is at once the character's moment. The actor commits an action and concerns herself less with the personality, identity, or fixed logos of those who commit these actions.

For Meisner, "impulse" is synonymous with "instinct;" in fact, it is the manifestation of instinct, the visible product we see that results from instinct. Spontaneous instinct bubbles up and drives human behavior. Hence, the "emotional impulse," not "emotional memory," informs his technique. Meisner asks: How can we develop the impulse and instinct that lies dormant in the novice actor? He understands that emotions would emerge from activities and our reactions to others. His technique for teaching acting is to remove emotion, psychology, or "character" from training. Instead he stresses impulse that will surface from the interchange of differences found in others. The repetition exercise was borne from Meisner's desire for the communal in acting and his emphasis on the spontaneity of the formative moment.

There are many stages in the word repetition game, but basically it consists of two primary levels, the mechanical repetition exercise and the repetition from your own point of view. The capacity to observe the physical characteristics of one's partner forms the basis for the mechanical repetition exercise, which has very precise parameters. Students perform it with partners. Students A and B sit in chairs, placed at a comfortable conversational distance apart, facing a student audience. Student A is instructed to begin the exercise by looking at the partner, Student B, observing the first characteristic of this partner's physical appearance which comes to mind, and stating it aloud. Student B listens to what Student A has just said and repeats it exactly. Student A then listens to what Student B has said and repeats it exactly, too. The first moment of this exercise is structured on the precept that one partner must be allowed to discover what is personally interesting about another human being and state this one observation aloud. If partner A says, "You are wearing a blue shirt," then partner B must respond by repeating exactly what has been said, which in this case would be, "You are wearing a blue shirt."

The partner who begins this exercise is asked to make a spontaneous observation of any one observable physical trait of the partner. The words Student A speaks become the blueprint by which the partners perform the two aspects of this exercise, listening and repeating. The word is not holy or authoritative but open to interpretation at the moment it is spoken. This is a living, organic exercise, which rests on the concept that its two participants are completely dependent on each other. There is no abstraction here, merely the concrete and material necessity of listening and repeating what one hears while simultaneously attending to the partner in order to read his or her behavior. The observations are interruptive, recursive, and looping in and through the partners all the time. This exercise reverberates with emotional fullness when it is performed skillfully.

The following is a typical example of the text that would emerge if Students A and B were to perform this exercise.

A: You have on blue jeans.

B: You have on blue jeans.

The text remains the same for a time. Eventually Student B hears a different meaning or sound from Student A, and the text can change. In these cases, Student A must repeat what is heard from Student B, not return to the initial text that began the exercise. Thus, the text can now be "Yes, I am wearing blue jeans." Or it is possible that Student B is getting tired and therefore, after five minutes of listening to Student A and repeating what Student A began—"You have on blue jeans"—Student B jumbles the words and responds by saying, "You have on blue pants." Student A must now repeat what is heard, saying "You have on blue pants."

Students become frustrated as they perform this exercise and this frustration forms an integral part of Meisner's grand design. There is a purpose for creating an exercise that causes frustration in its practitioners: Frustration is an emotional impulse that lies at the base of specific behavioral reactions. What initially appears to be boredom, when allowed to continue indefinitely during the course of this exercise, naturally transmutes itself into a catalyst for strong human reactions that are inadvertently emitted by exercise practitioners. These reactions form the root of the exercise. Of utmost importance here is that the "doing" and "reacting" is important, not the words or their meanings. Students empty the words of meaning and instead emphasize the act of listening to their partners and repeat the words as they hear them.

At issue here is the concept of reacting to the partner. Partners A and B are dependent on each other, and in this way the "self" is formed in the act of listening, not in any preconceived fashion based on character or psychology. Listening, which Meisner stresses is an act of "doing," coupled with repeating, forms a flow of sounds and text based on the one partner's capacity to react to the behavior of another partner. The actor reacts to the "presence" of the partner, to what might be called in Derridian terms the "trace of existence." For Derrida, "trace" is "not a presence but is rather the simulacrum of a presence that dislocates, displaces, and refers beyond itself."[12] One actor, in stating observations of another actor, dislocates and displaces the presence of the other, noting the latter's simulacrum within the living presence of the actor's gaze. Since we can never really be sure if our observations are correct, never really "know" for certain that what we observe is in itself factual, we are always working in a state of simulacrum—probing, inquiring, and guessing in our attempts to observe accurately. What is at stake here is not the "truth" of the observation but the blurring of identities, the endless destabilization of self while the self is being observed. The partners must react directly to each other; this direct reaction constitutes what Meisner terms a "connection" (*MA* 22) between partners. This connection, in turn, creates the self as fluid, protean, and malleable.

In the next phase of the repetition exercise, the repetition from one's own point of view, partners will move from mere connection to a fuller interaction that Meisner labels "contact" (*MA* 22). The contact between partners is based on the added dimension of reading each other's behavior. The term "reading behavior" refers to students' ability to "pick up" on the emotional impulses emanating from partners and to state them explicitly. This process of "reading" illuminates Derrida's explanation of reading: destable, protean, and proceeding spontaneously from moment to moment. In his discussion of Plato's pharmakon, Derrida writes that the theatrical cannot "be summed up in speech: it involves force, space, law, kinship, the human, the divine, death, play, festivity. Hence the new depth that reveals itself to us will necessarily be another scene, on another stage, or rather another tableau in the unfolding of the play of writing." He goes on to say that within explanations of events, "another scene slowly comes to light, less immediately visible than the preceding one, but, in its muffled latency, just as tense, just as violent as the other, composing with it . . . an artful, living organization of figures, displacements, repetitions."[13] Actors reading other actors (or audiences) will discover the same artful living displacement in the repetition exercise. They will discover a resistance to logic (logocentrism) and a focus centered on the irrational, on another person, on a past drifting through (fleetingly), and on a continual displacement of identity.

For advanced students, "point of view" is incorporated into the repetition exercise. Early on students are told that they do not have to repeat *exactly* what they hear. They must respond by reporting what they perceive, what they deem is the underlying action, thought, or impulse in the other actor. Students A and B are then told to keep the repetition going in a general sense until an instinct changes the dialogue. The following hypothetical example will serve to explain the exercise's dynamic:

A: Your shirt is pink. (*A is smiling.*)

B: My shirt is pink? (*B looks surprised.*)

A: Yes, your shirt is pink. (*A is not smiling.*)

B: My shirt is not pink. (*B sounds annoyed.*)

A: Not pink? (*A sounds defensive.*)

B: No, stupid, not pink. (*B attacks A by telling her off.*)

A: Are you calling me stupid? (*A's voice is loud and angry.*)

B: Yes, I'm calling you stupid. (*B starts to giggle.*)

A: Stupid? (*A, almost whispering, begins to smile.*)

B: Stupid! (*B has an authoritative tone to his voice.*)

A: I'm not stupid. (*A seems smug and self-assured.*)

B: You're not stupid. (*B seems to be reassuring A.*)

A: No, I'm not stupid. (*A seems reassured and happy.*)

Meisner's quote is worth repeating: He informs his students that there are two basic principles of the repetition exercise: "Don't do anything unless something happens to make you do it," and "what you do doesn't depend on you; it depends on the other fellow" (*MA* 34). In this way Meisner is actually exploiting Derrida's neologism *difference*, what Derrida describes as the "play [*jeu*] of differences."[14] The action depends on the differences perceived in "the other fellow;" this perception both defers to the existence of another and respects the distinctions of difference.[15] In his essay, "Structure, Sign and Play in the Discourse of the Human Sciences," Derrida allows us to see the possibility that structure need not be reduced to a fixed origin. Instead, he opens up the possibility that "[p]lay is the disruption of presence."[16] Meisner has created an exercise designed to teach his students that behavior, and in turn identity, is reactive to the presence of others and comfortable in the gray areas defined by Derrida. This presence disrupts any moment before or after; it forces the ephemeral nature of the moment to live out its being and then disappear into the mist. Moreover, it demonstrates the need to depend on the "presence" of partners for self-formation and the need to shake fixed foundations of an essentialized self. Partners are dependent on differences for self-understanding. Meisner encourages his students to grapple with the differences embedded in their identities. Each actor is entirely dependent on his fellow actors, or "the other," in order to accomplish the exercise. As a result, identity is developed interactively rather than rationally.

Meisner's repetition exercise can be seen as dialogue not of text but of behavior. Embedded within the parameters of the exercise lies the ability "to be oneself" only through the moment of performance. As we experience each moment of the repetition exercise, we experience the living interchange of differences. Moreover, what matters in this exercise is that we exist only in relation to how the other sees us and how we see the other and our surroundings. Another individual deconstructs us and we, in turn, deconstruct him or her. There is no objectification of the other, merely the possibility that one partner is asked to state observations as he or she sees it, without being held to an objective criterion of truth. To read the partner's behavior is to take a risk by saying what you think you see going on in the other person. Yet there is no assurance of truth, no guarantee that what you see is, in fact, actually happening as it appears. Meisner's work provides for a democracy and equality embedded in the concept that the other will always be different from the self and that the other is changing before our eyes. We, in turn, change as well.

Inherent in the practice of this exercise is the idea that "I respect you" and "you respect me." Therefore, being oneself in this exercise holds within it the possibility that I exist in a community of social democracy with the other, a community dedicated to the principle that each of us is different from the other. We are asked to look at the other human being who is in the exercise with us and remain in relation to that human being through the medium of repetition and reading behavior. The exercise brings together people of different circumstances, but it does not erase differences. We are charged by Meisner to use our instincts to read the emotional impulses of the other and to accept the self-consciousness of being observed as the other reads our emotional impulses. We therefore engage in the development of identity as a fluid activity.

The repetition exercise lacks a center, a closure, an origin, and an end to ground it in some universal truth. Although it is a structured exercise based on the concept that this interplay of emotional impulses, this "ping-pong game" of impulses, will sustain itself through the aliveness of the exercise, its premise lies in the fact that two beings interact. The interaction forms a spontaneous dynamic that excludes rationalist preconception.

At the risk of oversimplification, Derrida's formulation of deconstruction provides ways of looking at pairings that uncouple them from the central/marginal continuum. Structuralism has allowed us to see that in the Hegelian dialectic, the marginalized component can subvert the central component, overturn it, and establish a more fluid baseline. Derrida's poststructuralism suggests that we extend this idea of binaries of center/margin. In fact, in distinguishing differences we do away with binaries altogether, availing ourselves of dialogue and exchanges based on mutual respect and recognition.

By "free play" Derrida means that there is absolutely no finite point that grounds this play: no center, core, or anchor. This free play continues endlessly, as an end in itself, with no end in itself. Derrida believes that all human thought tends toward finding an origin and that this desire to ground thought emerges from anxiety or yearning to let the mind rest on some foundation as it grapples with any given thought. But Derrida asks us to accept the instability of groundlessness. He claims thought is free play of opposites that can never, or should never, be centered through hierarchical thinking. In this way he asks us to enter a kind of fragmented mental arena where "differance" exists. Simply put, *differance* is an aural pun on the French word "difference," which has two meanings, to differ and to defer.[17]

The intricacy of Derrida's thought is too complex to be clarified succinctly (if it can be clarified at all) in this brief chapter. All we need to understand here about *differance* is that it is, by and large, an organic, living concept that is always in suspension between two or more meanings. Thus when it is used in speech, the term, *differance,* is heard as "différence" (meaning difference) since the pronunciation of the two words in French is somewhat the same, but it can also be understood as having a double meaning, either "to differ" or "to defer." Derrida's *differance* is thus a living example of the anxiety inherent in our inability to ground thought, meaning, or intention in a play of binary opposites. *Differance* is the space between the free play of signs, the interstitial tension, if you will, that always lies suspended, anxious, and unsure, and that surrounds an infinite free play of signs that cannot be pinned down rationally.

All this brings us back to Meisner's repetition exercise, which serves as a literal "living proof" that Derrida's assertions about free play of signs exist in practice. Picture, if you will, our students, A and B, engaged in a lively repetition exercise, in which A says to B, "You make me sick," and B dutifully repeats, "You make me sick." Student A then repeats from his point of view by saying "You are jealous," to which B responds, "I'm not jealous." Using this simple example, let's assume that B is honestly not jealous of A in this moment (or at least thinks she isn't). Therefore, we can see that A calling B jealous was merely A's attempt to read the behavior, or the emotional impulse, of B in the moment, as accurately as possible. But A's observation has caused a disintegration of meaning, since B does not agree with the assessment. Yet A's observation cannot be dismissed entirely, since it reflects a sincere attempt to gauge an outward appearance. We can use this simple illustration to assert that the repetition exercise contains the anxiety inherent in the conception of *differance* and the free play of signs. The reality here in this exercise is that it matters not whether B is jealous or not jealous, or whether A's assessment is accurate or faulty, because there is no inherent value or logos to this emotional impulse. Actors are suspended, anxious, and unsure in a moment that spins away. The "jealousy" becomes a sign, a mere "free-floating" label applied to B by A. A's attempt to read B's behavior reflects the free play of identity, the reading of signs in the moment of "play." The jealous/not jealous reaction is not centered in any objective truth or logos, nor does it privilege one over another, but rather it hangs suspended as *difference,* a "difference" between two people who "differ" in opinion and "defer" to each other. Hence, this repetition exercise proffers a free play of emotional impulses, neither good nor bad, right nor wrong, but rather merely suggesting that emotional impulses exist in the here and now. The sign of jealousy exists as presence wanting to know itself, becoming but never being, if being is a grounding concept, and living only as a mere trace of existence, never anchored to a fixed truth.

For Auslander, being is a grounding concept, one that he attempts to break wide open using Derrida's deconstructive lens. Auslander has couched Stanislavsky in a grounding theory based on the workings of the actor's being, or subconscious. He has asked us to see the possibility that the actor's complex psyche is limited, at best, in its ability to be a container of emotions past or present, which can be dipped into for retrieval. Sanford Meisner has corrected our understanding of the actor's being and allowed us to see, through his repetition exercise, that the actor's emotions must "come into play spontaneously" and that they cannot be "consciously wooed." The actor exists in the present moment of performance, and the identity, or character, is derived in the presence of performance.

NOTES

1. Philip Auslander, "'Just Be Yourself': *Logocentrism* and *Différance* in Performance Theory," *From Acting to Performance: Essays in Modernism and Postmodernism* (London: Routledge, 1997), 28–38.
2. Ibid., 28. Auslander quotes from Jonathan Culler, *After Structuralism* (Ithaca: Cornell University Press, 1982), 92.
3. Auslander, "Just Be Yourself," 30.
4. Jacques Derrida, "Structure, Sign and Play in the Discourse of Human Sciences," *Writing and Difference,* Alan Bass, tr. (Chicago: University of Chicago Press, 1978), 279, 289, 292.
5. Jacques Derrida, *Of Grammatology,* Gayatri Chakravorty Spivak, tr. (Baltimore: John Hopkins University Press, 1976), 158.
6. Auslander, "Just Be Yourself," 30.
7. Ibid., 30–31.
8. Ibid., 32, 31.
9. Paul Gray, "Interviews with Vera Soloviova, Stella Adler, and Sanford Meisner," *Stanislavski and America: An Anthology from the Tulane Drama Review,* Erika Munk, ed. (Greenwich: Fawcett Publications, 1967), 208.
10. Rodolphe Gasché, *The Wild Card of Reading: On Paul de Man* (Cambridge, MA: Harvard University Press, 1998), 164.
11. Elinor Fuchs, *The Death of Character: Perspectives on Theater after Modernism* (Bloomington: Indiana University Press, 1996), 24.
12. Jacques Derrida, "Differance," *Speech and Phenomenon,* David B. Allison, tr. (Evanston: Northwestern University Press, 1973), 156. Derrida coins the neologism "Differance" as a pun on the French verb "différer," meaning both to differ and to defer. It refers to the continual slippage of meaning from sign to sign in linguists.
13. Jacques Derrida, *Dissemination,* B. Johnson, tr. (Chicago: University of Chicago Press, 1981), 142–43.
14. Derrida, "Differance," 130. Derrida explains: Differ[a]nce is "neither a *word* nor a *concept*" (p. 30). It is a middle ground, a strategy without a finality, an occult zone of a nonknowing. As soon as it appears, it disappears.
15. In Derrida's "Differance," he says that "everything is a matter of strategy and risk," a strategy "without finality" (135).
16. Derrida, "Structure, Sign, and Play," 292.
17. Derrida, "Differance," 129–160.

CHAPTER SIX

RECONCILING THE PAST AND THE PRESENT

Feminist Perspectives on the Method in the Classroom and on the Stage

Elizabeth C. Stroppel

Micropolitical practice encourages women to recognize the role of gender and sex-power relations as they apply to individual identity and positionality,[1] especially as these factors exist in the margins.[2] Through such praxes, feminists strengthen their political goals while simultaneously challenging the homogenous superstructure of male hegemony. Along these lines, the classroom is often perceived as a marginal space for women because of the superstructure's inclination toward male adversarial notions.[3] This situation is particularly apparent within the acting training classroom, where students must utilize their whole selves as instruments of enactment in order to participate.[4] In addition, part of the nature of acting techniques implies that such techniques are aesthetic tools, constructed from specific ideological bases.[5] Whether inadvertently or not, acting choices remain by and large aligned with the prevailing power structure. Acting methods as political choices, however, are generally not addressed within the average acting classroom. The focus in classrooms generally remains on developing a product rather than on investigating the politics of a process.

One acting technique that concentrates specifically on the steps taken to create a character from an actor's personal identity and experiences, yet with traditionally no attention paid to subsumed ideology or the politics of the choices made, is the Method. The American version of Constantin Stanislavsky's forty years of analyzing and codifying role development from a psychologically realistic basis stems largely from the American Lab Theatre of the 1920s and its students who formed the Group Theatre of the 1930s. The American version is, of course, a compilation of Stanislavsky's original tenets—acquired through translation and in developmental stages—and the renowned variations of American acting-teaching legends, such as Lee Strasberg, Sanford Meisner, Stella Adler, Uta Hagen, and others. Now reinterpreted by second- and third-generation acting teachers, the Method continues to evolve, expand, and diversify along with current cultural expectations. Or does it? In one form or another, the Method remains the dominant mode of acting training in the United States, albeit not without controversy. Many believe that it has remained static, due largely to its privileging of self over character.

Within the last few decades of the twentieth century, feminists have scrutinized and resisted the Method as a process of enactment for women. In the 1960s and 1970s, feminist theatres experimented with techniques that would put women's lives at the center of the acting process. They believed that the Method elided the female experience, both in its linear structure and in its resultant use in realistic texts that continued to privilege the male view of women.[6] Feminist scholar Sue-Ellen Case and others have singled out the Method, theoretically, as an entrapment for women. According to Case, the Method is based on Freudian principles that keep the female actor ensconced in a range of systems that deny her sexuality and compel her to pursue a line of action dissimilar to what she actually experiences in life.[7] With the demise of most feminist theatres in the United States during the politically conservative 1980s,[8] Case's treatise may have served as a published source for women in other areas to reevaluate the Method as a suitable acting technique for female actors. Realism came under strengthened attacks by

feminists and other cultural theorists during the postmodern era; however, counter defenses of realism also emerged.[9] Academics and practitioners alike explored even more intensively how the Method could be
replaced or repositioned within feminist consciousnesses. Brechtian acting, which allowed the actor to critique character and circumstances
through a distancing effect, arose as a strong alternative.[10] Yet many of
the Method's tenets still worked for women as they continued to teach
and act.

As an instructor of the Stanislavsky System at the Sonia Moore Studio in New York City for eight years, I engaged students in elements of
the Method: the use of truth, imagination, objectives, and sense memory
to attain a personal identification with character.[11] While this alone may
not seem biased against the female actor, I can think of exercises where
the choices of action and images created remained insensitive and preju-
dicial to women because gender perspectives went ignored. In my dissertation, "Acting Theory, Training, and Practice from Feminist
Perspectives," I sought ways of reconciling my own background in the
Method with newly acquired feminist cognizance. When I began this
task, I uncovered only a scattering of published information on the topic.
As a result, I went directly to the women currently exploring feminist
awareness within acting technique and performance. The information included in this chapter originates from one hundred women who teach,
act, direct, and otherwise engage in theatrical activity, practitioners from
both universities and professional venues. Establishing how feminism
critically uses the Method is the focus of this chapter.

At least two-thirds of the respondents I interviewed acknowledged
that their initial acting training came within some form of Stanislavsky's
technique as taught in this country. In addition, the majority professed
that a feminist perspective was a part of their lives, if not a conscious
choice of their artistic endeavors.[12] My analysis reveals that references to
Method acting training follows, for the most part, along three lines: an
obligation to expose students to traditional acting jargon; a need to put
Stanislavsky's work in context as merely one of the many paradigms of
acting; and the exposition of the detrimental effect that it could have on
women who empathized with their characters without recognizing the
potentially hostile structure lying beneath the surface of the text. The

observation that remains most clear about these conclusions is that the respondents do not adhere to any particular authority of acting techniques. Instead, many of them seek ways of accommodating feminist perspectives within prior procedures of acting with which they are most familiar as well as newer ones that they continue to explore.

The fundamental question for this chapter remains: Is the Method inherently antithetical to feminist thought and praxes, or can it be instilled with feminist consciences? Does a character created through a utilization of the physical and emotional self of the past, which unites self with character in textual circumstances and a linear ordering of actions, always disempower the female actor in performance? Or is the error to be found in the failure to interrogate the gendered and other socially constructed behavior that denies feminist embodiment in the present? These questions remain significant to feminist perspectives in the acting classroom and on the stage. In what follows, I will demonstrate some of the ways in which women respond to them.

Professor Joyce Devlin of Mount Holyoke College, for example, defends the truth in the Method as it relates to text and claims that sensory exercises, personalization, justification, circumstances, and other Method-based facets remain effective.[13] Devlin, nevertheless, uses alternative techniques, such as Suzuki movement, in conjunction with the Method elements mentioned above, in order to enable students to achieve the physical parameters of character in addition to the psychological.[14] While this eclectic procedure is not unique to feminists, what is unique is the attention paid by such instructors to the gendered actions and reactions that emanate from a heightened awareness of the female body and use of gesture within systems. For example, while Devlin praised the quick physical involvement of Suzuki, she also criticized the "male, warrior-like" effect that this type of training had upon her feminist sensibilities. The Method actress with a feminist sensibility can remain alert to images and selections of actions that tear down passive ways of behaving. This awareness helps to foster a renewed sense of identity in women's lives because of its intimate link to the performance of gender. However, reinforcing destructive images through the use of technique also could be detrimental. For example, under the guise of employing Meisner's repetition exercise, which seeks to encourage spontaneity in acting, one female teacher told me of whispering in an actor's ear that a terrible event had just occurred as a result of another actor's actions. This could be manipulative and contradictory to feminist concerns where ethics override the "successful" product at all costs. Rather than seeking to validate women's own emotional control as subjects, the particular construction of the repetition exercise has the potential to foster the false cliché of women as victims of their emotions. When used in this manner, and particularly if gendered tendencies of reactions remain unacknowledged, the exercise can do more harm than good.[15]

One way in which many women choose to deal with gender stereotyping while using the Method is to alert female students to selections of gesture, action, and so on, which may reinforce rather than challenge conventional notions of women. Feminist scholar Lisa S. Starks, in writing about the "asexual wommen's libber" image that often plagues women who proclaim their feminist agendas in this manner, particularly in academia, states that in reality "a feminist is one who studies gender in order to demystify the essentialist mythologies that trap men and women into determining gender identity as 'natural.' Rather than policing desire and prescribing 'politically correct' behavior (sexually and otherwise), the feminist strives to open up the range of possibility in terms of gender and equality and to encourage others to respect differences."[16] This examination process exists on a literal and representational level, so that an actor remains aware of how behavior plays upon her own body, mind, and emotions, in addition to how it may read to an audience.

Many of the interviewees attempt to insert an awareness of gender (often as a social construct) within realistic training.[17] Doing this enables students to be alert to ideological superstructures. Feminists who teach acting seek paths of maintaining identification with characterization—for both the actor and the audience—through realistic personalization. Nonetheless, they question choices that remain subsumed in stereotypical contexts. As students learn to determine critically how their beliefs dictate behavior, character portrayals open up to ideological and theoretical scrutiny.

When I first explored this topic at the Association for Theatre in Higher Education (ATHE) convention in Philadelphia in 1993, Chicago acting teacher Bella Itkin vowed to teach women and men in the same manner.

This mandate to teach equally coincides with other acting professors who claimed to adhere to equality in the classroom. However, the following year, I observed Itkin's acting technique in practice at the ATHE convention in Chicago, as she worked on the love scene between Masha and Vershinin in Anton Chekhov's *Three Sisters*.[18] Although each student received equal treatment, Itkin reinforced gendered stereotypes. She urged the male student to identify emotionally and physically with a stalwart colonel who tears himself away from the woman he loves by marching off to a career and family. In contrast, she enjoined the female student to identify with the torture of Masha's ensnarement as the victimized lonely woman with no choice but to resign herself to an empty life. As a consequence, the "universalized" approach advanced by Itkin perpetuates stereotypes and, in so doing, prevents tapping into creative work that could reach beyond clichés. Even if the circumstances of text—in their most obvious interpretation— seem to suggest this type of behavior, what can students do to counteract cliché depictions? The students in this demonstration became puppets manipulated by Itkin's ideological strings, instead of agents free to explore alternative possibilities through the use of evolving self-identity as encouraged by the Method. Conventional work might create an easily consumable product, but an acting environment should concern itself with broad awareness of social and political ramifications.[19]

In contrast to this predictable use of Chekhov's realistic text, Susan Mason of California State University—Los Angeles assigns scenes from *The Cherry Orchard* in which the women play Lopakhin and the men play Varya. She comments that within this cross-gender casting, women jump up, eager to embody and identify with the role of the upstart peasant who makes good, while very few of the men seem eager to enact the adopted daughter facing a life of servitude if Lopakhin does not propose to her. This situation indicates both female desire to take on more active roles that contradict the passive ones usually offered to women as well as male reticence to identify with inferior behavior. According to Mason, "all [the actors] experience playing both parts in terms of the subtlety of interaction."[20] This type of training offers students possibilities beyond mere stereotyped behavior. While many teachers conceded that it might be acceptable to begin sketching a role with stereotyped observation, they ultimately work with students in discovering the individual that lurks beneath the one-dimensional text through the use of self in all its contemporary observations. The Method, which encourages the use of self above the role, helps students envision ways in which they can subvert the gendered stereotypes in classical realism.

In dealing with each actor as an individual, and with how each individual has been conditioned to respond from a gendered perspective, the teacher can bolster students' ability to make choices that are politically and socially informed. In addition, race and other cultural determinants also factor in. This emphasis on gender and race is the basis of identity politics. At the very least, the recognition of the actor's performance of gender and other such constructed factors would serve as another inroad to help actors understand themselves, and thereby what they do and say "in" character, more keenly.

Feminist theatre scholar Elaine Aston writes that "Working from personal experience offers you not only a way in to the text, but also a way of resisting the 'here are the important, universal themes and messages in this play that you *ought* to address' approach." She adds, "as life experiences are conditioned by factors such as gender, nationality, race and class, we should think of the personal not just as the 'text' of an individual in isolation but produced by her or his social, cultural and material environment."[21] While the Method advocates the use of the personal in order to create the psychology of an individual, the Group Theatre developed the craft of Stanislavsky's work as a way of expressing its own sociopolitical beliefs. Many of the respondents in my work mentioned, for example, the need for actors to find and play the struggles within characters' circumstances to avoid acquiescing as victims. A number of them, however, noted that good actors do this anyway, denouncing the notion that this might be a tactic indicative of acting from a feminist perspective. The difference may be the cognizance of positionality of gender from a socioeconomic perspective and not merely from an individual standpoint. French feminist critic Teresa de Lauretis calls this "the practice of self-consciousness" because it analyzes and critiques women's social experiences in order to revise, reevaluate, and reconceptualize those circumstances.[22] Doing so allows actors to fight not only internal battles but also external ones that may victimize them. A number of the women revealed how overcoming obstacles, such as poor, working-class backgrounds, sexual harassment, and racial discrimination, has compelled them to recognize and resist oppression in the characters they create, and in very realistic ways.

Some of the respondents to my inquiry use an objective, socially critical eye to look at positionality as character and as performer in order to enhance the subjective, psychological vision. Once the subjective identity is established, the actor then begins to deconstruct her image. She looks at how her choices culturally signify and create meaning rather than merely reflect reality. The construction of character occurs when subjective-psychological and objective-social perspectives combine, reaching beyond our ordinary lives and into the realm of the extraordinary. Rather than being mutually exclusive, the subjective and objective acting choices become multilayered. After scrutinizing the cultural background, actors reinsert their identification with their characters. They can then provoke identification from spectators through familiar choices that on some level unsettle expected images. Still, the question essential to acting training is: Does such belabored attention to political self-identity interrupt the spontaneity sought by the Method?

Three noteworthy examples of positionality and identity strategy have shown how such strategies can be implemented. First, Jodie Hovland of Riverside Theatre sought to make the sister who cooks and nurtures the family in Brian Friel's *Dancing at Lughnasa* wanton and physically aggressive. Hovland, in general, noted that she usually explores nontraditional images for her female characters through expanding the range of her voice and body. For this character, she acknowledged the sister's sense of humor and longing for an adventurous life by personally identifying with that. Given her past, she also connected with the "tomboyishness" evidenced in the text, as, for example, her character's enjoyment of the "sensual physicality of tromping around feeding the pigs."[23] Hovland then made specific choices, such as a bold open-leggedness, to exhibit a character who fought against the type of culturally expected, "feminine" stances of the other sisters in the play. Her work helped to create a range of womanhood from both a psychological and a social level.

Second, Nan Brooks of Oasis Productions utilized the visually recorded behavior of Eleanor Roosevelt, such as a raised chin, severely straight back, and gently curved fingers with forefinger extended back toward her ear as a performance of gender for the 1940s.[24] She contrasted this contained physical demeanor with outspoken, direct address and tried to move a contemporary audience to effect social change, as Eleanor did through her national programs. In creating her character, Brooks identified personally with much of what Eleanor experienced in her life—for example, a childhood of neglect and the discovery of a community of women to support her. She captured this ex–First Lady's walk on painful "White House feet" by studying the effect of high heels and girdles on older women. Brooks's goal is to portray Eleanor as "not just an abstract figure, but a real woman struggling with the very contradiction of restriction versus her progressive, forward-looking actions" of historical impact.[25]

Finally, Rog Wall of Austin's Word of Mouth Women's Theatre identified with and separated herself from her portrayal of a 1920s lesbian in Claudia Allen's *Hannah Free* in order to contravene stereotyped images. Believing that taking care of the body is vital to feminist practice, Wall worked vocally and physically to enlarge her capabilities. She studied books and talked with people, especially to enact her character's spirit that at one point rises from a coma into a dance. Wall also brought a sense of yearning to be with her lover through her own contemporary lesbian body by seeking differences and similarities between her and the character. For example, personally unfamiliar with wearing a dress, she used that costumed awkwardness as an inroad into her character's struggle against the culturally specific wife and mother whom she played.[26] At the same time, Wall felt that her strength in the role came from justifying Rachel's position to stay at home tending her trees and flowers while her lover traveled the world, rather than playing the victim of social mores. For Wall this choice was as valid her own lifestyle in the 1990s.

The acting of Hovland, Brooks, and Wall imagines the space where women freely move in and out of socially prescribed behavior, based on their relational needs as historicized characters and as contemporary actors identifying with those characters. Perhaps because the interstitial space exists between expected behavior and that behavior which seeks to reconfigure expectations, some of what the actors accomplish may appear vague. Rather than obviating their intentions, however, their acting choices suggest the problematic nature—but not the impossibility—of efforts to include feminist perspective within realistically based Method work. As a result of their differing but subject-centered emphases, each

actress chose varying ways of projecting an awareness of female positionality. They all empowered themselves through their physical choices of
actions and gestures, thereby resisting the hegemonic nature of the narratives in which they found themselves inscribed.

Do these serve as examples of feminist acting? Elaine Aston argues
that feminist acting does not exist if "terms of form and content can be
assimilated into dominant artistic and political values, . . . with a mainstream technique like that of a Stanislavski based 'method' of performance." She classifies this type of "showcasing" of women's talents as
belonging to a "bourgeois feminist dynamic aimed at improving the position of women in spectators' eyes without any radical social changes."[27]
In researching this subject among one hundred women practitioners and
instructors in this country, I have analyzed and defined two categories of
feminist acting, namely "implicit" and "explicit."[28] The former involves
acting that occurs, for the most part, within a realistic framework but still
seeks to imbue characters with a sense of individual psychology and social critique. The latter implies the type of acting that breaks realistic
frames and exposes the constructedness of the acting process and the
characters created. It visibly highlights differences of gender, race, sexual
preference, and class as cultural representations rather than subsumes
them as natural reflections of society. Both are equally valid in their feminist intent and process, if not in their resultant product. Generally, both
also seek positive goals of self-actualization and self-determination rather
than merely to defy or destroy existing practices.

The previous acting examples are indicative of implicit feminist acting.
Hovland understood being caged into one-dimensional images of a particularized woman and fought against that through unexpected physical
acting choices and personal identification as a feminist. Conflict of character is complicated by a contemporary consciousness of the positionality
of women in relation to each other. Brooks uses a historical figure to
demonstrate the absurdity of behavioral limitations imposed on women
by specific cultures. Implicit acting necessitates that the actor be in control of her choices and attuned to the images that she creates through
them. And Wall, in investing her character with her personal identity
through her use of the dress, acts both inside and outside of gendered behavior and ideological manifestations. This personal identity and costume

exhibits the strength of performer and character, as both the physical and emotional power of the actor is balanced and capable of driving her performance. A complex, multifaceted figure of a woman, personally identified with the actor, is presented. Ultimately, implicit acting marks the work of an intelligent, thinking actor, alert to the images of gender and other differences and capable of embodying them.

A Method actor seeks ways of investing herself in the emotional, imaginative, and relational contexts of characters. More often than not, she privileges the self over the role in some form or another. For a feminist, this can be a beneficial way of performing. While taking on the circumstances of a character, the female actor can keep herself present as well through a critical, social eye on performance. If women remain alert to the images created by the choices of the evolving self—on both a literal, individual, as well as representational, collective level—they can utilize Method acting to develop characters who are feminist not only in bourgeois strength of actions but also in materialistic differences. Method practice can then work in spite of its alignment with an acting technique that originated a century ago.

NOTES

1. The term "positionality" refers to a person's placement in any given context, seen as relational and moving, and defined by gender, race, class, and other socially significant dimensions. See, for instance, Francis Maher and Mary Kay Thompson Tetreault, *The Feminist Classroom* (New York: Basic Books, 1992), 22.
2. See, for instance, Esther Beth Sullivan, "Women, Woman and the Subject of Feminism: Feminist Directors," *Upstaging Big Daddy: Directing Theatre as if Race and Gender Matter*, Ellen Donkin and Susan Clement, eds. (Ann Arbor: University of Michigan Press, 1993), 28.
3. Deborah Tannen, professor of linguistics and specialist in gendered conversational relations, describes how the classroom traditionally favors boys' language experiences more than girls, because boys grow up accustomed to participating in central activity with peers, whereas girls learn to communicate privately with selected friends. Tannen, "Teachers' Classroom Strategies Should Recognize That Men and Women Use Language Differently," *Chronicle of Higher Education*, June 19, 1991, 2: 2–3.
4. See my study, "Acting Theory, Training, and Practice from Feminist Perspectives," Ph.D. diss., University of Texas at Austin, 1997, 75–103, for

discussions on how female students grapple with not speaking as frequently as male students in the classroom and how some teachers purposively devise exercises to compel women to overcome such resistance.

5. Patricia Schroeder makes the point that realism is an aesthetic structure that may be implicated in the political ideology that led up to its construction but is not inherently oppressive because of an alignment with patriarchal values. See Schroeder, *The Feminist Possibilities of Dramatic Realism* (Madison, NJ: Fairleigh Dickinson University Press, 1996), 41.

6. See Charlotte Canning, *Feminist Theater in the U.S.A.: Staging Women's Experience* (New York: Routledge, 1996), 54; Sue-Ellen Case, *Feminism and Theatre* (New York: Routledge, 1988), 123; and Kathryn Carter, "A Phenomenology of Feminist Theatre and Criticism," Ph.D. diss., Southern Illinois University, 1985, 53.

7. Case, *Feminism and Theatre*, 122–23.

8. Canning, *Feminist Theatre*, 210.

9. See Shelia Stowell, "Rehabilitating Realism," *Journal of Dramatic Theory and Criticism* 6.1 (Spring 1992): 81–88; and Janelle Reinelt, "Realism, Narrative and the Feminist Playwright—a Problem of Reception," *Modern Drama* 32 (March 1989): 115–27.

10. See, for instance, Elin Diamond, "Brechtian Theory/Feminist Theory," *TDR* 32.1 (1988): 82–94; and Janelle Reinelt, *After Brecht: British Epic Theatre* (Ann Arbor: University of Michigan Press, 1994).

11. Sonia Moore professed to have taught the Stanislavsky System in its entirety rather than the American derivative known as the Method. She believed that her emphasis on Stanislavsky's final finding of the method of physical actions separated her teachings from Lee Strasberg and his emphasis on emotional memory.

12. I ran into opposition from some women when it came to labeling their theatrical endeavors as feminist. A number in the professional world, such as director JoAnne Akalaitis, believe that giving their work a feminist label prevents people from viewing their work as artistic. In the academic world, several women also refused the label largely due to job security.

13. Joyce Devlin, interview by author, July 28, 1994, Chicago, tape recorded at the Association for Theatre in Higher Education Convention.

14. Tadashi Suzuki trains actors to use their whole bodies to speak expressively by concentrating on the stomping of the feet and the control of breath. See Suzuki, "Culture is the Body," *Acting (Re)Considered: Theories and Practices*, Phillip Zarrilli, ed. (London: Routledge, 1995), 155–60.

15. Feminist theatres base much of their work around validating women's emotions as well as reassessing the stereotyped figure of the "hysterical woman." Alison M. Jagger refers to emotions that women and other subordinated people feel as "outlaw emotions," because they are incompatible with dominant perceptions and values. See Jagger, "Love and Knowledge: Emotion in Feminist Epistemology," *Women, Knowledge and*

Reality: Explorations in Feminist Philosophy, Ann Garry and Marilyn Pearsall, eds. (New York: Routledge, 1996), 180.

16. Lisa S. Starks, "Hyper-feminisms: Poststructuralist Theories, Popular Culture, and Pedagogy," *Gender and Academe: Feminist Pedagogy and Politics,* Sara Munson Deats and Lagretta Tallent Lenker, eds. (Lanham, MD: Rowman and Littlefield, 1994), 113.

17. Judith Butler argues that gender is a "social temporality," constructed through the repetition or performance of behaviors linked to cultures. This is salient to the materialist feminist position that seeks to understand how reality is shaped by such socially determined factors. See Butler, *Gender Trouble: Feminism and the Subversive Identity* (New York: Routledge, 1990), 139–41.

18. Bella Itkin, "Taking the Mystery Out of Sensory Technique," ATHE Convention, Chicago, July 28, 1994.

19. Deanna Jent's study confirms that acting classes claiming to free students physically, in order to develop characters from a more neutral basis of gestures, in fact, allow students to remain locked into gendered behavior when gender is ignored. See Jent, "Sex Roles in the Acting Class: Exploring the Effects of Actor Training on Nonverbal Gender Display," Ph.D. diss., Northwestern University, 1989, 191–92.

20. Susan Mason, telephone interview by author, May 24, 1994, Los Angeles, tape recorded in Austin, TX.

21. Elaine Aston, *Feminist Theatre Practice: A Handbook* (London: Routledge, 1999), 91.

22. Teresa de Lauretis, *Technologies of Gender* (Bloomington: Indiana University Press, 1987), 20.

23. Personal interview by the author of Jodie Hovland, compiled over the following dates: September 12, 1999 and September 22, 1994.

24. Brooks continues to perform this one-woman show. Personal interview of Brooks compiled by the author over the following dates: September 12, 1999 and 17 July 1994.

25. According to Brooks, this is how Eleanor Roosevelt referred to her consistently sore, high-heeled feet. As part of the show, Brooks offers to tour the audience through the Roosevelt residence, but not before she changes from heels to walking shoes, which still only slightly modifies her stilted stature.

26. Personal interview of Rog Wall compiled by author, June 23, 1994.

27. Aston, *Feminist Theatre Practice,* 65–6, 65.

28. Credit goes to Julia Pachoud of Augustana College for suggesting these terms. Personal interview of Julia Pachoud compiled by author, August 3, 1994.

PART II

PRACTICE

CHAPTER SEVEN

MINING MY OWN BUSINESS

Paths between Text and Self

Deb Margolin

It's good, right, and refreshing that I don't know anything about her other than her first name, which I couldn't spell if I tried. That's not true: I also remember that she was Russian and newly come to America, that she had a small son who was two years old but had the strength of a Titan, that she wore open sandals even in the winter to showcase her lavish pedicures, that she was an acting teacher halfway between old and young with a creaseless forehead and two curved lines around her mouth that seemed to put her sensuous lips in parentheses, who held some sort of salon twice a week in which actors were forced to do all sorts of strange, irrelevant things in pursuit of depth in their stage work. That's all I know.

I was invited to attend one of her acting salons in 1978. Knowing nothing at all about acting, which is what gained me entrée into this astonishing teacher's circle in the first place (she hated "actors"), I was just a poet with a listless, passionate body who was, unbeknownst to me, being considered as a possible collaborator for a nascent theatre collective. People often see more about us than we see about ourselves; that's the very predication of Drama.

I showed up breathless. Teacher was holding court in a loft on a Soho street on the seventh floor of a building with a dysfunctional elevator. I later learned that she did this deliberately, as she believed it was impossible to feign emotion or use the body falsely when struggling for breath. Although it was winter, I was hot from the trek up the stairs and nervous because some preconscious part of me knew that this was the beginning of my life.

In open sandals she greeted me at the door, and I was ushered in to a large, well-lit room. Seated around a table were about eight people of different ages and aspects, some of them in conversation but most of them in an anticipatory silence. As I was the last person expected, the session started at once. I don't remember what she said in the beginning; we began with some sort of vocalization to "loosen the voice from its held place," and then we commenced an exercise that, in retrospect, fully defined for me the nature and relationship of the Self to performance. The structure was this: Each actor was given a piece of text with which to work, from a play of the instructor's choosing. When it was that participant's turn, he or she stood up and began to recite the text, as neutrally as possible, and then, when our teacher said *change,* the actor was to drop the text and seamlessly begin talking about an important personal experience, until she said *change* again, and then the actor would return to the text. An actor would go back and forth between text and personal narrative many, many times, and eventually, as in a cartoon where two brawling animals look like a unified ball of fur, the actor's personal narrative would be recounted in the cadence of the author's text and the text of the play would take on the color of the actor's personal experience. The actor arrived at a secure, significant, repeatable emotional plateau, at once layered, simple, and entirely compelling.

Our teacher knew exactly when to tell the actor to *change;* it was right at the fault line between habituation and habit. She crushed the distance between the text and the Self with her bare hands. She maintained that acting was simple: One needed only to say one thing while thinking another.

There's almost nothing to say about acting. Acting is an emergency, and in an emergency you do whatever works. What you do in a fire drill may bear no resemblance to what you do in an actual fire, but your odds of survival are greatly improved by a past *enactment* of the drills. And so we have the Method and lots of things, pro and con, to say about it.

There's almost nothing to say about acting. Acting is just a particular, heightened way of living, for an hour or two, in which isolated, identified elements of the Self are channeled into a specific, prearranged journey or vision. It could be argued by a lively determinist that life offstage has exactly the same strictures: We live *as if* we were making choices and charting our own courses, when, in fact, somewhere off-site, it's all been written; it's been preconsigned. Onstage or off, we need merely present a believable case for a vital and free will, the only difference being that the former argument is conducted publicly and the latter, privately.

This is where the distinction, as I understand and practice it, between Theatre and Performance becomes relevant, even if only for an instant. Performance Theory is often engaged in an analysis of various aspects of the Self *as* Performance, i.e., gender and sexual practice, race, class, and so on. I think these lively discussions arise due to the most essential difference between the actor's use of him- or herself in the Theatre versus in Performance, and that is *the visibility of the actor's tools.* We are taught, as actors, to blend seamlessly with the character. Method is all about finding ways to go inside a character—ways for the actor to integrate herself fully inside a character, to limn the character with the deepest personal elements while remaining herself invisible *in the act* of doing so. Performance, on the other hand, relies on and takes part of its meaning from *not hiding;* from creating a series of transparent layers between the actor and the character, thus managing to create not only a character but also a dialectic on the *choice to enact this character at all.* Such dialectic has an instant and tacit political component to it, and characters that society might not consider worthy of the stage are suddenly supercharged by and *indistinguishable from* the visible desire of the actor to present them.

As an accidental and founding member of the Split Britches Theater Company, a three-woman repertory theatre collective, I received my early education in theatre with these precepts at the vanguard. Peggy Shaw and Lois Weaver, whom I met at the Russian instructor's salon in the late 1970s, were working on a piece about Lois's ancestors, three women who lived in the Blue Ridge Mountains of Virginia. Weaver was intrigued by the lives of these "forgotten" women; folklore had it that they lived in one room, although they had a whole house; that they never changed their clothes, choosing instead to wear layer upon layer constantly; and that they had cows and pigs and chickens in the room with them. Weaver took a tape recorder down to the home-place and interviewed people about the lives of these women, and she brought these recorded sessions back up to New York. From her relatives' reflections, she and Shaw and several other women began trying to piece together a view of these women's lives.

Most generative for me was their "Method" for creating the women's *inner lives*. Although Weaver was classically trained in the theatre, having studied with Jerzy Grotowski and others, and Shaw was trained on her feet in the raw streets of Europe with Hot Peaches, an all-male gay theatre troupe, both women arrived at the same "Method" for creating truth in character: that of bridging gaps in the understanding of character (whether the playwright was Shakespeare or they themselves) with purely personal narratives. What they didn't know, they vowed to create out of themselves, out of their own desires to speak, to live. Weaver explored images of childhood eroticism within her character, Cora, a woman described by the relatives as "not quite right in the head." Shaw, as Della the caretaker, imagined her character as a lesbian with no word for lesbian, no knowledge of a precedent in her realm of desire. As a "real-life" lesbian couple, Shaw and Weaver had many avenues closed off to them; through the embodiment of the characters in the Blue Ridge Mountains, they were able to speak of those anguishes, to reclaim the stage for three old ladies we might have found too old or uneducated to be "attractions," and to explore lesbian sexuality as it may or may not have existed in the lives of two of the women in the play. Ultimately, the sexual orientation of the real women was less important than the depth and political importance of Shaw and Weaver's commentary on sexuality embedded into the text of the play. They filled in the gap between fact and fiction with their own passions (an inherently political methodology when you let it show), which is exactly where conventional Method's usefulness, it seems to me, begins and ends. Lee Strasberg said: "How can I paint unless I am willing to confuse my own feelings with what I am doing? I then have to have the skill and the means to make my vision, my feeling, my thought apparent to other people who don't have my personal attitudes. But I can only work out of my personal attitude. How else can I work?" (*SS* 184).

Shaw and Weaver scoped me out during those roundtable salons, and decided I was the quirk and language freak just right to complement their desire to use the theatre to invent and present the truth out of themselves. I began working with them as a writer, borrowing their faith in the political power and inherent poetics of blatant uses of personal experience in the creation of text, and found myself *mining my own business* in writing monologues for characters who were, on the surface, nothing like me at all. The next thing I knew, I was *in* this play about the three women; I don't even know how that happened, playing the eighty-something senile Southern Baptist aunt of the other two. I was, at the time, a twenty-something razor-sharp Jewish nerd with glasses. Now as an actor, just as I had been as a writer, I was encouraged to fill in the distance between myself and my character with whatever I had in my lexicons of silence that was yearning to be made manifest. For me, that was madness, the solitary nature of mind, the way the body belies the mind; other things too ineffable to say, things that I was able to express only through the act of portraying this old lady.

Split Britches employed an acting Method we referred to as Multiple Choice acting, which meant that in the course of a performance, you had many different sources to draw on for depth of field in maintaining the life of a character: You had affective memory, you had the very moment in which you found yourself, you had your relationships with and responses to others onstage, you had the behavior of the audience, you had the valence of the language, you had the inherent problems of the situation (both as defined by the imaginary circumstances of the play and by the real effort of performance), and you had other emotional sources that came and went. Although choices changed moment-to-moment or performance-to-performance, the result was a consistent engagement with the act of performing that made for a repeatable vitality.

I was discovering then how authorial acting is, how we *write* a play through our *acting* it; conversely, as a writer, I was coming to see how inherently kinetic language becomes; how considerate of the body, both her own and that of the actor, a writer must be to achieve character successfully. Excellence also underwent a redefinition: How *well* a line was spoken or an action was taken had to do with how articulately the *desire* to speak or act was conveyed.

It may be interesting to note that, except during the filming of *Split Britches* for Public Television in the late 1980s, I used almost no makeup at all, made no attempt to literally transform myself ahead in age sixty years. I let my yearning to speak and be seen do that for me, and it worked, after a fashion. That "fashion" is the state line between Theatre and Performance: Very flimsy. Strasberg said:

> You yourself have moments of despondency, of not knowing whether you can act, of not knowing whether you can get an acting job, of worrying whether you should get some other job, of being worried about what the hell is the matter with you. And we say that the actor can somehow share these moments with the character. We say that this kind of life can be brought alive within you, the actor, and that you can thus bring it alive within the character in the scene who is not an actor but a poet. We say that when you have succeeded in bringing alive this kind of creative moment, you don't have to worry about what you will act—writing or dancing or anything else—because you can then do any scene involving that kind of moment. If it is a writing scene, you will be able to write. If the character is someone who wants to dance, instead of doing a definite dance and giving an obviously exhibitionist and performing value, you will be able to allow the music to affect you in some kind of rhythm that retains a human value because precisely what movements will happen from it are not known in advance. [*SS* 272]

I will leave definitions of Method acting to the scholars, but I feel clear for myself that Method is all about the problem of redistributing autobiography. We cannot perform what we do not imagine, and we cannot imagine that which is not within us to be conceived. We have nothing but ourselves, which is the same as to say there is nothing to say about acting. Split Britches, the theatre company, was often described as "radical" in its aesthetic, in its approach to creating character, to creating theatre. The jagged juncture between actor and character was the metaphysical site of our performances, and it felt dangerous to some critics, as if we ourselves might burst forth out of the play at any moment and infest them with life, with tragedy, with sex. I think we were just Method actors who didn't bother to clean up. We conducted our fire drills during the fire, and we survived those fires together for fifteen years.

I bet Lee Strasberg would have laughed his head off at Split Britches' antics. Say whatever you want. Scholars will argue. Strasberg would have laughed. Method is criticized for being too self-centered, for being too shallow of text analysis, for emphasizing character at the expense of the play, for emphasizing the actor over the character or the character over the actor, for contradicting itself. Strasberg was a great acting teacher who was *willing* to contradict himself, which is what made him such a great philosopher of theatre. Theatre just isn't the kind of precise science that might make it sane, reasonable, and consistently repeatable upon experiment. It seems to me that Strasberg stressed all the right things in training actors and that those things contradict each other a great deal of the time. You can disappear if that works, you can hang out there if it doesn't. What matters is: Can you breathe life into this character or not?

NINETEEN EIGHTY SOMETHING

Some gadget freak friend had installed a telephone in my bathroom. The bathroom is supposed to be a place of baptism, privacy, and relief, not a place to order a pizza. It was late; I was expected at the theatre in forty-five minutes to perform in a funky, exciting downtown venue on a bill with four other artists. I had chosen a demented comic monologue in which a parched, middle-aged, sexually tone-deaf woman trying to sell vacuum cleaners breaks down emotionally every time she attempts to discuss the solving of household problems. At one point the hapless saleslady holds up a newspaper headline reading DEFICIT OCCURS IN A VACUUM, and she shrieks: Is that what I've got in here? *The fucking deficit?*

In the bathroom, putting on makeup. The light was best in there. When the telephone rang, I was raking my eyelashes with clotty black mascara; I reached for the phone with my left hand. It was this man; I can't remember his name, not any part of it. He was calling because three months prior I had answered a personal ad he left in some free newspaper in which he called himself a Jewish Guy. That got me: Jewish Guy. He introduced himself, and I said:

Look. I have a show in half an hour. I'm a performer. An Actor. I've got a show in a coupla minutes and I can't talk to you now. Here's what you do: You get in a cab and you come down to Ludlow Street. My name is Deb Margolin. You sit in the audience and you watch for me. If you like what you see, you hang around after the show. You don't like it, just get lost. It'll be like a police lineup. I'll never know you; I'll never know which man you are. Every man in the audience will be like you *to me. I'll see you later. Or not.*

And I hung up.

It was so late I had to take a taxi. What a hardship! The city skyline streaming like phosphorescent liquid on the two sides of my peripheral vision—my accelerated heartbeat rushing toward a moment. Arrived at the theatre ten minutes before curtain, greeted my colleagues, quieted down, breathed deeply. Realized I had forgotten to look at the huge, motley audience for *my Man*. Vowed to do it while performing. Someone else went on first and had a wonderful time, came back aglow, covered in sweat. I was up next. Back in those days I always asked the emcee to announce me by name and by the fact that I get a headache the minute I cross the state line into New Jersey. *Now I live there*. I heard the state line announcement, saw the stage manager set my vacuum cleaner; she winked at me, the stage went dark.

That's the last thing I know. That's not true: I know that I did that whole monologue just for Him; just to entertain him. I did this monologue just as I always had, except that the subtext was radioactive, more ridiculous, and deeply erotic. The personality disorders of this middle-aged, unmoist woman were subtly altered, making her into a sort of languishing, executive, Jewish Blanche du Bois. When I lifted the vacuum, its weight was sacred, it was his weight: It was *my* weight, I was selling myself, my body. My hands extended outward in familiar, well-rehearsed gestures; suddenly, instead of the nervous, self-betraying hands of the solitary eccentric, they were hands newly on someone's cheekbone, questing behind a lover's ear, the flat of the lover's back. I looked for this man not with my eyes but in my work. I heard people laughing, but the lasting laughter was, I think, mine.

He hung around after the show. He was boorish and unpleasant. I blew him off and went home.

CHAPTER EIGHT

STANDARDS AND PRACTICES

Doug Moston

There are many ways to study acting. Ultimately, the teacher must ask herself: What does good acting look like? The answers are personal and subjective. They depend on standards and practices. Ask an audience member if she likes actor X and she might say, "No, I don't like him." An actor in a Shakespeare play, for example, pours out his soul to express his personal pain and conflict. We admire his ability. Many are impressed with his emotional flexibility. Yet others, while acknowledging the actor's talents, are troubled by the performance. They feel that the actor has obscured the magnitude of the character because of the actor's direct expression of emotion. In this case, emotion is actually an obstacle to the character's quest for his objective. What we see, then, are differing standards.

Let us turn to stage acting and, in particular, the way it was approached by Constantin Stanislavsky. Stanislavsky divided the work of stage acting into two categories, work on the self and work on the role. With these two goals, we seek to balance an actor's instrument and craft. Instrument work can be defined partly as work on the Self. It helps the actor express all the feelings and behavior without editing or censoring impulses.[1] Craft allows actors to create what needs to be convincing in the performance, what needs to be believed. These are the given circumstances of the play and of the actor's faith in them.

In examining three phases of Stanislavsky's work—the psychological, the imagination, and the method of physical actions—it is interesting to observe how teachers and students extract what they need in order to validate their own particular biases. Lee Strasberg emphasized the psychological; it was his way of utilizing Stanislavsky's system, given his assessment of American acting. He focused on affective memory, emotional recall, and personal, even private, exercises, throwing the focus on the production of behavior, feelings, and emotions. When those feelings and emotions arose in an actor who was simultaneously pursuing the character's actions and objectives, his efforts were successful, according to most actors and observes. However, when actors tried to exploit their emotions in the name of authentic behavior, Strasberg offered sharp personal critique.

Some acting courses, classes, and workshops are terrifying, if not dangerous, because the director or teacher bores into the actor's psyche in the name of art. Such behavior is a cheap imitation of Strasberg, Stella Adler, and Sanford Meisner, the consequences of a desire to imitate attributes of great teachers but without substance or originality. The results are the development of trusting actors or students, diligently trying to comply. Along the way, their dignity is compromised as well as their creativity and art. This crime is often perpetuated in the name of the Method, and should be rejected out of hand.

After assessing actors' strengths and challenges, a teacher might look to balance instrument and craft in individuals. For example, some actors might be emotionally available, easily expressing anger, sadness, joy, and other feelings. However, they may be unable to coordinate this inner life with their character. In this instance, the students need craft work. Some actors instinctively understand the character, what the character needs, and what choices to make that will illuminate the character. However, despite their ability to make choices that elicit behavior, the behavior is not fully expressed. These actors would need work on their instruments—the emotional and felt behavior—that stretches their expressivity. One set of exercises classically used by Lee Strasberg to stretch both instrument and craft is sense memory.

Actors can be trained, using the sensory exercises, to employ the memory of their five senses to respond to stimuli. They can have a genuine conditioned reflex without the original stimulus, which is called the object. They can, in effect, create a reality that doesn't exist in the present. In rehearsal and in homework, actors can create all of the circumstances so that their senses respond to objects (whether real or imagined), creating the character's world for themselves and the audience.

Sense memory is not returning to the past to remember your dead pet so you can cry in a scene. This is a misunderstanding of the work. Based on Dr. Ivan Pavlov's turn-of-the-century experiments in Russia, sense memory is a technique that helps actors believe a reality that in fact doesn't exist in the present. Pavlov, a pioneer in human conditioned response, found that a dog would associate the sound of a tone or a metronome with food. When the sound accompanied food, the dog would salivate. Once the dog had been conditioned through repeated experiments, it would salivate when hearing only the sound, and no food was necessary.[2] This conditioned response helps actors achieve real sensory experiences that are, in fact, nonexistent.

How do actors believe what isn't actually there? How can actors look at a painted flat upstage and respond as if it is the front wall of Elsinore Castle? How can an actor look at someone they don't get along with offstage and love him as their father onstage? The answer is: Actors can *condition* themselves to respond sensorily to the circumstances of the play. One way is to endow the fictional elements of the play with elements of their own experience. Stanislavsky calls this the "magic if." This is his way of using semantics to get actors' "truth-sense" to work for them. For example, if you try to tell yourself that you are in love with the actor playing opposite you, and you're not, your truth-sense will kick in and say, "Are you crazy? You don't love him. You don't even like him!" But if you simply respond to him as if he were someone you *did* love, or did love once, you are not resisting your truth-sense. The actor might say: "No, I don't love him, but I can do what I would do *as if* I did." This is very different from pretending. Pretending implies that it isn't actually true. But to actually do what you do when you are in love is, by definition, active, and actable.

Simply put, if you have ever smelled a familiar fragrance, heard a familiar song, tasted a familiar flavor, or seen a familiar item from long ago and found yourself instantly transported back in time, you have experienced a sensory effect. Sensory work is not a crazed notion of angst-ridden torment but a vital experience that is used by all artists. It is as if your emotions understand what is happening to you before your brain can make sense of it. The sensory object unintentionally becomes the stimulus for an emotional effect. Sense memory is a way of controlling that phenomenon and using it artistically to create the character's world onstage.

This is not an exercise to be used for creating emotions directly. To use it this way would be to second-guess human nature by preconceiving which emotion should be created in the first place. Don't go directly for the result, but trust your process and the result will emerge *in the moment*. *In the moment* has become a Method cliché, which means it had a noble genesis that, at some point, lost connection with its origin. It means, literally, living in the moment, and not anticipating the next action.

Stanislavsky's system was a way of finding inspiration in our work as actors, directors, and playwrights, instantly expressing the original thought without censoring interference. This is the goal and the art. The objective of actors is, in part, to match their own truth to the truth of characters. But how do actors use their truth to create characters? Two primary elements form the basis of this necessary synergy.

The first element of this formula is to believe the play's circumstances. These include place, time, relationship to other characters, illnesses and/or physical restrictions, past, present, future, fears, challenges, dreams, and the psychological characteristics involved. The second element is a strong personal choice, a stimulus that impels actors toward theatrical action, actively doing what the characters do. While most teachers and practitioners may feel this is obvious, the Method is, again, often misunderstood regarding this point. Teachers explain it and students nod in understanding, but instead of really focusing on their process as discussed, students focus on the result (an emotion, a conclusion, or an obvious action that lacks strong conviction). They exploit their own emotions in the name of art. If they manage to tap into a real feeling, they have a personal catharsis, usually at the audience's expense. Actors should choose to *do* rather than to *feel*.

Another technique that uses sense memory as a basis is *substitution*. In employing substitution, actors replace a fictional element of the play with one from their own lives. Controversy surrounds this tool because, like sense memory, it has frequently been misunderstood. The most prevalent misinterpretation asks: "How can an actor focus on her partner while substituting his face with someone else's, which in effect cancels him out? She can't be properly involved in the scene, genuinely relating to her partner." If true, this technique would be an excellent reason to avoid substitution. But this is not what substitution is. Substitution, efficiently, creatively, and responsibly used, is a way of connecting an actor to her partner, strengthening the relationship, not denying it. It is dependent on the actor's choice and how it is applied. Consider this example.

If your attention is on your choice at the expense of your partner, you miss the point of substitution. You miss an opportunity to negotiate the scene in the moment. You can't focus on the scene if by virtue of your choice you are otherwise engaged. But if you choose something personal from your own experience and find that element in the actor(s) you're relating to in the scene, you are supplying through substitution the element that truly makes you need to deal with your partner(s). For instance, if you're playing Ophelia (Act III, scene I), you must give Hamlet, your former lover, back his letters. What choices might you make as to who Hamlet is to you? The obvious choice would be to talk to the actor playing Hamlet as if he were a former lover. It might work. But it might not. The logic of emotions and behavior is different from intellectual logic, and in using intellectual logic we sometimes miss the logic of theatrical action, which leads to theatrical behavior. The simpler the choice, the easier it is to execute, with less margin for error. Perhaps you've never had a significant other that you have felt particularly special about. Maybe you don't really know what love is. Suppose, then, that you return a special present that was given to you by your mother. Could you approach the actor playing Hamlet as if you were dealing with your mother under similar circumstances? Of course! It isn't difficult. You simply *endow* the actor with those attributes you found in someone special. Once you develop the habit of substitution, the choices begin to come to you rather quickly, and you commit to the give-and-take of the scene without missing a beat.

The most useful way of going about making choices that serve the play is to structure your time with lots of questions during rehearsal. In the creative process, questions are far more important than answers. It is the act of questioning that propels you into your process. The answers will be evident in your performance. The process of asking questions through exploring various choices focuses your attention and commits you further. It is in itself active. Consider the example of Hamlet. Is Hamlet seeking revenge? Why? Is Hamlet actually seeking the truth? Why? Is Hamlet trying to regain control of the country? Why: Because he hates his uncle? Or is it because he is suffering from grief, betrayal. These questions are a beginning. They should be posed in rehearsal through doing. Don't merely think it, do it. In the last analysis, you may decide that Hamlet is seeking revenge. But now you will play a Hamlet on many levels, creating a role that is as complex as the author intended.

Another Method process based on sense memory is *affective memory*. Affective memory, also called emotion memory, or emotional recall, is a technique that asks an actor to re-create all of the sensory elements of a past emotional event in order to explore behavior for use in a scene. More than any other exercise, this is the most misunderstood. In the hands of some teachers, it often becomes psychotherapy. Some teachers suggest that when properly trained in the use of affective memory, actors can push the right emotional buttons in themselves. This is anathema to my own understanding and use of Stanislavsky's System. In 1936, Stanislavsky, in a talk to actors and producers at the Moscow Art Theatre, said, "There is only one system-creative organic nature. There is no other system."[3] "Pushing buttons" violates the principles of organic nature that were so emphatically embraced by Stanislavsky; it, in effect, causes actors to seek catharsis as an end in itself. Actors become addicted to the experience of their own emotions (their own button-pushing) at the expense of action.

Affective memory can be used effectively as an instrument exercise. Sometimes actors may have difficulty expressing an emotion. If they feel the need to explore the expression of that emotion, affective memory may be of some value. This use of affective memory is different from an actor deciding to use a specific emotion at a specific point in the scene. The character's emotion originates from the actor's belief in the circumstances coupled with his or her genuine desire to take action. The actor is trying to surmount an obstacle. To replay a so-called past emotion is like painting leaves green. The resulting emotional color is cosmetic. Fertilize the soil with nutrients and the leaves will be green organically.

Sometimes difficulties arise in teaching affective memory because a teacher will suggest an event for a student to use. The teacher may have some personal knowledge about the student's past. This can be dangerous because the student may not be psychologically ready to deal with some of the stimuli touched upon. It is important that students be allowed to make their own choice of what to use. Students must know why they are doing the exercise. Using the exercise to explore behavior is one thing. Using it to create emotions for emotion's sake is to use it improperly. This technique is part of an actor's homework. Affective memory, like sensory work, is Pavlovian. Once affective memory has opened the instrument for expression, actors must trust that the trigger for that expression will be the character's action. They shouldn't make choices to make them "feel," but should make choices to make them "do."

After students have learned to be in the moment, then they must make choices to string these moments together. Doing so is working *moment to moment*. I have been exploring different ways to give students the experience of acting moment to moment through a teachable and repeatable technique. One is a craft tool I call *action to action*. Two actors go onstage to negotiate their scene. Students and teacher not only break the scene down into beats, or units, but also into subbeats. These subbeats are simple, physical actions. For example, prior to a job interview, the father straightens his son's tie. The actor playing the father must complete a physical action that is understandable to the audience before advancing to the next beat. The effects of this exercise have helped actors to be physically aware of their characters. As a result, the audience knows precisely what is happening.

We must also respect the audience. The audience is always a character in the play. Audience members are there; to pretend otherwise would be fundamentally untruthful. It is the playwright, the creator of the character, who designates the audience as part of the given circumstances by choosing to tell the story in the form of a play. Therefore, if the audience is a character, a part of the given circumstances, actors must factor into their performances the audience's needs from one evening's performance to another. Actors should also make certain that acknowledging the audience does not have a deleterious effect on their performances. Audiences are as different as the various characters actors portray. The relationship between actor and audience significantly affects a particular performance.

When working on choices for a role, it is important to cast the audience. If they are treated as some amorphous enemy (we killed 'em last night), actors miss an important opportunity to develop their characters fully. In dealing with the audience directly, either through asides or soliloquies, actors should make choices as to whom, and what, audience members are to them. There is no such thing as a soliloquy or monologue for an actor. It does not exist. A soliloquy is always a scene. It could be between actor and audience, between actor and God, or between actor and actor. A soliloquy is done for the audience, never at its expense. Whichever choice actors make regarding who the audience is to them or the character, it will inform their behavior and communicate that much more vital information about the play, the character, and the circumstances, as well.

Method training, in a necessary attempt to focus students on the dramatic tasks at hand, frequently calls for the construction of the "fourth wall." This idea of the "fourth wall" unfortunately tends to create, for some, the notion that the audience is to be ignored. Toward the close of the nineteenth century, electric lighting changed the relationship between actor and audience. Audiences sat silently in the dark pretending to observe life through the fourth wall. Actors were confronted with footlights that prevented them from seeing the audience. Because they couldn't see the audience, they turned to talk to each other. But this was not the case in Shakespeare's time. Understanding the relationship between actor and audience is a vital factor in applying the Method to Shakespeare.

Since my earliest awareness of the Method, I have heard and read that it fails to work well for acting Shakespeare's plays. After years of attending sessions at the Actors Studio, I believe I know why this is. Modern actors are used to working in a specific sequence, creating behavior first in order to find the character. Behavior is their stock-in-trade, what they market. The Method works with Shakespeare if the order is adjusted in this way: Let the words do the work in directing you to do precisely what Shakespeare says the character does. The appropriate behavior will result.

In playing Shakespeare, actors still need an objective and need to believe the circumstances of the play. Actors need, moreover, to do convincingly what characters do. For example, a modern actor may interpret Constance, in *King John,* as being distraught at the loss of her son, Geoffrey. This preconceived idea might cause her to try to create that emotion for dramatic effect. Unfortunately, she may do this precisely when the character actually wants to avoid expressing emotion in order to accomplish her objective. If Constance proclaims that she is not mad and then becomes hysterical, she will appear mad to us and to those around her. How often, in real life, do we feel intense emotion and work to distance ourselves from it, or simply, perhaps, desperately try to hide it? The poor mother on the evening news who is pleading for her missing children is trying frantically to suppress her own emotion in order to get her message out clearly to the public. Stanislavsky advises actors to play the objectives and find the obstacles that prevent access to their goals. In this instance, emotion is the obstacle.

If the character is supposed to speak verse eloquently, connecting clause after clause, articulating complex thoughts and ideas using intricate language, and the modern actor has no experience in doing this, how is she to follow the directions in Shakespeare's text? Elizabethan theatre was an oral and an aural theatre. People went primarily to hear a play, rather than to see it. Today we see acting mostly in television and on film, which tell stories visually. An actor's quick glance at the end of a short television scene tells us what the character is feeling, wants, or is frightened of, or that a commercial is imminent. How do we get today's actors, trained for a different standard, to do what is warranted in classic theatre?

In my Classics, Period, and Style classes at the Actors Studio Master of Fine Arts program, I use an exercise called the *passion workout.* It offers actors the opportunity to express themselves with words, many words. The exercise is accomplished in three phases. Often several weeks may elapse between each phase. First of all, actors choose a topic that they will speak to the class about. They will speak for seven or eight minutes. The topic should be connected to something they feel passionately, something they might sell listeners on, something so infectious that, even though listeners may never embrace it, they embrace the actor's love of it, whatever it may be. Second, actors must use words to reach listeners, to connect listeners to them, and perhaps, to change the audience as well. Third, as they express themselves, actors articulate personal, complex thoughts using complex language and gesture, suffused with their passion. Their language is often rich in metaphor, simile, wordplay, and alliteration. The exercise necessitates this way of speaking in order for actors to achieve their objective: To sell the listeners on this item, this event, and this idea. As the teacher, I rarely intercede except to keep actors on track in terms of their salesmanship or their effectiveness in reaching and involving the audience. Objectives and actions are the key to this exercise. Afterward I moderate commentary from the class. This is important: We discuss form, never content. We are watching, or perhaps I should say listening, for new patterns of thought expressed as new patterns of language. In this exercise, judgment deters extemporaneous expression; hence, all judgment is eschewed. We are seeking effective communication; right or wrong is not a useful focus. The work in class is a means of making thinking effective through language. In his book *Lateral Thinking,* psychologist Edward de Bono puts it this way: "The purpose of thinking is not to be right but to be effective. Being effective does eventually involve being right but there is a very important difference between the two. Being right means being right all the time. Being effective means being right only at the end."[4]

During an actor's passion workout, students often take notes and are excited to report back wonderfully constructed, lyrical phrases that an actor is totally unaware of. At the conclusion of Phase 1, or Passion 1, as we call it, we discuss what the actor will do for Passion 2 (the next phase of the work).

In Passion 2 actors repeat the same topic. However, this time I adjust the circumstances by making them more specific. Now actors are asked to address the class as if they are a specific person. This is designed to cause actors to condense their speech by planning carefully, perhaps referring to notes, changing their former demeanor. During Passion 2, one student spoke passionately about her love of snowboarding. We learned about the sport but, more important, we learned about *her.* For her adjustment sometime later, she chose to discuss her participation in this sport with her mother. She told her mother, and us, about how dangerous it was. She spoke about a young instructor who, after a near-fatal accident, is now a quadriplegic. She needed her mother to understand that she was compelled to do this, to take this kind of physical risk, in order to live, to feel alive. Another student chose to speak about her childhood sexual abuse.

Her objective was to save others from her fate, to protect us from these circumstances. Her adjustment for Passion 2 was to repeat the same story in Washington, D. C., before a Senate subcommittee on child abuse. She had made notes, created a lectern, a pitcher of water, a microphone, and so on. The intense emotion she began to feel was palpable in the room. But her objective made her choose stoicism; that is, she had to remain articulate and clear despite her underlying feelings. The information, she knew, was far more important than her feelings at the moment. Again discussion was sensitively moderated, focusing solely on her use of rhetoric, her ability to persuade or dissuade listeners using words and gesture infused with genuine, organic passion.

In Passion 3, actors use a classical monologue that they have selected using what they learned in Passion 1 and Passion 2 as a preparation. They begin again as they had for Passion 1. When they connect with their objective and the audience, they may move into Passion 2 in order to formalize their actions. They continue to express themselves, this time using their monologue instead of their unscripted narrative. For example, the actor who spoke about snowboarding chose to play the part of Polyxena in *Hecuba*. Although she is sad because she will never see her mother again, she tells her that it is an honor to lay down her life to save her country. In this instance the actor pursued the same objectives she used twice before but this time she used her classical monologue. The actor connected with her circumstances and, using sensory work, created her mother. She spoke to Hecuba in the same way she spoke to her mother in the exercise—this time, using Euripides' words to express her deepest feelings. We as listeners could easily see how the experience she went through in Passions 1 and 2 informed her portrayal of Polyxena. Even though we had heard her exercise twice before and were familiar with the monologue, we experienced her Polyxena behaving as if for the first time.

It should be pointed out, however, that the choice of topic in Passions 1 and 2 does not have to parallel the subject of the classical monologue used in Passion 3. The objective and actions that were vital in Passion 1 and 2 have served their purpose. The mastery of the language and the personal actions and objectives that become expressed through the monologue allow actors to use themselves to create living, breathing characters who express themselves through complex language.

When we understand what characters are really doing, and how they do what they do, we have a means to prepare for the role. An actor playing a surgeon today would spend time with a doctor or in a hospital. An actor playing a sports figure would learn something about the sport. Actors who play the classics also must have the tools to enable them to drive these long speeches of complex verse, speeches in which one sentence, one complex thought, sometimes is composed of thirty lines of verse. In Shakespeare, the character is the language. The techniques of internal behavior and external verse technique must harmonize seamlessly if we are to *embody* real characters before real audiences. Some actors do it instinctively. Some need instruction. It can be taught. It can be learned. But it must be practiced, and it must become the standard.

NOTES

1. For a detailed discussion of terms used in the chapter, see Doug Moston, *Coming to Terms with Acting* (New York: Drama Publishers, 1993).
2. For further information on Pavlov's work, see, for example, James G. Holland and B. F. Skinner, *The Analysis of Behavior* (New York: McGraw-Hill, 1961).
3. David Magarshack, "Preface," *Stanislavsky: On the Art of the Stage,* 2nd ed. (Winchester, UK: Faber and Faber, 1950), 1.
4. Edward de Bono, *Lateral Thinking* (New York: Harper and Row, 1970), 107.

CHAPTER NINE

REDEFINING ACTING

The Implications of the Meisner Method

Brant L. Pope

U ntold wealth would be mine had I a dollar for every prospective student of the Florida State University/Asolo Conservatory for Actor Training who claimed to have studied "a little Meisner." This superficial spin on the Meisner technique causes me to wonder how a physics professor would respond to an applicant who boasted of studying "a little gravity." Perhaps for some, Meisner training is like a special spice that a chef has on his shelf, and when he cooks up a "Meisner dish" he uses the Meisner spice; then when he is finished cooking the dish, he goes back to the "regular" stuff. For an acting conservatory that defines itself as a Meisner program, these preliminary impressions of our methodology are rather humbling. While it is certainly possible to reject the fundamental tenets of Meisner-based work, it is difficult to comprehend how principles this radical and transformational (once adopted) could be inconsistently applied to dramatic material. So, as the physics professor might say, if gravity works, it works all the time.

It is important to make clear at the outset of this chapter that only Sanford Meisner taught the "Meisner Method." When I say that Florida

State University's Asolo Conservatory is a "Meisner" program, I am actually suggesting that our faculty has developed its own method of teaching acting that has been greatly influenced by the work of Meisner.[1] We have developed our process from the basic presumptions of Meisner's teaching. Therefore, what I am proposing as Meisner-based work is actually our interpretation of that work and represents nothing more than that. Indeed, the subject of this chapter is less the application of what Meisner actually taught and more of what we believe is the logical implication of his core teaching. In other words, our work is an extension of what Meisner developed. This extension builds on his emphasis on action and in particular his work that focused attention of the actor not on him- or herself but on the "other." The implications of this emphasis and focus on our understanding of character, conflict, and a basic definition of acting constitute the thrust of this chapter.

The radical nature of Meisner's work is expressed in the core principle of *doing* and the manner in which this alters the basic definition of acting. The emphasis on doing, or action, as opposed to the expression of emotion is the primary characteristic that differentiates Meisner work from that of the other master teachers of Method acting in the United States. Further, a commitment to doing suggests that the central focus of the actor's attention is now on the other actor(s) and *their* response to what is being "done to them."[2]

It is difficult to underestimate the importance of this shift in perspective from self-consciousness to other-consciousness and the way in which it changes the entire conception of the acting process. From the very first repetition exercises, the Meisner approach emphasizes working off the other person, thus suggesting that it is the other person who is the source of the actor's inspiration and stimulus in performance. This concentration (perhaps obsession is the better word) with the other encourages shared and unselfish energy (behavior) that flows from the actor for a particular and specific affect on the other actor(s). Seen in this way, then, acting can be defined as behaving truthfully in imaginary circumstances. Sharing energy makes acting so much easier and joyful because it is such a pleasure to make real contact with another person onstage and see in that person's eyes that he or she is actively listening and fully taking into account what you are doing and feeling. By placing primary importance on the behavior of the other person(s) in a scene, the Meisner approach removes the overlay of self-indulgence that has often been associated with Method acting.[3]

The primary difficulty with acting processes that concentrate the actor's attention on his own character rather than on the ensemble is that it violates the central principle of how it is we come to know and evaluate other human beings. By what means do we come to understand someone's personality and thereby judge his or her character? Is it not by observing the person's behavior toward other people? After we have seen multiple interactions between the individual and other people, a certain pattern or consistency of behavior has become obvious. This pattern we then judge and label "his or her personality." A goal of our approach to acting would be to re-create the same opportunity for the audience to come to a decision about the "character" of the individuals in the play. Another way of saying this is that our goal is to focus not on emotions but rather on human interactions that allow the *audience* to assign meaning and experience emotions. If the actor is concentrating on his own feelings and is attempting to access his inner life, how can he possibly be engaged in a meaningful encounter with another individual? Absent an engagement with another person, how can the observer ever have any idea what the character in the play is thinking or feeling? Because the individual is communicating with another person, he is (without being self-conscious) clarifying his feelings before an audience. It also becomes obvious to an actor that the best way to access his own feelings is to concentrate on activating the emotional life of someone else.

Yet so often actor training seems to discourage an honest interaction. Attempts to play state of being, the demonstration of character, and the total disregard of the energy coming from the other character(s) are the most glaring symptoms of this self-focus. The genius of Meisner, in our view, is the way in which a concentration on the other can solve so many acting problems. I would like to examine several closely related difficulties and suggest how a Meisner approach can offer the actor a successful resolution. The first situation is a virtual pathology in acting that the master teacher Manuel Duque calls "playing the problem." By this he means that actors are aware of their characters' dilemma or problem and feel the need to "play" the problem and let the audience know what the characters are experiencing. The last two issues suggest a redefinition of conflict and character in light of the Meisner emphasis on the "other."

PLAYING THE PROBLEM

A useful illustration of these ideas can be found in the famous bedroom scene between Biff and Happy Loman in Arthur Miller's *Death of a Salesman*. Biff Loman has once again returned to the family home occupied by his father and mother. A traumatic confrontation with his father during his high school days has caused Biff to reject the values espoused by his father, Willy, and also resulted in the complete breakdown of their relationship. Unable to find a new set of principles by which to live, Biff has unhappily bounced from job to job and returns home in a desperate search for some direction in his life. His brother, Hap, is equally unfulfilled in his retail career despite adhering to Willy's dictums for success. They spend the night in their old bedroom sharing frustrations and anxieties. Restless and unable to sleep, the boys are caught up in their own inner turmoil. These are the circumstances that the actors must convey to an audience.

The actors face a difficult task in performing the scene because often their natural instincts, as well as the director's instruction, will in subtle ways encourage them to "play the problem." Most non-Meisner methods of training actors will focus on getting actors in touch with how the characters are feeling in this scene. The director often reinforces this by asking the actors to produce the "quality" (or mood) of the scene in the mistaken belief that some direct way of "portraying emotions" exists. The inability to resolve feelings of anger, failure, confusion, and yearnings for fulfillment is Biff and Hap's problem. The dilemma arises when actors then "take on" their character's problem and in effect demonstrate this problem for the audience.

Meisner's approach to the scene focuses actors not on their character's problem but on the other character and encourages the actors to ask: "What problem does the other character have, that I am going to resolve?" Countless times in directing this scene I have said to the actor playing Biff, "What are you trying to get Hap to do?" (What is your objective?) This is often a befuddling question because the actor is so aware of Biff's problem that he has thought of the scene in completely inactive terms. So, the frequent response is something like, "I am *venting* my frustrations on him," or "I am *sharing* how lost and mixed up I am." This answer betrays the fact that the focus is on the self, not the other, guaranteeing that the scene will be mired in mood, atmosphere, and other forms of "stewing in their juices." Venting and sharing are synonymous with playing the problem because they are attempts to convey the character's internal state of being. The result will be both ineffectual and monotonous.

Actors should be encouraged instead to see the scene in terms of developing changes in the other person. A more helpful question might be to ask the actor playing Biff: "What important thing *happens to your brother* in this scene?" This question compels Biff to view the scene in terms of Happy's behavior and not his own problem. The actor could be lead to conclude something like: "This is the scene in which Hap finally admits that he isn't happy and fulfilled either." Now Biff can organize his energies to make this change happen to his brother. His emotional problems (frustration, self-doubt, and anger with his father) become not what he plays, but rather constitute the emotional motivation for changing Hap. As is true in life, Biff is using what we call "covering energy" in an unconscious attempt to mask his deep inner feelings. It is through the observation of this energy that an audience understands intuitively what feelings motivate Biff's behavior. The more effectively Biff tries to change Hap's perspective and behavior, the clearer Biff's problem will become to the audience. Thus by not "playing the problem," the actor is successfully portraying the problem.

By examining a key moment from the scene we can see a demonstration of this principle. Here is Biff's response to Happy (Hap), who asks if Biff is content working in the West:

> BIFF, *with rising agitation:* [. . .] whenever spring comes to where I am, I suddenly get the feeling, my God, I'm not getting anywhere! What the hell am I doing, playing around with horses, twenty-eight dollars a week! I'm thirty-four years old, I oughta be makin' my future. That's when I come running home. And now I

get here, and I don't know what to do with myself. I've always made a point of not wasting my life, and everytime I come back here I know that all I've done is to waste my life.[4]

Our approach to acting this scene will inspire the actor to find ways in which this monologue is about Hap rather than Biff. To the observer (i.e., the audience), this monologue discloses Biff's recent activities and communicates his frustration, confusion, and agitation. Methods of acting that encourage emotional self-indulgence serve only to reinforce the obvious; thus the actor will merely "play the problem" contained in the words. A more effective approach might be to persuade the actor to see that Biff is saying these things to alter something in Happy; thus, changing Happy in some specific way becomes the purpose and objective of the monologue. It also adds a sense of ensemble play, reinforcing the give-and-take (talking and listening) that results when actors are working as part of a larger whole.

It is a significant challenge to persuade the actor that the following line is about Happy and not Biff: "What the hell am I doing, playing around with horses twenty-eight dollars a week, I'm thirty-four years old, I ougtha be makin' my future." Yet despite the fact the words appear to be about Biff, the action played by Biff must make Happy feel and/or do something. The words are made active (and thus about Hap) if they produce an energy that makes Hap feel the same way Biff does, or perhaps even forces a similar admission from Hap about his own confused, unfulfilled life. With this approach in mind, we redefine the speech as the moment when Biff uses his life story to shock Happy into revealing his own despair. The actor has thus manipulated the words to serve his objective and allowed the audience to see his character's "problem" by focusing his energy on solving his brother's troubles.

From Biff's perspective, Happy's problem is that he can't or won't admit that he is as discontented as Biff. By making Hap aware of his problem and gaining this admission, Biff reveals his own feelings of isolation, confusion, and frustration. Biff attempts to find a kindred spirit in his brother, and the two men reinforce feelings of affection for each other that each feared was impossible. This synergy between brothers allows the audience greater insight into the emotional circumstances about which the characters are unaware—namely, that they are reinforcing each other's aimlessness, ameliorating their feelings of guilt about their lack of success, and avoiding shouldering responsibility for their father's emotional troubles.

The primary goal of our training is to teach actors to see the text as a series of opportunities to change the behavior of another person instead of a vehicle for producing emotion onstage. The energy expended in attempting to solve the problem of the other character(s) produces emotion as a by-product. The audience can then observe what the character is feeling as it is happening in the moment of exchange and not in the actor's "dredged-up" experiences of past emotions.

The same process holds true for the actor playing Happy. Like Biff, Hap is filled with self-doubt and frustration about the course of his life. Biff's problem, from Happy's perspective, is somewhat more evident in the lines themselves when Happy says: "where's the old humor, the old confidence?" From Hap's perspective, Biff needs to admit that what he most wants is to come home to the city life and "beat this racket."[5] If Happy can get Biff to commit to this goal, it not only affirms the choices he has made in his life, but it also greatly eases his own feelings of despair and doubt. If Happy focuses his energies on getting Biff to do what he wants, the audience in turn will acquire a balanced understanding of what Hap is actually feeling. The audience will notice that it is not merely a question of what Hap "feels" but rather a question of what *Hap wants Biff to feel.*

As noted before, many approaches to acting focus on getting actors "in touch" with how their characters feel about the situation. Meisner's emphasis on the reality of doing refocuses the actor's attention and urges him to see the dialogue as an opportunity to restore his relationship with his brother. When Happy says, "my apartment, a car and plenty of women and *still, goddammit, I'm lonely,*" the *doing* of the line must be to extract some response from Biff. The script supports this intention when in the next line Biff says, "listen, why don't you come out West, *with me.*" By getting Hap to focus on Biff's behavioral change, we have in a subtle way redefined the acting process.

This redefinition is the result of seeing acting as doing something to others instead of emoting. The often-heard disparagement of Method acting is that it is almost always aimed at the self-absorbed "stewing in the emotional juices" or playing the problem. Techniques such as emotional recall, affective memory, or others that have as their purpose the conjuring up of emotions for their own sake are ultimately devoid of the dynamic quality that Stanislavsky calls action, communion, and adaptation.

REDEFINITION OF CONFLICT AND CHARACTER

A second extension of Meisner-based work is a redefinition of the concepts of character and conflict. The rehearsal of a play most often begins with a discussion between the director and actors regarding the characters that will be created. Operating from the observer's perspective (i.e., the audience, the reader, the critic, etc.), the director identifies characteristics associated with the individuals dramatized in the script. The director conveys traits of personality to each actor, traits that in turn become the goal of each actor's creation. In effect, actors are being asked to make this "selected" personality observable to the audience.

This attention to personality traits leads to a multitude of acting problems. First, it places the actors' focus on themselves and in effect condemns them to play a replication of what the director has determined to be the characters. It is the director who makes value judgments about the individuals presented in the script. For actors to "portray" characteristics violates our understanding of human beings. People are largely unaware of how the world views them; thus for actors to give their characters this kind of insight is contrary to reality and common sense. Yet time and time again actors are making valiant efforts to "show" audiences character "types" by adopting attitudes and moods they associate with their character's personality. Playing attitudes and qualities is a trap resulting from an improper focus on the self.

It is the audience, however, and not the actor that makes the judgments that determines character. The job of actors is not to demonstrate character traits but rather to incorporate the "point of view" (self-concept and worldview) of the characters and to produce behavior consistent with that point of view. The important difference between this and what the director has given the actors is that characters' points of view are the way in which they see themselves and others, whereas the director is giving the actors the observer's judgment about the individual. By adopting the way their character sees the world, actors can concentrate on the behavior of the other people in the play instead of feeling the need to "be" the character. Understanding this "point of view" (which is the actor's definition of character) allows actors to discover how their character views other people in the play, which helps to clarify relationships. In other words, actors are characterizing the *other people* in the play. The manner in which they do that reveals their character's mindset (point of view) to the audience and *allows audience members to make judgments about the character.*

Death of a Salesman provides another excellent example for applying this definition of character. Happy's character is revealed by the way he relates to Biff. His conception of Biff, therefore, is crucial to determining his behavior. The question "What kind of character is Biff?" is best answered by Hap's point of view because *only Hap conceives of Biff in this way.* This conception (point of view) is a deeply held predisposition toward his brother that will cause Hap to "characterize" Biff in a certain way. Consider the following possible points of view that Hap might take toward Biff:

1.   Biff is really hiding his intense desire for success and wants my help to get it.
2.   Biff is virtually suicidal and is reaching out to me for help.
3.   Biff has never taken me seriously, is jealous of me, and treats me like a child.
4.   Biff knows a terrible secret and I've got to find out what it is.

These four versions of Biff are distinct and will require Hap to behave in different ways. Each choice requires different behavior, thus producing a different "character," not because Hap is different but because *Biff is perceived as a different character.* If Hap actually fears that Biff is desperate and possibly suicidal (number 2 above), the need to find solutions for Biff's dilemma will be greatly intensified. His point of view regarding Biff mandates that he provide strength and direction. The observer (the audience) viewing this energy directed toward Biff will attribute certain qualities to Hap. The point here is that if the director tells the actor playing Hap to produce a more sensitive, caring Hap, the actor can fulfill the director's demands without playing the quality or mood of "sensitive." From this standpoint, then, character is something that is revealed to the audience through relationships rather than demonstrated through attitudes.

The Meisner focus on the other actor also suggests a redefinition of the conception of conflict. Conflict is something both actors and directors are trained to find because it is through conflict that we understand dramatic action. Difficulties occur when actors understand conflict from the perspective of the observer rather than that of their character's needs. From the director's and the audience's view, conflict takes place when characters are set against each other. It is not surprising, then, that many actors will "play the conflict" rather than the objectives.

Conflict arises as a result of action and cannot be the action itself. Focusing on the other continues to be the key to understanding conflict. Conflict is the *result of two people trying to change each other*. The emphasis here is on the word "change" because changing the other person is the principal action. The actor must concentrate on doing whatever is necessary to alter the behavior and outlook of the other person. When both people are fully engaged in this effort, conflict will result. In addition, the potential for change can exist only when the actors have learned to play *positive* energy in conflict situations. If the energy directed at the other person is negative (i.e., venting, mocking, being sarcastic, etc.), it will be unproductive, failing to change anyone.

It is impossible to overstate how difficult this conception of conflict is for actors to learn. For example, when presented with a fight scene, every instinct in the actors' body urges them to vent, attack, yell at, destroy, or in some other way punish the other person because the script "says so." Often it seems contrary to good sense to tell actors to play positive energy in a scene replete with harsh language. But although the scripted scene will appear negative, actors cannot relinquish their responsibility to play positive actions just because the words are negative. Actors are encouraged to understand that *positive energy means effective energy* because it contains the possibility of changing the other person. In other words, if actors are producing behavior that can in some way result in productive change in the other person, they are using positive energy. Playing anger or any other quality implied by the words will not result in any change in or engagement with the other character.

The purpose of acting schools ought to be the teaching of a process or *way of working* that will enable actors to respond creatively to direction in any period or style of dramatic literature. However, left to their own inclinations, most untrained actors attempt to do their work by reproducing what they have seen or imagined. No real creativity and certainly no art is attained by mere copying. The propensity to demonstrate character is often reinforced by both conventional Method training and the director in rehearsal, leaving actors trapped inside a world of imitation and self-indulgence. A Meisner approach creates a process of liberating actors' creative energies, giving them an artistic focus and purpose. Once the energy is focused outward, the character's internal life becomes evident to the audience for whom the entire theatrical endeavor is created.

NOTES

1. Most of the terminology in this chapter, such as "playing the problem" and the concept of "playing positive energy," is the work of Manuel Duque. Duque, a student of Sanford Meisner, spent most of his career at Pennsylvania State University and served as Head of Acting at the Asolo Conservatory from 1981 to 1985. Jim Wise, the current Head of Acting at the Conservatory, also deeply influenced the ideas in this chapter, especially the concept of "point of view."

2. Some understandable confusion may arise from the frequent use of the words "actor" and "character" in illustrating specific ideas. In saying that the central focus of the actor is on the "other," I am suggesting that this means the other human being(s) *on the stage*. My use of the word "character," therefore, does not mean the literary figure in the text but rather the actor impersonating that individual on the stage. Thus, trying to "change the other character" means that the actor is attempting to alter the behavior of the living being standing on the stage with him or her.

3. Larry Silverberg, in *The Sanford Meisner Approach* (Lyme, NH: Smith and Kraus, 1994), says: "What I want you to know is that acting is not emoting. Again, *acting is not emotion*. Acting is doing something. Of course acting demands of us the ability to access our own rich emotional life and the way in, the organic way, is through meaningful doing" (4).

4. Arthur Miller, *Death of a Salesman* (New York: Dramatists Play Service, 1980), 14–15.

5. Ibid., 13, 16.

CHAPTER TEN

SIGNIFICANT ACTION

A Unifying Approach to the Art of Acting

Jean Dobie Giebel

Constantin Stanislavsky biographer Jean Benedetti comments that Stanislavsky "was always moving forward, revising and modifying his methods so that no single formulation seemed satisfactory for very long."[1] Therefore, when reevaluating his System, we ought to consider not only what he stated (and often later contradicted) but what he ultimately intended to achieve. Early in his work, Stanislavsky explained that his goal was to develop a system of acting as a means to inspiration: "What I wanted to learn was how to create a favorable condition for the appearance of inspiration by means of the will, that condition in the presence of which inspiration was most likely to descend into the actor's soul. As I learned afterward, this creative mood is that spiritual and physical mood during which it is easiest for inspiration to be born." But how, he inquired, "was one to make this condition no longer a matter of mere accident, to create it at the will and order of the actor?" (*MLA* 462) My intent here is to answer Stanislavsky's ultimate question with the theory of *significant action*, a unifying approach to acting that enables the actor to induce the "creative mood." I will relate (though not limit) significant action specifically to the American Method through theories on the physiological process of emotion and inspiration, and offer examples of how to practically apply the ideas introduced to both analysis and performance. Finally, I will demonstrate how the concept of significant action unites actor and audience in the creation of dramatic illusion.

Stanislavsky is often credited with the *methodology* of modern actor training, based on the philosophy that the art of acting can be taught systematically. If, as Stanislavsky wrote:

> It is impossible to own [the creative mood] at once, then one must put it together bit by bit, using various elements for its constructing. If it is necessary to develop each of the component elements in one's self separately, systematically, by a series of certain exercises—let it be so! If the ability to receive the creative mood in its full measure is given to the genius by nature, then perhaps ordinary people may reach a like state after a great deal of hard work with themselves. [*MLA* 462]

Fueled by a popular fascination with modern psychology and the advent of naturalism, Stanislavsky's work created a new paradigm of actor training. He shifted the nineteenth-century emphasis on physical and vocal technique to what he referred to as "the *emotional side of* creativeness," adding "I do this purposely because we are too prone to leave out feeling" (*AP* 248).

Stanislavsky's emphasis on a strong portrayal of human emotion carried over to the American Method acting technique. In his account of the development of Method acting, Lee Strasberg wrote: "This voyage begins with my awareness of the central problem of the actor: How can the actor both really feel, and also be in control of what he needs to do on stage?" Through his work at the Group Theatre, at the Actors Studio, and at the Lee Strasberg Theatre Institutes, Strasberg believed he addressed this problem and also discovered the answers to a second problem: "How can the actor make his real feelings expressive on the stage?" (*DP* 6). Stella Adler, a Group member who developed her own version of the Method, responded to the question of expression by stressing physical action. Still, the basis of her technique lay in the actor's ability to exist imaginatively within the given circumstances of the play: "Imagination refers to the actor's ability to accept new situations of life and believe in them. From your imagination come your reactions to the things that you like and dislike. If you cannot do this, you had better give up acting. Your whole life will depend on your ability to recognize that you are in a profession where your talent is built on imagination" (*TA* 20). Another noteworthy teacher to come out of the Group, Sanford Meisner, emphasized imagination and situation, defining good acting as "living truthfully under imaginary circumstances" (*MA* 15). Meisner also recognized the importance of emotion, developing exercises that were meant to train actors to work as a composer writes music: "A composer doesn't write down what he *thinks* would be effective; he works from his heart." For Meisner, acting is not intellectual but rather "emotional and impulsive" (*MA* 36–7).

Following the lead of Strasberg, Adler, and Meisner, many conservatory and university actor training programs in America narrowed their focus to these three aspects of what are commonly referred to as the "internal" processes of acting: emotion, imagination, and impulse. Emphasis on physical and vocal technique continued to fade and, over the years, so did theatricality. However, today's training programs are again searching for a new paradigm. Charged by the need for theatre to redefine itself as something other than cinematic naturalism, new training techniques such as Viewpoints, best known through the work of director Anne Bogart, are generating interest among actors and educators. Although the Viewpoints may be applied to naturalism, the technique is most often connected to postmodern abstraction. This particular technique feeds highly theatrical productions by following an "external" path to creativity through emphasis on physicality and exploration of spatial composition. The value of this or any other creative method is not in question here, only the limitations imposed by *any* particular approach. If university acting programs see as their mission the training of flexible performers, they must teach techniques that apply to a variety of venues. For training to function practically, programs and departments must recognize that these various approaches need not be mutually exclusive. Not only can actors be exposed to a variety of different acting techniques, these techniques can be taught in conjunction. A unifying theory, which I have developed to support this type of training, is *significant action*.

Significant action is the symbolic form of drama that expresses human feeling. I define "symbolic" along the lines of philosopher and semiotician Susanne Langer, who asserts that symbolism is "any device whereby we are enabled to make an abstraction."[2] Langer suggests that works of art have a tendency to dissociate from actual reality and thereby create "the impression of an illusion enfolding the thing, action, statement, or flow of sound that constitutes the work." She refers to this illusion as "semblance," the function of which is "to give forms a new embodiment in purely qualitative, unreal instances, setting them free from their normal embodiment in real things so that they may be recognized in their own right, and freely conceived and composed in the interest of the artist's ultimate aim—significance, or logical expression."[3] In theatre, we refer to semblance as the "dramatic illusion," which abstracts physical or mental activity to act symbolically. The symbol is referred to as an "action." A composition of actions in a dramatic presentation creates a semblance of life, or the illusion of vital existence.

"In art," Langer states, "forms are abstracted only to be made clearly apparent, and are freed from their common uses only to be put to new uses: to act as symbols, to become expressive of human feeling."[4] The phrase "human feeling," however, encompasses something much larger than merely emotion. Webster's Dictionary defines the word "feeling" as an *emotion, idea, awareness,* and *physical sensation.* Actors who create works of art express a complex combination of all the aspects of "human feeling," which take the form of the dramatic illusion. This combination of emotion, idea, awareness, and physical sensation releases the "creative mood."

Candace Pert, a neuropharmacologist and AIDS researcher, reveals the physiological process of the "creative mood" by confronting the "James-Cannon debate": Is emotion originated in the body and then perceived in the head, as maintained by philosopher and physiologist William James, or originated in the head to be passed down to the body, as held by his student, psychologist Walter Cannon? Resolving the issue, Pert maintains that emotion is the result of the mind and body working together, communicating via proteins called neuropeptides, which she refers to as the "molecules of emotion." By using the model of the body as an information system—not unlike a computer network—Pert explains that communication may initiate at any nodal point and effect the entire system. "Emotional states or moods," she says, "are produced by the various neuropeptide ligands [substances that selectively bind with receptors on the surface of a cell], and what we experience as an emotion or feeling is also a mechanism for activating a particular neuronal circuit—*simultaneously throughout the brain and body*—which generates a behavior involving the whole creature." In other words, neuropeptides "bring us to states of consciousness and to alterations of those states."[5] The origin of emotion lies in the communication of the mind *with* the body, or the "internal" *with* the "external." Where the communication begins is not an issue, only that it occurs.

Once communication is established, the whole mind-body system recognizes the experience as an emotional state. This explains the effectiveness of the Method's emotional-memory exercises, in which physical sensation is engaged to intensify an emotional experience. Strasberg developed these exercises in the belief that "recreating or reliving an intense emotional experience at will" (*DP* 114) was the manner in which an actor should induce inspiration. Pert, however, suggests that inspiration has its own emotional state. "When I use the term *emotion*," she writes, "I am speaking in the broadest of terms, to include not only the familiar human experience of anger, fear, and sadness, as well as joy, contentment, and courage, but also basic sensations such as pleasure and pain, as well as drive states studied by the experimental psychologists, such as hunger and thirst." This includes not only measurable and observable emotions and states but also what Pert calls "an assortment of intangible, subjective experiences that are probably unique to humans, such as spiritual inspiration . . ."[6]

To induce inspiration, then, or the "creative mood," is to induce a particular emotional experience. This experience is characterized in theories on creativity by two differing emotional states: fear and joy. The duality of the "creative mood" was initially brought to my attention while attending E. Katherine Kerr's professional actor training classes at Playwrights Horizons' Theatre School in New York.[7] Her class was the first time in my journey as an actor that I encountered training centered on a process for performing rather than for preparing a role. She identifies the creative process as a dual experience of discomfort *and* release, or "breakthrough." Kerr describes the process as similar to birth, in which the actor experiences discomfort analogous to that of the contracting womb, discomfort that grows until "breakthrough" occurs.[8]

A "breakthrough" correlates to the release of dramatic tension, which exists between the theatrical present moment and the impending future. In her chapter on dramatic illusion, Langer writes: "It has been said repeatedly that the theater creates a perpetual present moment; but it is only a present filled with its own future that is really dramatic." This sense of destiny, in actual life, occurs "only in unusual moments under peculiar emotional stress,"[9] emotional stress characterized by measurable physiological changes including quickening heartbeat, rising blood pressure, and an increasing intensity and constriction of vision. All these changes, states psychologist Rollo May, are neurological changes that relate directly to what psychologist Walter Cannon described as the "flight-fight" mechanism and which May defines as "the energizing of the organism for fighting and fleeing. This is the neurological correlate of what we find, in broad terms, in anxiety and fear."[10]

Artists such as Viewpoints advocate Anne Bogart find the root of their work in these neurological changes: "The energy of individuals who face and incorporate their own terror is genuine, palpable and contagious. In combination with the artist's deep sense of play, terror makes for compelling theatre both in the creative process and in the experience of the audience."[11] In contrast, Stanislavsky's description of the "creative mood" is "exceptionally pleasant, especially when it is compared with the state of strain to which the actor is subject when the creative mood is absent. It can be compared to the feelings of a prisoner when the chains that had interfered with all his movements for years have at last been removed" (*MLA* 463). Stanislavsky observed the "creative mood" in himself and his fellow actors correlating with the lack of tension; however, his description of the experience is not of relaxation per se but relief. May adds to Stanislavsky's observation by describing the creative experience as one of joy: "joy defined as the emotion that goes with heightened consciousness, the mood that accompanies the experience of actualizing one's own potentialities."[12]

Combining Bogart's fear with Stanislavsky's joy creates an emotional duality we can correlate to the experience of artistic selection. The actor encounters the experience of both fear and joy in the performance of a theatrical "moment." Langer defines the theatrical moment, unlike a moment in actual life, as living in a "tension between past and future."[13] This tension climaxes when the character must make *a* choice on how to act, and the actor must select *which* choice will produce the abstraction, the expressive symbol. Dramatic tension builds as the actor watches and listens, waiting for the information necessary to make the most expressive selection and thereby create the release. Therefore, acting that incorporates the physiological process of mind-body communication with an awareness of dramatic tension induces the "creative mood." The actor is *physically* involved in an action grounded in the given circumstances, that action has *intellectual* and *emotional* resonance, and the actor's *awareness* is focused on searching for an expressive release of dramatic tension.

To apply this concept practically, I employ modified versions of Sanford Meisner's improvisation exercises. These exercises allow students to experience the function of dramatic tension in the creation of a theatrical moment. For example, while involved in an activity that is grounded in a high-stakes imaginary circumstance, the student is met with an obstacle: A second student enters the playing space with her own high-stakes imaginary circumstance, and requires assistance. Neither student is allowed to ask questions, which complicates the situation. Once the first student realizes the needs of his partner, he must make a choice: agree to aid the second student or return to his activity. This choice creates a new situation, and so on.

The structure of this exercise may then be applied to a beat (a theatrical moment defined by playing a single action in pursuit of an objective). When analyzing a role, the student must determine what information the character is lacking, or what is *un*known. The choice of action, or beat shift, results in a release of tension when this information is received and the selection made. The action pursued in turn creates a new tension, propelling the drama forward. This method of analysis correlates to Langer's definition of rhythm in music, as a "setting up of a new tension by the resolution of former ones," and consequently determines the rhythm of performance. In addition, Meisner's repetition exercises develop the skills the actor must employ once the structure of dramatic tension has been discerned. The skills of watching, listening, and waiting for the impulse to act are essential to the dramatic illusion. They create what Langer refers to as "the constant illusion of an imminent future."[14]

Meisner, through repetition, sought the "inner impulse," which he believed to be the source of "organic creativity" (*MA* 37). However, reaching an inner impulse is not enough for an act to assume significance. Art requires selection in the creation of form, with form in this case being the dramatic illusion. As a result, the actor's range of possible action must be defined by an awareness of the audience, an awareness that is a necessary element to the production of a theatrical event. The tension that arises in the dramatic illusion is one built on the need for the actor to make not merely an impulsive choice but an expressive one. This awareness must not be employed to play *to* the audience but rather to play *with* the audience, to invite the audience, as director Peter Brook writes, to assist in the production:

> With this assistance, the assistance of eyes and focus and desires and enjoyment and concentration, repetition turns into representation. Then the word representation no longer separates actor and audience, show and public: It envelops them: what is present for one is present for the other. The audience too has undergone a change. It has come from a life outside the theatre that is essentially repetitive to a special arena in which each moment is lived more clearly and more tensely.[15]

The abstraction of human feeling in an expressive act is complete when the actor incorporates the assistance of the audience, through awareness, in the selection of the act. A form is then created that transforms the perception of both artist and audience. This creation is achieved through the performance of significant action: Action that is conceived in the "creative mood" and born in the union of actor and audience within the dramatic illusion.

NOTES

1. Jean Benedetti, *Stanislavski: An Introduction* (New York: Theatre Arts Books, 1982), 50.
2. Susanne K. Langer, *Feeling and Form* (New York: Charles Scribner, 1953), xi.
3. Ibid., 45, 50.
4. Ibid., 51.

5. Candace B. Pert, *Molecules of Emotion: The Science Behind Mind-Body Medicine* (New York: Simon and Schuster, 1997), 145.
6. Ibid., 131–32.
7. E. Katherine Kerr is an actress, writer, and teacher. She was nominated for a Drama Desk Award for her performance in *Laughing Wild* and won an Obie Award, a Villager citation, and a Drama Desk nomination for her three roles in *Cloud 9*. In addition to regular classes, she teaches a two-day workshop titled "The Creative Explosion."
8. Kerr, "The Creative Explosion: A Simple Guide to Brilliant Acting/Action," unpublished MS, 65.
9. Langer, *Feeling and Form*, 307–08.
10. Rollo May, *The Courage to Create* (New York: Norton, 1994), 44–45.
11. Anne Bogart, "Terror, Disorientation and Difficulty," *Anne Bogart: Viewpoints*, Michael Bigelow Dixon and Joel A. Smith, eds. (Lyme, NH: Smith and Kraus, 1995), 15.
12. May, *Courage to Create*, 45.
13. Langer, *Feeling and Form*, 308.
14. Ibid., 127, 310.
15. Peter Brook, *The Empty Space* (New York: Touchstone, 1968), 140.

CHAPTER ELEVEN

BURDENS OF REPRESENTATION
The Method and the Audience

David Wiles

It is not true that your center of attention is in the center of the stage. Since you are playing for an audience the center of your attention must be expanded forward to the center of that audience. You know that and the audience knows it too.

— *Erwin Piscator*, Objective Acting

Who is the Audience?

— *Joseph Chaikin*, The Context of Performance

What is the relationship in the theatre between the actor and the audience during performance? This relationship is as fundamental as that of actor and actor. It is affected by the composition of the audience and by the personal and social facts of the actor's life. I don't believe that Method acting adequately addresses the actor/audience relationship. To the degree that it doesn't, the Method is incomplete as a means for training actors to perform in the theatre.

My training as an actor is rooted in the Method. I have encountered the limits of that training in trying to live in the "world of the play" while performing in the world of race. I walk into a theatre as an African American actor. I bring with me the historical, political, and social complications of race, as do my audiences. The African American intellectual and activist W. E. B. Du Bois theorized that every African American lives with the double consciousness of being both an "American and a Negro,"[1] a person and a problem. I bring that double consciousness with me onto the stage. I am aware of my race when I perform, as my audience is aware, regardless of play or role. I am also aware of the racial makeup of my audiences and aware of how the performance experience differs when the audience is largely black, largely white, or racially mixed. I belong to a racially defined cultural community, and my performance is affected both by what I am portraying and whether I'm portraying it within or outside that community.

In this chapter I will discuss some experiences in which the problem of the actor/audience relationship has been complicated for me by the burdens of race. Those experiences have led me to begin to apply the Method's principles of analyzing texts and developing stage relationships to the exploration of the actor/audience relationship in the context of culture and race. Every actor brings personal and cultural issues into performance. So does every audience. Here I make suggestions and pose questions regarding the actor/audience relationship that can be useful to those of us who teach and create theatre.

All Method actors work from a form of double consciousness, treating the fictional circumstances in the text as if they are real. We think our characters' thoughts, experience our characters' emotions, and engage in our characters' relationships while simultaneously remaining aware that we are performing. We become what a teacher of mine called "actor/characters." At the center of every Method approach to acting is our imaginative, emotional, and intellectual relationships to the "given circumstances." But what is our relationship to the actual circumstances of performing itself and, above all, to the audiences we perform for?

The issue is made more complex for me by race. I perform a role while "performing race" and performing those aspects of myself not solely defined by race. I do so in dialogue with the text, my partners, and the audience. As a Method-trained actor, I know who my character is and who my partners are in the world of the play. But who am I in the world of the performance, and who is the audience? My primary dialogue is with them, and race is part of the dialogue. If I am to engage in a truthful dialogue with everyone in the room, I need to consider these questions.

Actor/director Joseph Chaikin advocated that "every performer . . . make a secret choice . . . as to 'who' the audience is" and asked "to whom does the actor personally dedicate his performance?"[2] Chaikin offered the self, parents, lovers, critics, and casting agents as possibilities. Everyone on Chaikin's list has been part of my secret audience at one time or another. But my introduction to theatre came during the civil rights and antiwar crusades of the late 1960s. I became involved in theatre at least in part because I thought it was a way of making a difference.

I once saw the black South African actors John Kani and Winston Ntshona perform a play they created with Athol Fugard, *Sizwe Banzi Is Dead.* The story involves the struggle for dignity and survival under apartheid. They performed it with a rage I might have expected but also with a depth of humor and joy that came as a shock. It was a model of the kind of theatre I wanted to do, deeply felt, a pleasure to see and important.

Not long after I saw *Sizwe Banzi Is Dead,* I was involved in a drama school production of its companion piece, *The Island.* The play is set on Robben Island, the prison where South African political prisoners, including Nelson Mandela, were held. We performed the play for two very different audiences, one in prisons, one at drama school. The play follows the fourth-wall convention until the final scene, when the two prisoners leave their cell to perform *Antigone* for an audience of prisoners and guards. The audience in the "prison" is the audience in the theatre, a perfect metaphor for the South African audiences the play was created for.

Most of the inmates in our prison audiences were men of color, the majority of them black. I felt I was performing for members of my community. The prisoners who saw the piece were moved by it and moved by the fact that we had come to perform for them. In the postshow discussions, they taught us a great deal about prison life that informed our later portrayals of it. All of us felt as if we had accomplished something worthwhile. We knew why we were doing the play and whom we were doing it for.

The school audiences presented a set of different conditions. They were composed of friends, faculty, fellow students, and people with cultural and political ties that gave them a vested interest in this particular play, including members of a South African studies institute. The stakes were different. We cared about the opinions of our friends. The faculty and the directing students controlled our casting in future projects, and I was not the most sought after actor in school. Here was a chance to make a mark. I was looking forward to pursuing a career in New York after graduation, and there were professional actors and directors in the audience whose help might be useful to me. Simply put, I felt the need to impress them.

There were also South Africans in the audience, including, during one performance, a man who had worked with us on dialects. His brother was on Robben Island at the time. I regarded the two groups as different audiences—one composed of our peers, who had come to see a play and to see us in it; the other composed of people who didn't know us or care about our careers, but who had come to see *this* play. For me, the situation was filled with the two primary pressures in the theatre, impressing the audience and serving it, getting on in the world and making art. My training provided an obvious answer to the dilemma. Live in the world of the play, relate honestly to my partner, and express the character's emotional truth. The problem lay in doing this work while *my* emotional truth included the issue of who was watching us and why. It isn't that the Method asks me to forget the spectators. It simply doesn't offer tools for forging a relationship with them. It suggests instead that my relationship with the audience will be taken care of by immersing myself in the character's life. It will not.

In this case, I consciously chose to perform the play for the South Africans in the audience. They became my community. In the play-within-the-play section, I addressed the South Africans as prisoners and our friends and colleagues as guards irrespective of race. I made those I felt a need to impress the enemy in order not to pander to them. My performances were honest. My acting was no better than I was capable of at that point, but for the first and one of the only times since I didn't care. What praise I remember was for the play.

German director Erwin Piscator was, with Bertolt Brecht, a principal architect of the Epic Theatre. Piscator saw the actor and the audience as a unit, partners who, with the other actors onstage, formed a triangle. He criticized Stanislavsky for freeing his students from their fear of the audience by directing their attention to the center of the stage. Piscator saw the audience as part of the play, and the actor's attention had to "be directed constantly towards the center of the theatre." He regarded Stanislavsky's "magic if" and the idea of the fourth wall as devices that were "untheatrical and . . . not absolutely honest" because the audience "can never be non-existent." Piscator thought that the fourth-wall convention in which the actor never meets the eyes of the audience was "humiliating for the actor."[3]

The idea of the fourth wall, once a revolutionary concept in the theatre, has become so internal to Method practice that unless it's being "broken," it is rarely discussed. The idea has become a largely unexamined assumption of Method training. The institutionalization of the concept may have to do with the extent to which the Method has been used to train actors for film and television. The Method training I've experienced and most of the texts I've read treat acting as essentially one art form practiced in two mediums, on camera and onstage. Chaikin pointed out that the most important difference between acting in film and acting in theatre is that "those who attend and those who perform are both present."[4] Race and all the other inescapable socio/political facts shatter the fourth wall by asserting their presence into whatever theatrical "reality" is being presented. Piscator's ideas required the actor to "describe the composition of the audience" and to know "what makes it what it is."[5] He wanted his actors to know what messages they were sending and for whom they were intended.

The artists in political and ethnic theatres often regard themselves and their audiences as members of the same community. South Africa's anti-apartheid theatre had a clear conception of its intentions and of its audience. There are performance artists who know with some precision whom they make their work for. African American theatre tends to reflect communal concerns as much as it reflects individual ones. In these kinds of theatres, practitioners think consciously about who comes to see the work.

The audience is as specific as the play. But I have never rehearsed in a mainstream theatre and heard a discussion of who comprises the audience that went beyond its demographics and the general tenor of its taste.

The relationship with the audience affects every relationship on stage. "The relationship of actor to actor is inseparable from the relationship of actor to audience," wrote Chaikin. Each of these points, he adds, "need[s] to be answered by the particular text performed and by the decisions taken on the text by the actors . . . in order to avoid letting these relationships fall into an unexamined pattern."[6] For example, I once played the role of the Sergeant in Romulus Linney's *2*, a play about the Nuremberg trial of Hermann Goering. In one scene Goering calls the Sergeant, who is black and one of his guards, a nigger. In another the Captain, who is white and standing guard with the Sergeant, calls him "boy." The moments are there to point out the ironies that attended Americans putting Goering on trial for his treatment of racial and ethnic minorities. Both moments are meant to be humiliating for the Sergeant. In the first he starts to attack Goering physically but is brought up short by the presence of his superior officers, none of whom comments on the insult. In the second, he has just offered to do a favor for the Captain, who replies by insulting him.

I reacted with anger in both moments but found it difficult to express any shame. I've always refused to reveal any emotion apart from anger in response to racial insults. But that response, though truthful, was wrong for the play. A black man who responded angrily to a white person's insult in 1945 courted trouble. To do so in the military, to a superior officer, guaranteed it. Nor would our audiences get the point if I responded in a way they found justified and, in the present day, common. I understood that. My problem lay in what I was willing to do in front of the audience, not in my interpretation of the text. Our audiences were largely white, sometimes entirely so. I was, without realizing it, *refusing to be humiliated in front of them.* When I knew there were African Americans in the audience, I laughed the insults off in defiance and swaggered offstage on my exits to gain their approval and to show them that I hadn't been hurt. I had active and conflicted relationships with our audiences that changed depending on who was in the house from show to show.

The director Lee Breuer contends that all actors have a personal story to tell that governs the choices they make in performance. My difficulty involved a need to defend my personal status as a black man subjected to a public racial insult (being called a nigger in a play is still being called a nigger). The story I needed to tell about those moments was different from the story of the play, and even though I had done my text work I didn't see it. Once I understood that, the tension I felt during each performance as I approached those moments eased. I stopped preparing for them. Since neither insult was "expected" in the action of the play, I was caught undefended and shamed. I could permit my humiliation to show in service to the play and to the audience but not before I became consciously aware of which story I was telling, the playwright's or mine. The performance in 2 is the first time I can remember that I've ever expressed any shame onstage. The fact that it happened where it did, not in a cell in Nuremberg in 1945 but on a stage in South Carolina in 1999, made the experience that much more powerful.

It is rewarding to create theatre in which the actors and the audience are engaged in a dialogue about what everyone knows to be common concerns. Sometimes the dialogue is a literal one. In most of our theatre, we expect the audience to remain quiet apart from laughing and applauding at the end. It wasn't true in Shakespeare's time. It isn't true in children's theatre now, nor is it true for any audience that comes from another tradition and doesn't accept or hasn't been taught this *rule*. This is particularly true in African American theatre.

James Earl Jones once complained in a National Public Radio interview about the behavior of some audience members during the Broadway run of August Wilson's *Fences*. The audiences were racially mixed. Some of the African Americans talked during the play, to each other and to the stage. I saw the production and was in one such audience. There were black audience members who reacted vocally and emotionally to what they saw and heard. They took sides and passed judgments on the behavior of the characters. The play was about people they knew, situations they recognized, and the communities they lived in. They had transformed the theatre into something like the black church. They were, in their level of engagement, ideal.

I was torn. I wanted to join them but in the mixed house I behaved "properly" out of respect to the actors. I behaved in accordance with the conventions of the "general," though not in this case the majority, audience. I've been in similar situations in performance and not known how to react. If actors permit themselves to react to *what* audience members are saying as opposed to the fact that they are saying anything at all (and in this case some of the cast probably did), they can feed off those responses and not become distracted by them. As long as there is an audience in the room, its members are a part of the actor's circumstances. Attempting to ignore their behavior because they are not part of the character's circumstances creates a tension-ridden and pointless double bind. Responding doesn't require violating the fourth wall if that's the convention being followed. Not responding requires segregating the emotional responses, separating those of the actor from those of the character, expressing some and suppressing others. It requires responses that are incomplete and, in terms of Method principles, dishonest. It denies Stanislavsky's idea that the actors and the audience are in communion. An audience that is willing to behave in the theatre in the same way it behaves during worship deserves a high level of respect.

I bring race and a host of more individual issues to performing for an audience. Whether that constitutes creative wealth or limiting baggage doesn't depend on transcending my issues or overcoming them in therapy. It depends on my ability to recognize them and use them in my work. For other actors the primary issues may include gender, religion, ethnicity, class, all intermingled with personal history. The list is long. All of our identities come with narratives that must be reconciled with the dramatic narratives we perform. If not they will influence our work in ways we can neither control nor understand.

Actors need to know how the stories we tell conflict with the ways we need to represent our communities and ourselves onstage. Above all, we need to know to whom it is we're talking and what we have to say to them. We need to define our relationships to our audiences as we define them to other characters in the play. The Method provides analytical tools for this if the tools in use are extended to investigate the actor/audience relationship. We may already know an audience for a particular play better than we realize if we think beyond the consumer survey categories of age, class, and race that pass for audience analysis in so many institutional theatres. We can create an image of our audience during the rehearsal process by asking ourselves who might be compelled to see this particular piece of work. What are the audiences' conflicts in life? What are our intentions toward them in performing the play? How do we want to affect them, what do we want them to think and feel? What is the nature of our relationship, and what will be its result? These questions are often left to directors and dramaturges while actors focus on "character." Actors can ask them too and pose them onstage one performance and one audience to the next.

Jazz improvisers often speak of playing a solo as telling a story. Miles Davis once said that his solos consisted of what the audience made him play. It suggests an intimacy and a circle of communication in which everyone in the room influences what happens. If actors using the Method's techniques for listening and responding to one another can both hear the audience and sense what its emotional experience is whether it is voiced or not, then the way lies open for using what's received in shaping the performance. The actors can respond spontaneously to anything they sense will feed the moment. The play can become a living dialogue that changes moment by moment, one performance to the next, based on the emotional experiences of everyone in the room. The actor/audience relationship need no longer be a source of tension but of creativity. That would amount to the deepest use of the theatre's capacity for empathy, something that only the presence of human beings permits. The audience will understand that it is being listened to and that its presence matters. Everyone in the theatre might find the intimacy that results from that compelling. We might create a sense of community that would replace what we so often have now, actors and audience, us and them.

The issues involved in the actor/audience relationship are at least as old as the Method itself. My ideas have been deeply influenced by training, working, and teaching with Shakespeare & Company. The company's aesthetic is rooted in an exploration of the actor's self in relationship to the audience. Shakespeare & Company's artistic director, Tina Packer, has said that theatre is the place for "saying the unsayable." Her statement is a commitment to the idea that if a culture talks about the things it commonly avoids, change can occur. If the dialogue is to be a real one, audiences must be treated as members of the company. But this cannot happen unless our awareness of audiences becomes part of the way we train, rehearse, and perform.

NOTES

1. W. E. B. Du Bois, *The Souls of Black Folk* (1903; New York: Signet Classic, 1995), 45.
2. Joseph Chaikin, "The Context of Performance," *Actors on Acting*, T. Cole and H. K. Chinoy, eds. (New York: Three Rivers Press, 1947, 1970), 665.
3. Erwin Piscator, "Objective Acting," *Actors on Acting*, T. Cole and H. K. Chinoy, eds. (New York: Three Rivers Press, 1947, 1970), 302, 303.
4. Chaikin, "The Context of Performance," 666.
5. Piscator, "Objective Acting," 302.
6. Chaikin, "The Context of Performance," 666.

CHAPTER TWELVE

PRACTICING THE PARADOX

Addressing the Creative State

Peter Lobdell

Contrary to the conventional understanding that the actor only performs one thing at a time, he must actually be concerned with a number of problems. He must also have a clear comprehension of where his major concern is at each moment, plus the order of significance of all the other objects that must be attended to at the same time. All this depends upon the actor's ability to control, divide, and adjust his concentration. The talent of the actor functions only to the extent that the concentration is trained. Concentration allows the actor to focus on the imaginary reality demanded by the play; therefore, concentration is the key to what has been loosely thought of as imagination.

—*Lee Strasberg*, A Dream of Passion

In light of all the observations that the Method limits actors to their small personal selves, and all the knee-jerk associations of the Method with crude psychoanalysis, I submit that the Method encourages actors to understand their experiences, both in life and in the studio, as particular theatrical metaphors that create their characters' behavior onstage. Creativity is metaphoric. Finding connections is the essence of creativity. The Method's exercises foster those connections by tuning actors' psychological instruments.

In this chapter I develop two fundamental points about practicing the Method. First, the Method supports actors' abilities to live actively in the center of a paradox—namely, they are at once the character and not the character. They must live simultaneously within the imaginary given circumstances of the play and on the actual stage—allowing both and denying neither. Second, the Method trains actors to invent behavioral metaphors that illuminate their characters. Strasberg's assertion that *concentration is the key to what has been loosely thought of as imagination* is central to my argument. I will frame my position around an extended discussion of actors' imaginative use of their senses.

Strasberg contends that relaxation "is only a preamble to the actor's central concern: the need for concentration. Everything the actor does is a two-sided action. Relaxation is connected to concentration" (*DP* 125). Most people understand concentration to be a mental focus on the task at hand that eliminates distractions. Actors' concentration is extraordinarily active. Their attention moves from the words of the script to the character's impulses to speak, from personal connections with those impulses to inner and private imagery that gives the words life and personality to the physical score of the performance, and from fellow actors' expressions to the audience's responses. Actors maintain their concentration by moving their attention swiftly, fluidly, and precisely. Concentration is the result of the speed and particularity of actors' attention. Actors do not admit to "distraction" as the very nature of their concentration encourages their attention to move from stimulus to stimulus.

While attention to a task often is accompanied with muscular tension—thread a needle and notice how much neck and shoulders you use—actors' concentration can exist only within a relaxed and energized physicality. Actors learn to release tension in the muscles. Muscular ease allows their attention to flow freely. Like water flowing powerfully through a hose, actors' energy flows through their bodies; tension is a kink in the hose.

The simplest relaxation exercise asks actors to place their attention on the smallest possible muscle group at the top of their head, to lift the muscle ever so slightly on an inhale and to let it go on an exhale. Actors move their attention systematically down their body, lifting and letting go, ending with the muscles of the feet. At first this exercise takes a long time, but with practice actors develop the ability to relax very quickly.

They learn to release the muscles by paying attention to them throughout the day. The goal is not to create some strange and altogether useless flaccidity, but rather to permit energy to flow absolutely freely through the body—always sufficient to fill the moment, but never tense.

In life we tense our muscles to control pain. Onstage, we "bite the bullet" emotionally to a plethora of imaginary sensations as demanded by the given circumstances of the play. Muscular tension interferes with actors' imaginative realization of these sensations. Uta Hagen underscores the importance of these imaginative sensations to actors. The actor, she says, "learns that, at will, he can induce specific, imagined stimuli to produce organically correct behavioral response in order to arrive at the essence of experience."[1] If tension in life can serve to stifle actual sensation, then tension will inhabit the "imagined stimuli" onstage all the more.

The term "sense memory" implies that memory is the active principle in the exercises. I substitute the term "sensory work." If I ask you to remember your phone number, you will have it in a flash. However, if I ask you to visualize your number as it is written in your date book, the shape of the numbers, the color of the ink, the texture of the page, you are doing an act of the imagination by re-creating the details—the particular details here and now. Sensory work is not a function of memory alone; it requires imagination through the senses in the immediate moment. Critics of the Method often accuse sense memory of making actors self-absorbed, of encouraging actors to concentrate on their sense memories at the expense of the action onstage. This criticism falls short when one considers actors' concentration and how it works. Actors' attention must move to maintain concentration. An actor's private sensory object is as important as his acting partner's slight frown. Sensory work, the actuality of the rehearsal, and the stimuli outside the given circumstances simultaneously attract actors' attention. As a result, they move their attention swiftly among these "objects." I encourage my students to acknowledge distractions as they rehearse in class. If an ambulance siren shrieks in the distance, I want the actor to turn her head—to pay attention to the siren for the slightest moment. Once actors can observe all the events surrounding them, they can choose to acknowledge the stimulus or move on. If they pay attention for an instant, the distraction will not break their concentration.

Teaching sensory work can be delicate. At all times actors' privacy must be honored. Actors may try to show that they are working well, essentially miming the imaginary objects. The teacher must discourage that impulse by reinforcing at once the private nature of the work and at the same time insisting that the sensory work, in this context, is an exercise. Sensory work finds sensation at the nerve endings; it is not meant to communicate shape. If anyone walks into the studio at that moment, he should see actors doing sensory work, not handling invisible objects. As actors become more facile, the exercise can be moved into rehearsal as a tool to approach the given circumstances of the play. Sensory work is like the pianist's scales and dexterity exercises. Method acting teacher Doug Moston contends:

> The most creative uses of sense memory are not the literal ones you do in class on a weekly basis. What you use are the results you get directly from the exercises. That's not to say you will go directly for the result. Rather you will use many of the processes that get you to each respective result. You will trust your powers of observation and your sense of wonder and curiosity. They in turn will stimulate your concentration. That will allow you to create and combine stimuli, the effects of which you've already begun to explore.[2]

Sensory work invites actors into the essential paradox of acting by asking them to re-create the sensations of an imaginative condition, or *if*—for example, *if* you are walking in the rain. Actors know that they are dry, but they work to create the specific and particular sensations of rain. Their concentration and imagination focus upon the rain flowing down their cheeks, on the wet seeping in at their neck, and on the splash of their feet. The teacher must help actors to avoid indicating the experience—shaking the rain off the hair, for instance. Rather, the teacher watches for actors' concentration to deepen. Subtle changes in actors' behavior happen when they inhabit the sensory experience. They tilt their head to change the angle of the flow of the rain across their cheek. If they shake their head to explore the sensation of the raindrops scattering, they do so experimentally, focusing on the imaginary experience. Actors' concentration and imagination flow freely.

The next step of this work asks actors to notice how the behavior created by the sensory work feels. The actors' life within the imaginary sensory experience fosters movements and adjustments. The speed of their concentration and the freedom of their impulses allow them room to experience the behavior. The simultaneous re-creation of sensation and the private observation of feeling that is catalyzed by even the smallest movements foster their creativity. Shaking the rain out of the hair may suggest a gesture of sudden puzzlement by a particular character—shaking confusion from the mind like raindrops. On one level, sensory work allows actors to explore the logic of the play's given circumstances; on another level, the sensory work is metaphoric and connects actors to the characters' experiences and particular behaviors. Acting teacher Duncan Ross maintains that in this approach, the "ideas of 'internal' and 'external' are misconstructions. The movements of a limb and the bodily activity of which the image is a sign are both presentations of consciousness, both known to the organism by the activity of the central nervous system."[3]

In acting vocabulary, I distinguish between "action" and "task." An action is the character's tactic to move toward achieving an objective. A task is the actor's tactic for solving an aspect of the character's behavior. This double mentality for the actor—willingly moving between the character and the self, accepting both and denying neither—lies at the heart of the paradox of the actor's work. Often tasks are sensory. For example, an actor must react to bad news in a letter. The given circumstances suggest to the actor that the letter be viewed with caution. She handles it with care. She opens it slowly. She may choose to endow the letter with a powerful smell, say the smell of garbage left too long in the kitchen. She allows herself to meet the re-created sensation openly. The actor working simultaneously on the level of the character and on the level of her acting problem creates a metaphor: The letter contains news that stinks of old garbage.

Metaphors encourage actors to find their particular and individual creative choices. For example, I have actors work sensorily on a large knife. When they are concentrated, I ask them to hold the imaginary point of the knife an inch from another actor's face. Often both actors are uncomfortable. If I ask one to cut the other, the first has to overcome the imaginative reality of the knife if he or she is to use it—even though there is no actual knife. There is no *why*, and therefore often the actor with the knife will summon an indication of an emotion to permit the action. If, however, I take the actor aside and suggest that the knife has magically become a banana, a homicidal maniac is born. Not knowing the secret, the class is shocked. In another example, an actor who has a touch of vertigo playing an awkward young man waiting to meet his blind date may find that sensorily standing by the rail of a high balcony will serve as stimuli for his creative imagination. The warmth of the early spring sun on his face can create a grateful prayer. For actors the imposition of metaphors is everywhere when they need to use them creatively.

The special sound, images, smells—the things that delight us, that appall us, that sicken us and nourish us—are the private and special objects of sensory work. These sensations, or objects, are useful to actors and are at the heart of the Method. I use one such object as an example in teaching. I loved the Flash Gordon serials as a kid. Most especially, I loved *Flash Gordon Conquers the Universe*. The score of that serial was Franz Litz's *Préludes*. As I describe the sensory exercise to my students, I will tell them about Flash, Dale Arden, Doctor Zarkov, and Ming the Merciless. I will tell them my object—the music. As I begin to re-create the music in my mind, especially the strings, I give myself permission to soar into the strange happiness of my kid self. I beam. Occasionally I will tear over with a feeling of joy at living. I know it's acting. But herein lies the paradox, for I do it openly and fully for my students. As an actor I can move my attention from those strings to my students and explain my sunny tears, and back again to Ming's shriek, "The earthman must die!" over the music. I am both submerged in my sensory work and alive to the students before me. I move back and forth freely, responsive to my sensations, to my students, and to the circumstances surrounding me.

The sensory task has a three-fold effect: First, and most important, the task enables actors to concentrate. Second, the active re-creation of sensation in the nerves encourages actors to move physically, exploring the sensations and responding to them. Finally, as actors move, they are aware of experiencing movements. The experience creates the metaphor. If I work sensorily with a long-stemmed flower growing out the top of my head, I might discover, within the sensory exploration, a sense of moving with privileged and upper-class sensuality. I can use that movement and behavior as an aspect of character.

Actors never describe the sensory task to others. In the secret lies the power of the task. If the audience knows the knife is a banana, the thrust into the victim's body is a prank, not a crime. Secrets fuel actors' presence. When I waited to be introduced for my audition for *Equus* center stage at the Plymouth Theater on Broadway lit only by a ghost light, I worked on a shower exercise to concentrate and to relax. I did the exercise because I knew I would feel paradoxically vulnerable, naked and dripping, and powerful at these private sensations. I used the shower as a task to solve the problem of my nervousness and to make an emotional connection as I waited to be introduced.

Actors investigate the acting problem—the posture of the character, a particular gesture, an entrance or exit, a reaction—through the task. For instance, to solve a mincing dandy's gait within the context of a stylized political fantasy, I might explore walking across hot sand. I re-create the Sandy Hook beach of my childhood in its searing dryness on my moist child feet to experience a hurried gait here and now. The sensations encourage me to walk in a way I ordinarily don't. The sensory work gives me permission to move with confidence. Although I know there is no sand, I still re-create the sensation, unconcerned with the result. I discover the quick lifting of my feet as I walk by doing the exercise—always preserving freshness and spontaneity.

Another example is the "place" exercise that layers actors' awareness of their surroundings with their deliberate attention to the details of an imaginary environment. First, actors do a relaxation exercise. Once relaxed they might be directed to steer their imagination toward a room from their childhood home. Although the intuitive impulse at this suggestion is to remember a place, the more precise action is to look down at the floor, or to feel out with the buttocks for the texture of the seat, or to reach out with the mind's ear to listen for an imaginary sound—each impulse activated without anticipation. The doing of the sensory reach, within the conscious category of "room from a childhood home," often results in an imaginative perception that was not "remembered" yet is experienced in the moment. This subtle, but important, distinction encourages actors to trust their creative imagination. Don't anticipate, just do the sensory work.

In the place exercise, actors work with discrete sensory detail. For example, one finds himself in his bedroom when he was five. At his feet he visualizes a ping-pong ball on the imaginary carpet. He re-creates the details of the ball: its color, texture, and shape. Then he moves his attention to the carpet: its colors and texture. Then he focuses on the edge of the carpet and the floor. Each imaginary object contains the next inquiry within it. Again, the movement of attention creates concentration.

The place exercise is private; no one needs to know where actors have placed themselves imaginatively. Although at first actors may close their eyes, they will later be encouraged to work with them open. For example, in the child's bedroom exercise, the actor will learn to allow the visualized bedroom floor to coexist with the studio floor, to put the playpen just in front of the instructor's desk, to listen for his mother's voice while paying attention to the sounds that exist for all the actors in the studio. In his memory and his reality, he will move his attention from the imagined footsteps of a brother to the grunt of a nearby actor. He will pay attention to the light from the playroom window and when his attention is drawn to another actor standing up, he willingly looks and then places his kid's bed just in front of the other actor. *These two realities coexist.*

The imaginative and the real are not fighting for the actors' attention; rather *they create and allow both to exist simultaneously.* The two interpenetrate and support each other. Actors are not isolating themselves within the sensory work; but rather, and most significantly, they allow the sensory work to influence their perception of the actual surroundings and vice versa. So, if actors work upon a private place that has strong emotional connections, those feelings condition their behavior within the public space. I sometimes describe sensory work as a colored gel on a light. It colors the illumination, casting imaginative choices on the stage.

Critics charge that the Method asks actors to use themselves as the material for their characters. While that point of view begs the question of where else they can look, the charge is also misleading because it ignores the creative and experimental nature of the Method. The Method does not ask actors to use only what they know, although certainly it does help them make the most of the many sides of themselves. The training teaches actors to use sensory tasks as metaphors to discover and experience creative ways of behaving. The Method trains actors to develop processes of active and physical imagining. It encourages them to experience many paths before making a choice. The Method reinforces risk taking and teaches actors creative courage.

NOTES

1. Uta Hagen, *A Challenge to the Actor* (New York: Charles Scribner, 1991), 77.
2. Doug Moston, *Coming to Terms with Acting* (New York: Drama Publishers, 1993), 115–16.
3. Duncan Ross, "Towards an Organic Approach to Actor Training," *Educational Theatre Journal* 20 (1968): 260–61.

CHAPTER THIRTEEN

THE HEART AS CENTER
Entering the Body and the Creative State

James Luse

As an actor, no matter what my appearance, no matter what my ability to transform myself through costume and makeup, at the center will always be myself.
— *Constantine Stanislavski,* Stanislavski and the Actor

I have mentioned before that we have many locks in our bodies. For instance, our fingers can be so locked that they do not take part in our actions. All of these locks can be opened by our understanding of the imaginary center, if it is developed until the whole body becomes free.
— *Michael Chekhov,* Lessons for the Professional Actor

"Relax! Connect the moments and thoughts! Breathe—you're not breathing! Will you get centered? You're not centered! Stop forcing! Don't hit it over the head!" In rehearsal, audition, and performance, these inner and outer voices clang and echo in the actor's consciousness. Eventually they become: "Why are they coughing? Am I that horrible? There! Someone coughed, or rustled a program!" Unfortunately, this poisonous rumination occurs while the actor is delivering a soliloquy or monologue or living an intimate moment onstage. "You can't imagine the horror of knowing you're acting badly," muses Nina in Act IV of Anton Chekhov's *The Seagull*.

Where are the solutions? How can actors return to total faith in and commitment to the onstage reality, once their concentration has abandoned them? Teachers, directors, and coaches demand their ensembles be *centered, relaxed,* and *grounded,* but so few offer paths or keys to attaining or sustaining Stanislavsky's treasured *creative state.*

From Stanislavsky's formula for "the inner moving picture" and his use of "self communion" come glimmerings of a trail out of the darkness of self-consciousness and judgment.[1] The key lies in a combination of the physical, mental, and imaginative processes of Lee Strasberg, Kristin Linklater, F. M. Alexander, and that immortal purveyor of imagination, Michael Chekhov. All four teachers of relaxation and creativity employ Stanislavsky's principles of concentration, observation, faith, and imagination. They simply take Stanislavsky further by inviting actors to enter their own physical mechanism—their body.

Through the establishment of his theories of inner "radiation" and "atmospheres" between 1938 and 1955, Michael Chekhov pointed the way for actors, performers, and public speakers to achieve relaxation, refined concentration, and increased belief. Chekhov, whom Stanislavsky had christened "the ideal student," took Stanislavsky's discovery of the "actor's physical center" from the solar plexus (*AP* chap. 10), and moved it to the physical region of the upper chest (*On the Technique of Acting,* chap. 4). Chekhov describes the increased flexibility, power, freedom, and breath that are attained by operating from this center. However, his written process fails to make clear the physical and intellectual steps necessary in creating the emotionally incandescent relaxed creative artist who confidently lives in their body. From his many inspired exercises in *Lessons for the Professional Actor* (1985) and *On the Technique of Acting* (1991), teachers and students of the Chekhov technique have arrived at various step-by-step procedures to attain integration of body, mind, imagination, feeling, and will.[2] The following two exercises are cornerstones of physical, intellectual, and psychic awareness that I have refined through application in both performance and in laboratory.

INITIATING INCREASED CORPOREAL
AND ENVIRONMENTAL AWARENESS:
BECOMING "PRESENT"

The celebrated actress/teacher E. Katherine Kerr has originated a process of scanning through the body and indexing the external and internal sensations. Kerr refers to this as "getting present." It is an invaluable system for recording one's personal truth in the moment. To initiate the process, actors must freely and honestly admit all of the physical feelings they are experiencing in the current instant. These include aches, pains, exhaustion, skin irritations, postnasal drip, sore throat, cramps, heat, perspiration, indigestion, lightheadedness, dizziness, nervousness, heartbeat, and breathing. An efficient variation of the exercise involves the following.

Once actors have investigated the physical sensations throughout their body, they are asked to describe them with vivid, neural exactitude. These descriptions are relayed to a partner and are coupled with the intention of sending agreement or making a pact. Eventually actors are encouraged by the partner or themselves to travel to the salient sensation in or on their physical being. Once this is located, actors are asked to approach the sensation with their inner point of concentration, or "mind's eye." Using the full rules of precise imagination employed by Stanislavsky, actors then speak aloud how the sensation appears. Its shape, color, hue, shadings, depth, and volume are all depicted audibly. Another configuration of lines and color may replace the formation the sensation originally assumed. These events are to be promoted. All images are valid and significant in laying the foundation of actors' truthful relaxation.

Ultimately, actors are invited to enter and become this descriptive object or scene that is a product of their corporeal neural awareness and imagination. By transforming themselves into this object inside their body, actors are now "present." That is, they are acutely alert and aware of the concrete surroundings outside them as well as activated and energized within their bones, muscles, and skin. The ensuing exercise is a fusion of the Chekhov and Stanislavsky processes in order to arrive systematically at Michael Chekhov's "ideal center in the chest."[3]

ESTABLISHING THE HEART AS THE WORKING CENTER

An operating center of the body may be defined as the location from which all thought, movement, desire, feeling, and behavior spring. To establish the center for yourself, you must enter the body. You will imaginatively visualize and register with your senses the bones, skin, muscles, fluids, and organs that surround your chosen center. For example, to enter the heart with your imagination and your mind's eye, first touch the middle of your sternum with your middle finger. Close your eyes. Place your concentration on that point of physical contact between your fingers and the skin covering your sternum. What are the textures? What is the temperature? Gently press your sternum. What pressure do you detect in the bone? Increase your force slightly. What occurs to the bone, lungs, and trachea? Release the pressure. What are the sensations on the sternum, the skin covering it, and in the organs beneath it? How does breathing alter under pressure and when it is released?

Repeat the above activities, but now travel with your mind's eye to the place of contact on your sternum. Travel beyond the bone with your mind's eye and enter your trachea, your lungs, and the surrounding tissue. As you push into and through your sternum, what are the sensations? Aching? Painful? Constricting? Puncturing? Warm? Remain behind your sternum with your point of concentration. How does the backside of the bone appear? What do you see? Turn your point of concentration and gaze into your lungs and trachea. Describe aloud the shapes, colors, lines and forms that you are witnessing within this chamber of your chest. Do not speak clinically or literally. Abdicate technical responsibility. Be careful not to edit yourself. Any shape, color, texture, line, arrangement of objects, or landscape of figures is valuable, and worthwhile, and must be validated.

Some who have entered their chests and hearts have merely perceived bone, muscle, tissue, cartilage, and organs. Still others are in an enclosed environment or inside a room. If this occurs, you must ask yourself for the light and shadow of the perimeter of the space or of the walls. Let design and colors penetrate. Many students have registered fields, bodies of water, streams, rivers, flowers, animals, architecture, and people. Others trace flowing abstract shapes, rays and rivulets of color, explosions of light and dark, and fluttering showers of gold or silver. Allow yourself to view a Jackson Pollack, Henri Matisse, Salvador Dali, or the luscious chiaroscuro of Caravaggio, da Vinci, or Rembrandt. Possibly you may glimpse the symmetry and vibrancy of the Venetian Giovanni Ballini.

View the images behind your sternum with a full, lively imagination, free from judgment. Any and all images are valid and productive.

Making contact with the vertebrae exactly opposite the sternum may also enhance the initiating physical stimulus of touch. From your location behind your sternum, travel with your point of concentration through your lungs and trachea and enter your vertebrae. Now touch the vertebrae to which you have imaginatively and mentally traveled. With your mind's eye meet your fingers on the outside of your spine. What are the sensations, textures, and temperatures of this encounter? Rest on your vertebrae and then eventually pass through them and enter your spinal column. What are the images? Is there a particular location? Allow the stimuli that you receive to change. Never try to control what you see or touch at any point in the exercise.

Extend a cord between the sternum and the vertebrae opposite it. Now move with your mind's eye to the left. As you journey between the ribs and shoulder blades under the trapezius, realize you are entering the chambers of the heart. While you are crossing the threshold of the heart, pause to absorb the cartilage, tissue, bone, and muscle in your path visually, aurally, kinesthetically, and tactilely. You will discover the heart wall beneath the left set of ribs, which extends from your sternum.

To note the unique textures, temperatures, gravitational forces, and visualizations aligned on the left side of the chest, try to journey to the right side. Beneath the right set of ribs, the nerve endings, organs, density, hollowness, mass, and contours are completely different.

Return to the heart. Step into its various chambers. It is essential to experience and record all sounds, images, textures, temperatures, boundaries, and tautness of surfaces. These may alter at any time, but the location of your point of concentration is constant. That images, textures, and environments may keep transforming is evidence of eternally changing cells and patterns of growth within our bodies.

Remember to describe the experience orally to a partner or an object and to articulate the altering stimuli. If you are entering the heart as a center in preparation for a particular scene or exercise, the contents of your heart will be influenced by your identity in the scene or exercise. Bear in mind that the inner objects of your heart may have no immediate discernible logic. Embrace the contents they unfold: Do not be quick to judge or categorize. There may be rolls of silk, satin, or bloody rags residing within the innermost recesses. Also within the most intimate hollows one may discover jewels, beacons of light, sweets, precious objects, books, boulders, tools, knives, or panoramas similar to those demonstrated living behind the sternum.

Remain with your point of concentration in the center of your chest. Embrace the eternally transforming scenes and feelings that have been awakened. Now open your eyes and observe the world outside your body and your center. With your point of concentration staying in your center, touch, view, smell, and listen to the external world surrounding you.

Now try executing simple activities with the impetus, vision, and knowledge of the activity occurring in your center first. These can be sitting, walking, lifting, and carrying objects or entering and exiting a room. What sensations occur in your veins, in your heartbeat, in your nerve endings, and on your skin when you perform the activities in this manner? How does the external physical environment appear? How do your surroundings register to the touch or smell as you move, breathe, and execute physical tasks? If you remain within your sternum center or your heart center at all times, you will be experiencing a heightened awareness of touch, sight, and hearing. Concentration, memory, and imagination will become increasingly facile and enabled. You are entering Stanislavsky's creative state.

Michael Chekhov has developed the use of this "ideal center" by asking his students to imagine that they have arms, legs, and a head growing from the heart or from beneath the sternum.[4] Practicing this technique allows actors to create and conjure desires, decisions, and obstacles from deep inside their body, instead of intellectually and physically forcing, indicating, or "telegraphing" behavior.

Transferring the origins of thought, idea, vision, and impulse from the brain to the heart requires drill. Every rehearsal may commence with breathing, stretching, and yoga and then progress to the just-described meditations of entering the body with the "mind's eye." Let's return to the journey of the inner visualization to solidify the heart or chest as the center of thought, will, and action.

Record the inner moving pictures in the heart or chest center. Let these images lead to your point of concentration living in the blood, bone, and tissues of your arms, legs, and neck as you execute activities, blocking, or movements of a text or production that is in rehearsal. Landscapes, panoramas, and chains of scenes may continually alter, as long as they are initiated in the center. Since you have entered your center through speech, continue describing the qualities of your center orally. Now gradually transfer your descriptive speech to scripted dialogue. Incorporate this speaking with action or need to an outer object, such as a scene partner, props, or furniture of the setting.

INCREASED ACTIONS AND THE CENTER[5]

Now we will engage physical activities with the journey of inner visualization. Enter your heart. Speak your journey aloud to a partner who is doing the same. Now, using finely tuned faith and imagination, take your right hand and reach into your heart chamber. Be sure to adhere to the previous process of describing everything you touch, see, hear, and smell as you perform these steps. Let your hand tenderly blend with your skin and ribs as you perforate the left side of your chest. Your point of concentration is now in the middle of your right hand, which is now in the center of your heart.

What are you touching? What do you see? Rich fabric? Tapestries? Aged wood? Engravings? Hieroglyphics? Jewels? Stones? Are papers, books, or documents there? Are there toys or bric-a-brac? Is anything broken, tarnished, or scarred? What about heirlooms or neglected keepsakes? Do you perceive any blossoms, greenery, or forests? Do landscapes, vistas, or portraits present themselves? Or are there galaxies and solar systems?

Articulate orally all that your senses give you. Let your imagination soar. Limits or confinements are not permitted! Offer all of the sensory details to your partner. Coat and cover your partner orally with your vivid, graphic discoveries. Extract a piece of your heart. Hold it in your hand. See it. If the piece transforms, allow it. Take the fragment and place it in your partner's heart, describing the visual and tactile details the entire time. Take care to place your hand with your gift on your partner's chest, over the heart. Remain in that position. Travel into your partner's heart through your hand. What do you see, smell, hear, and/or touch inside your partner's heart, now that you have created a mixture? What are the images inside your hand?

Return to your own center. What do you see inside your own center, now that a fragment of it is inside someone else?

What just happened? You enacted the "physical actions," or active verbs of pledging, swearing, vowing, bestowing, uplifting and promising (among others). Now try the same order of movements and images from your center while you are speaking a Shakespearean sonnet or love poetry.

The exercise is completed. Michael Chekhov said: "We must at least *believe* that there is *something going on in us continuously*. Will this not increase in us our activities, our self-confidence, our ingenuity, our originality and our ability to grow day after day? We must never stop."[6] By actively employing the ongoing life of the heart center, dialogue, activities, behavior, and objectives of actors may live vibrantly, spontaneously, imaginatively, and creatively. By performing Michael Chekhov's exercises, there are fewer opportunities for faith and commitment to be shattered by the inner and outer voices of doubt.

NOTES

1. In *An Actor Prepares (AP)* Stanislavsky outlines a fundamental process of stimulating creative imagination (chaps. 4 and 10). He continues with *developing focus* and *observation* with effective exercises and theories in chapter 5. Jean Benedetti, *Stanislavski and the Actor* (New York: Routledge, 1998), contains recently translated exercises from the Stanislavsky Opera Studio (1936–1938). These studio drills inject vibrancy into the initial theories and exercises of *An Actor Prepares*. They heighten the physical experiences of "being in the body" through activities, images, visualization, and sensory awareness.

2. Michael Chekhov's theories of the invisible body and the use of the imagination as a picturing tool used before dialogue and movements are executed were first introduced in his book *To the Actor. On the Technique of Acting* is an updated edition of *To the Actor* and contains further explanation of the mind or point of concentration residing within a "center" in the body, not in the head. See *To the Actor* (New York: Harper and Row, 1953); *On the Technique of Acting,* Mel Gordon, ed. (New York: Harper Collins, 1991); and *Lessons for the Professional Actor,* Deirdre Hurst du Prey, ed. (New York: PAJ, 1985).

3. Chekhov's and Stanislavsky's theories of concentration on outer objects and inner sensations in the body come together in *Lessons for the Professional Actor*. This series of class notes and lectures from Chekhov's New York Studio has been transcribed and edited by Chekhov actress, teacher, secretary, and personal assistant Deirdre Hurst Du Prey.

4. In *Lessons for the Professional Actor,* Chekhov describes how behavior can emanate from designated centers in the body. Detailed notations occur in the chapters entitled "Twelfth Class" and "Fourteenth Class."
5. Psychologists Willis Harman and Howard Rheingold have discerned a similar heart meditation exercise employed in ancient Yoga traditions and the Byzantine Church. See Harman and Rheingold, *Higher Creativity: Liberating the Unconscious for Breakthrough Insights* (New York: Penguin, 1984).
6. Chekhov, *Lessons,* 157.

PART III

FUTURE

CHAPTER FOURTEEN

THE METHOD AND THE COMPUTATIONAL THEORY OF MIND

Rhonda Blair

Feel the truth within yourself.

—*Stella Adler,* A Technique of Acting

In this post-postmodern moment, it is time to engage Stanislavsky and the Method and observe key terms such as action, emotion, and given circumstances afresh, reexamining the general principles underlying them.[1] The various "Methods," as taught by Stella Adler, Sanford Meisner, Lee Strasberg, and others, remain the foundation for much of the actor training in the United States, but their ideas have been weakened by misunderstanding on the parts of actors, acting teachers, theorists, and even the master teachers themselves. They have been challenged by the rise of postmodern theories; mistrust of Freudian views of psychology and humanist-modernist views of identity; critiques of realism, representation, and mimesis; and the impact of performance modes resistant to psychological realism.

Criticisms come from various perspectives. Within the field of actor training, there are charges that the Method's views of emotion and feeling are too narrowly constrained; that some variations on the Method "lose the name of action" in their emphasis on an ego-based psychology and actors' hard-to-define inner "authenticity"; that its view of the self is overly Romantic; that it leads to self-indulgence; and that it is applicable only to forms of psychological realism. The Method can bring to bear counterproductive perspectives that compartmentalize emotions, physicality, and explicitly analytical aspects of the work from each other, or certain Method teachers valorize one of these aspects at the expense of another. Emotional authenticity, technical virtuosity, and critical acuity are sometimes viewed as being in conflict with each other or vying for primacy in the actors' performances. Some acting teachers in the United States give a limited "emotional," antitextual reading to Strasberg, which can lead actors to narcissism and overabsorption with the "self." Models that emphasize personal emotion without a broader context prevent some of the Method's fundamental tools (e.g., given circumstances and "magic if") from being applied effectively. From the perspective of some postmodern theories of performance, the Method gives way to private narrativity, a closed sense of character, and psychological realism; it reifies a nonexistent "self" at the expense of ignoring socially conditioned aspects of identity; it is applicable only to specific Western theatre forms; it colludes in mechanisms of representation that serve the ends of decadent late capitalism, reinforcing an ahistorical, noncritical, sentimentalized or sensationalized view of experience; it is part of the humanist project of universalizing experience; and, along with realism, it is inherently patriarchal and misogynist. The Method risks consigning us to a naive, anti-intellectual investment in narrative closure, "realistic" mimesis, and continuity that erases difference and ignores social critique.[2]

Thus, the Method is abused on two fronts: First, actors misread it to support an anti-intellectual, ahistorical attachment to a private, psychotherapeutically centered perspective that claims actors need only access their "authentic feelings." Second, theorists misread, also, rejecting the Method as too subjective and noncritical; they assert actors must be more skeptical about identity and emotional appeal (e.g., empathy and identification). What actors' naive "authentic" feeling and theorists' ultimately "self-authenticating" theories have in common is that neither of them can be pointed to physically, even as they rise out of public and personal historical and material conditions. Neither of the criticisms can actually be touched. Instead, they live somewhere in people's minds.

Given this, I would like to consider the Method from the perspective of some current research in cognitive science and its links to evolutionary biology. Rather than investigating psychotherapy, instinct or inspiration, or postmodern theory and politics—though my project is avowedly political—I want to demonstrate how selected principles of the Method, first stated in the 1920s, reflect and even embody basic characteristics described by cognitive science. I do not assert science as an absolute or objective authority, but I believe an examination of the Method in light of current "thinking about thinking" and its relationship to behavior could be useful in helping us keep the baby while throwing out the old bathwater.

Stanislavsky, Strasberg, Meisner, and Adler, in one variation or another, describe the actor's goal as being "to live truthfully," emotionally and physically, in imaginary circumstances. Stanislavsky described the actor's fundamental aim as the creation of the "inner life of a human spirit, and its expression in artistic form," which the actor accomplishes by "living the part" (*AP* 14). Central to the approach is "reaching the subconscious by conscious means." Lee Strasberg stated that the purpose of his exercises was "to train the actor's sensitivity to respond as fully and vividly to imaginary objects on stage as he is already capable of doing to real objects in life" (*DP* 123). Sanford Meisner's exercises "were designed to strengthen the guiding principle that [he] learned forcefully in the Group [Theatre]—that art expresses human experience" (*MA* 11). Key to this for Meisner is what he calls "true emotion," embodied by Eleanora Duse's very real blush in her performance in *Magda*—"the epitome of living truthfully under imaginary circumstances, which is my definition of good acting" (*MA* 15). Stella Adler said, "You must be truthful in what you do or say. Feel the truth within yourself. The most important thing is for the actor to sense his own truth" (*TA* 12); at the same time, the actor must be careful to distinguish between "the truth of life and the truth of the theatre" (*TA* 7). While we have a sense of what these teachers mean by "truth," the term is so subjective as to be highly suspect and subject to criticism. Nonetheless, these four masters devised ways of manipulating principles of action, imagination, attention, emotion, and sense memory to help the actor reach what Stanislavsky called the *inner creative state,* a complete engagement with the work.

Stanislavsky describes a relationship between the conscious and unconscious in a way similar to that of the other three teachers. His language both concretizes and mystifies, making the conscious and unconscious seem completely separate and at war with each other, as in "we are supposed to create under inspiration; only our subconscious gives us inspiration; yet we apparently can use this subconscious only through our consciousness, which kills it" (*AP* 13). He views the conscious and subconscious as entities rather than as sentient processes that are physiologically interlocked. Today's acting theorists must now exchange this image of a split structure of consciousness for the idea of a complex consciousness that inhabits the entire body, in which voluntary and involuntary behaviors are not so cleanly separated from each other. There is nothing in this notion that contradicts the Method; I am merely rearticulating its terms. Cognitive scientists, neurophysiologists, and psychologists are proving that Stanislavsky, seventy-five years ago, began intuiting something fundamental about how we, as human beings and as actors, work.

Stanislavsky names motivated action, supported by given circumstances and imagination (*if*), as the core of the actor's work. He is adamant that the actor begins not with feeling but with "some bit of action," since "feelings are the result of something that has gone before" (*AP* 41). He is also adamant that the actor directs all of her attention "to the 'given circumstances.' They are always within reach," while emotions are "of largely subconscious origin, and not subject to direct command" (*AP* 51–52). Similarly, Meisner, Adler, and Strasberg all start with something other than emotion—Meisner with action (or "doing"), Adler with the script's "given circumstances," and Strasberg with specific objects and experiences, in terms of both sense and affective memory. All of these are kinds of specific "information" about what has happened in the past or what is happening now in the actor's environment or experience. As a result, in spite of the slipperiness of the Method's goal—"emotional truth"—the methods employed by Strasberg, Adler, and Meisner are concrete and emphasize the material and physical.

INFORMATION, ACTION, AND THE
COMPUTATIONAL THEORY OF MIND

We are organisms, not angels, and our minds are organs, not pipelines to the truth.

—*Steven Pinker, How the Mind Works*

The materiality of the Method reflects the computational theory of mind's assertion that information is the key component of our mental lives. In *How the Mind Works,* philosopher and linguist Steven Pinker posits that this theory allows us "to connect the ethereal world of meaning and intention, the stuff of our mental lives, with a physical hunk of material like the brain."[3] He provides a foundation for understanding the actor's basic problem: how intelligence, desires, behavior, and body connect. It also helps provide a counter to the two faulty perspectives described earlier: first, to that of theorists who minimize the role of biology (and the emotion and instinct embedded in it) and who view humans primarily in terms of immediate environment and choice, and, second, to that of actors who focus on a too-narrow reading of the Method, minimizing its material and historical (in the broadest sense) aspects.

The computational theory roots us in a physical realm that links symbols, neurons, sense organs, belief, and behavior. Except for neurons, all of these terms are used in one way or another by great acting theorists from Stanislavsky and those following him to Grotowski and Brook. For Pinker, the computational theory of the mind holds that:

beliefs and desires are *information,* incarnated as configurations of symbols. The symbols are the physical states of bits of matter, like chips in a computer or neurons in the brain. They symbolize things in the world because they are triggered by those things via our sense organs, and because of what they do once they are triggered. If the bits of matter that constitute a symbol are arranged to bump into the bits of matter constituting another symbol in just the right way, the symbols corresponding to one belief can give rise to symbols corresponding to other beliefs, and so on. Eventually the bits of matter constituting a symbol bump into bits of matter connected to muscles, and behavior happens. The computational theory of mind thus allows us to keep beliefs and desires in our explanations of behavior while planting them squarely in the physical universe. It allows meaning to cause and be caused.[4]

This theory does not posit people as "machines" or "computers,"[5] but rather it emphasizes that we act and behave in certain ways, based on how we process information. It is a way of looking at how the mind is designed, based on a genetic program. This program determines how our brains develop and how we learn, including how we learn to "act." Brain development and the various ways of learning are products of natural selection, which is

> not a puppetmaster that pulls the strings of behavior directly. It acts by designing the generator of behavior that package of information-processing and goal-pursuing mechanisms called the mind. Our minds are designed to generate behavior that would have been adaptive, on average, in our ancestral environment. . . . Behavior is an outcome of an internal struggle among many mental modules, and it is played out on the chessboard of opportunities and constraints defined by *other* people's behavior.[6]

Behavior that is adaptive is designed to accomplish or prevent something, to achieve a goal, which is *action* in the Method's sense. "Opportunities" and "constraints" defined by "other people's behavior" are analogous with "objectives," "obstacles," and "given circumstances." From this perspective, key parts of the Method are fundamentally Darwinian and biological, not necessarily Romantic, modernist, humanist, psychological, Western, and spiritual. If this theory is correct, it means that the appeal of the Method is due not necessarily (and only) to the hegemony of various kinds of realism and habits of representation and mimesis but to the fact that it reflects how we function organically. From this perspective, self and behavior are grounded in our being as physical organisms while also being affected by culture and conscious choice.[7]

Based on his study of Ivan Pavlov's experiments in reflexology and Théodule Ribot's writing on the relationship between sensation and emotion, as well as on his own experimentation and observation, Stanislavsky found a way to begin connecting behavior, body, emotion, and intelligence, centered around the idea of a character wanting or pursuing something. This idea of connecting behavior and characters' wants, or objectives, was carried on by Strasberg and Adler, and particularly by Meisner's emphasis on "doing." The concept of motivated activity is also central to Pinker's definition of intelligence, encapsulated in a response to a humorous, but thought-provoking, question he posits to get at basic questions of mind: "What makes a good alien?" The answer, Pinker surmises, unites behavior, desire, and will:

> [One], they have to have intelligent but impenetrable responses to situations. You have to be able to observe the alien's behavior and say, "I don't understand the rules by which the alien is making its decisions, but the alien is acting rationally by some set of rules." . . . [And two], they have to care about something. They have to want something and pursue it in the face of obstacles.[8]

This definition of intelligence means de facto that a creature has will, desire, and objectives. This is not to say that actors are necessarily inscrutable aliens, but this view does reflect core elements of the Method and even uses its terminology: wanting and pursuing something, and the negotiation of obstacles in that pursuit. In acting, desire is central and operates on two levels: the level of the character and, more important, the level of the actor—the one actually doing the acting. Stanislavsky and his American followers intuitively understood this. Stanislavsky notes: "At the heart of every unit lies a *creative objective*. Each objective is an organic part of the unit or, conversely, it creates the unit which surrounds it" (*AP* 116–17). Moreover, an objective had to be both believable and "have attraction for the actor, to make him wish to carry it out" (*AP* 120). Stanislavsky understood desire as being a central component of intelligence and behavior. Within this framework, emotions are responses that grow out of an intelligence-based "wanting" grounded in a particular environment. When Strasberg, Meisner, and Adler follow Stanislavsky's dictate that *"all action in the theatre must have an inner justification, be logical, coherent and real"* (*AP* 46, emphasis in original), they are applying the key characteristics of intelligence to describe a central aspect of the actor's work. "We have to want something," says Pinker, "and pursue it in the face of obstacles."[9] In short, in the Method's sense, intelligence is acting.

Intelligence has components of desire and action that manifest in relationship to information, belief, and other aspects of context. Information that we gather from our environment and what we believe about that information set up our desires and, accordingly, the actions we take. To be sure, the information available in a particular environment to a particular individual constrains belief and, thereby, action. However, the point is that there is a direct correlation between information and behavior. The Method embraces this formulation: desire equals objective; behavior equals action; information equals given circumstances; and belief equals imagination and "if." The equation presents intellect and action in a way that reinforces the organic "rightness" of the acting teachers' attraction to the Method's cluster of terms while clarifying some of the mystifications of its language. The Method's key elements grow out of intuitive psychology and biology. They are in our very hard-wiring.

The Method is, at its core, relational and physical. It is ultimately about wills acting through and on physical bodies. This fact ties it to principles of object psychology, which focuses on how humans (and other animals) perceive and "compute" the characteristics of objects as a basis for understanding and behavior. This perspective can be dismissed as "Newtonian," but it largely determines how we make choices in the course of a day; for example, one objective cannot pass through another, objects move along continuous trajectories unless hindered, objects are cohesive, and objects move each other by contact only. (If you are tempted to raise quantum or postmodern objections, please visualize two cars and one intersection, not two quarks, or two children with one toy, not two subatomic charms). This view sets the foundation for the two fundamental metaphors of thought and language that are connected to how we perceive and negotiate objects—metaphors involving *location in space* and metaphors of *force, agency, and causation.* These two categories of metaphor link motion (i.e., an object existing at one point or locus, capable of moving to another point or locus) and desire. That is, "[s]pace and force pervade language."[10] In essence, "the elements of mentalese are based on places and projectiles," on our need to place ourselves and objects in particular relationships to each other and our need continuously to negotiate issues of force and causation.[11] The Method is also permeated by metaphors of locus and agency. Its use of given circumstances

(e.g., Adler's "who," "what," "where"), of action vividly imagined and enacted (the foundation of Meisner's approach), and of objects and experience (in Strasberg) is an extension of this fundamental structure of
human consciousness.

MENTAL REPRESENTATIONS, IMAGINATION, AND EMOTIONS

*Self-betrayal, magnified to suit the optics of the theatre, is the whole art
of acting.*

—*George Bernard Shaw*

Spatial relationships and force are represented in the mind by mental representations, or symbols, and much of the Method has to do with how the
mind constructs and uses these symbols. According to Pinker, the computational theory of mind posits that these mental representations com-
prise our mental life and are "arrangements of matter that have both
representational and causal properties, that is, that simultaneously carry
information about something and take part in a chain of physical events."
These symbols have both narrative (informational) aspects and dramatic
(causal-behavioral) ones. We have several kinds of representations in our
heads—most important are visual images, grammatical representations
(spoken language), and mentalese.[12] The latter is the language of thought
itself, which carries information along mental modules and which we
might relate to terms such as "impulse," "instinct," or "insight." To call
mentalese a preverbal or metaverbal modality may not be completely accurate in scientific terms, but it could be useful to think of it metaphori-
cally in this way.

Mentalese is an active component in all levels of consciousness. This
perspective emphasizing symbolic representations views the brain less in
terms of unmediated stimulus-response (which would relate more to
some simplistic descriptions of the Method and to principles of associa-
tionism, reflexology, or behaviorism in ways that risk diminishing the
role of cognition and analysis) and more in terms of a field of conscious
and subconscious internal representations existing between input and
output layers. Consciousness is composed of the awareness of a rich field

of sensations—a kind of general sensory awareness. This awareness then becomes refined as portions of sensory information fall under what Pinker calls "the spotlight of attention."[13] Whether something falls under this spotlight depends on its importance to our interest and well-being. This is the material of mental representations.

I am struck by how "spotlight of attention" resonates so closely with the Method's concepts of circle of attention and point of concentration. These key concepts—connected primarily to vision, but also to the other senses, especially in Strasberg's sensory exercises—relate to how the organism negotiates its environment, or "given circumstances," in order to maximize its ability to prioritize and accomplish its goals. Stanislavsky anticipates the computational theory when he describes the links among attention, desire, and creativity, noting that simple attention is

> intellectual in origin and is especially useful in collecting attention which has strayed. . . . To grasp your object firmly when you are acting you need another type of attention, which causes an emotional reaction. You must have something which will *interest you* in the object of your attention, and serve to set in motion your whole creative apparatus. [*AP* 89, emphasis in original]

When we consider what constitutes mental representations, the issue of emotion arises, since these representations encompass the linguistic, imaginational, sensory, and emotional aspects of awareness. They constitute consciousness. The computational theory posits that the main features of consciousness are *"sensory awareness, focal attention, emotional coloring, and the will"*[14] (emphasis in original), which are perceived and processed as a series of mental representations. These four traits reflect the Method's sense memory and observation, concentration, attention to emotion, and action. The Method basically uses the main features of consciousness to provide the actor with a technique for constructing a string of symbols in order deliberately to trigger things to happen in the body, that is, to access the unconscious by conscious means.

In the cases of both the computational theory and the Method, Pinker maintains that these representations are to be understood as "a set of symbols corresponding to *aspects* of the world" and not as "a lifelike photograph of the world" (emphasis in original).[15] In short, they are not replications of a kind of external or idealized "reality" but intensely individual interpretations of phenomenal experience. This correlative nature of mental representations is key to understanding the personal way that symbols work; they allow (or even require) each of us to perceive and respond to our world in individualized ways. This is more than a conventionally psychological interpretation; it provides a way of understanding how the mind filters and transforms experience by connecting sense data and past experiences through stringing together sets of symbols. This explains the unique ways in which general principles of the Method can work for each person. Stanislavsky draws this together in describing the actor's process:

> We must have, first of all, an unbroken series of supposed circumstances in the midst of which our exercise is played. Secondly we must have a solid line of inner visions bound up with those circumstances, so that they will be *illustrated* for us. *During every moment we are on the stage, during every moment of the development of the action of the play, we must be aware either of the external circumstances which surround us (the whole material setting of the production), or of an inner chain of circumstances which we ourselves have imagined in order to illustrate our parts.* Out of these moments will be formed an unbroken series of images, something like a moving picture. As long as we are acting creatively, this film will unroll and be thrown on the screen of our inner vision, making vivid the circumstances among which we are moving. [*AP* 63–64, emphasis in original]

In a discussion of mental representations, Pinker notes that "Images drive the emotions as well as the intellect." He continues: "Ambition, anxiety, sexual arousal, and jealous rage can all be triggered by images of what isn't there." He cites one experiment in which "volunteers were hooked up to electrodes and asked to imagine their mates being unfaithful"; the results were substantial changes in skin conductance, muscular contraction, and heart rate.[16] These results are not surprising to any acting teacher worth her salt; they confirm the links the Method describes among body, imagination, and emotion. Images (elements of mentalese) are connected to fundamental structures of language, which are embodied in metaphors of place and agency. This structural connection clarifies the murky relationship between reality and imagination in the Method. Stanislavsky talks about the need to be lifted "out of the world of actuality and into the realm of imagination" (*AP* 46), saying that "There is no such thing as actuality on the stage. Art is a product of the imagination" (*AP* 54). But he also speaks about the need for theatrical action to be *real* and for actors to be believable. In the same way, Meisner's credo states: "The foundation of acting is the reality of doing" (*MA* 16). Stanislavsky begins to articulate the relationship between "reality" and "art" in describing the relationship between *if* and given circumstances:

> *If* is the starting point, the given circumstances, the development. The one cannot exist without the other, if it is to possess a necessary stimulating quality. However, their functions differ somewhat: *if* gives the push to dormant imagination, whereas the *given circumstances* build the basis for *if* itself. And they both, together and separately, help to create an inner stimulus. [*AP* 51, emphasis in original]

Stanislavsky discusses how *if "arouses an inner and real activity"* by "natural means" (*AP* 47, emphasis in original). We can even see how imagination measurably affects emotional *and* physical feeling, as in the subtle but quantifiable changes in people's physiological responses when they are asked to imagine their spouses being unfaithful. "If" is a way to activate the individual's sentience and thereby the body's ability to react more fully and expressively.

Emotions and passions are set off in the mind, initiated not by inchoate impulses but by specific mental representations, images, and ideas. Within this framework, emotions are automatic or deliberate strategies for accomplishing objectives; they are the organism's responses that grow out of an intelligence-based "wanting" grounded in a particular situation. Emotions drive our strongest goals connected to basic issues of survival and reproduction, mobilizing us to action. Even the "amok state," a terrible loss of self in which the person uncontrollably does great violence, is, according to Pinker, "chillingly cognitive. It is triggered not by a stimulus, not by a tumor, not by a random spurt of brain chemicals, but by an idea."[17] One need only think of Othello's violent passion and actions, all inspired by an idea—not a direct experience or fact—that Desdemona has been with Cassio. To cite a terrible example from life, Eric Harris and

Dylan Klebold ran amok, wreaking havoc at Columbine High School, because of violent configurations of images, beliefs, and ideas constituted (consciously or otherwise) out of their experiences and imagination. Emotion is triggered primarily by information and its interpretation, not by energy. The emotion linked to the idea gives rise to what Pinker calls the goal, the objective:

> An animal cannot pursue all its goals at once. . . . The animal must commit its body to one goal at a time, and the goals have to be matched with the best moments for achieving them. . . . *The emotions are mechanisms that set the brain's highest-level goals.* Once triggered by a propitious moment, an emotion triggers the cascade of *subgoals and sub-subgoals that we call thinking and acting.* Because the goals and means are woven into a multiply nested control structure of subgoals within subgoals within subgoals, *no sharp line divides thinking from feeling, nor does thinking inevitably precede feeling or vice versa.* [emphasis added][18]

To clarify the Method, we must clarify the place of emotions in our behavior. To abusers of the Method who overvalorize emotion, the preceding describes how emotions are not separate from intellect but how thinking, feeling, and acting are essentially indivisible. To postmodernists reluctant to ascribe any "natural" power to emotions, it describes how emotions are, in effect, the seat of the will—the thing that mobilizes mind and body. This concept mirrors Stanislavsky's structure of superobjective (or through-line of action) and smaller objectives, or units of action, that is, "nested," prioritized, life-preserving goals driven and energized by feeling. However, it differs from Stanislavsky in that it is as much about sub-or unconscious goals as it is about conscious ones. It describes how the brain works emotionally on all levels. This, of course, is the actor's problem: how to access and employ consistently the materials of both the conscious and unconscious parts of the mind; in this regard, the theory supports Strasberg's emphasis on sense and affective memory as a way of giving rise to powerful, motivated action.

Emotions and passions are not in opposition to the intellect but are its cohort and even its mover; the passions are a partner and tool of our intellectual processes. The purposes of emotions include energizing and reinforcing the will and, importantly, signaling to others the seriousness and believability of our threats and promises. Passions are built into our body-minds to strengthen our ability to defend ourselves and to make us scarier or more appealing to others; the brain for Pinker *"contrives [emotions]* as a negotiating tactic, like a terrorist with explosives strapped to his body." The brain selectively sacrifices "control" and reason because doing so is an effective tactic:

> The passions are no vestige of an animal past, no wellspring of creativity, no enemy of the intellect. The intellect is designed to relinquish control to the passions so that they may serve as guarantors of its offers, promises, and threats . . . The apparent firewall between passion and reason is not an ineluctable part of the architecture of the brain; it has been programmed in deliberately, because only if the passions are in control can they be creditable guarantors.[19]

Emotions function as "doomsday machines" (to use Pinker's analogy), guaranteeing various kinds of behavioral quid pro quos. This reframes the Method's problem of reaching the unconscious by conscious means: Actors need to do something that human beings are not supposed to be able to do: to feel, or appear to be feeling, powerful emotions spontaneously and "uncontrollably." If strong emotions are indeed a kind of doomsday machine, actors' neural networks are required to interrelate and work in ways that were not intended. An actor's job is to get past this physically encoded—not merely psychosocial—firewall on cue. It could be helpful if actors viewed emotions as physiologically grounded tactics—conscious or otherwise—that are responses to specific information (given circumstances) rather than essences or "truths" of an intangible and merely cultural self. Humans have developed increasingly refined skills for discerning trustworthy ("real") emotions are untrustworthy ("fake") ones. Evolution has played a trick for, in order to guarantee "trustworthiness" or believability, it has placed the responsibility for some of these feelings in the limbic system, a part of the brain generally beyond our control. As a result, many strong emotions, such as fear and anger, involve facial and other muscles that cannot be completely controlled voluntarily. (Think only about the subtle but powerful differences between a genuine smile and a social one.) This cognitive bypass makes an actor's emotions "false" at least to some degree, since they start from a conscious and manufactured place. Meisner, Adler, and Strasberg developed their Methods as a means of negotiating an end-run around the cognitive and limbic systems' firewall.[20]

The cornerstone of Meisner's method, the repetition exercise, is firmly rooted in the principles of concentration and directed activity (focal attention and behavior), given circumstances (information), and imagination (mental representations). It is built on focusing on an activity and responding meticulously to a scene partner, for the purposes of immediacy and emotional specificity in negotiating a relationship and getting past the evolutionary "firewall." The repetition exercise demands skills in assessing the other's feelings and motives—seeing and listening to the other "animal" in a focused, moment-by-moment way, and alert, as Pinker observes, to any "twitch of inconsistency that betrays a sham emotion."[21] To understand Meisner's point fully, we must translate some of his problematic language. He distinguishes between "instinct" (the source of good acting) and "the head" (the source of bad acting), constantly reiterating "Don't think—do" (*MA* 27–31). This "doing" equates "thinking/the head" with conscious, planned analysis and "instinct" with impulses/intuition, in essence splitting emotion from thought; this emphasis has led to valid criticisms of his method as being anti-intellectual. However, if we understand Meisner as saying that, *in the moment of performance*, we must give priority to action, given circumstances, and responsiveness rather than to planning (and this is, in fact, what he is saying), then the psychophysical rightness of his method becomes obvious. Adler uses components similar to Meisner but stresses them differently, giving primacy to the circumstances of the play, supported by imagination and concentration. She emphasizes the use of environmental information and the construction of a series of vivid, personal mental representations as a way of unlocking the actor's being.

Strasberg presents a provocative challenge. He has consistently been painted with the brush of emotional indulgence and excess, and has been rejected by Adler and Meisner, especially in regard to his emphasis on "affective memory" (*MA* 10). After decades of disavowing Strasberg, I am surprised and not a little chagrined to find myself now serving as a defender of at least some elements of his approach, having gone back to look more closely at his writing. When Strasberg describes his Method, he begins not with emotion but with close attention to objects, moving from physical to internal ones. While some theorists tend to focus on Strasberg's emphasis on affective memory extensively, its use is, in fact, inseparable from physical sensation, sense memory, and imagination. At its core, Strasberg's approach is physical and specific. The sequence of exercises, he says:

> proceeds from the simple to the more complex; from objects that are in our immediate environment to objects that reside only in our memory; from objects that are external and clearly observable to objects that are internal and depend on our inner concentration to be recreated. We move from single objects of attention to combinations of a number of objects. Thus, the actor is prepared for the variety of problems that he will have to deal with in the scene and in the play. [*DP* 124]

Like Stanislavsky, Meisner, and Adler, Strasberg begins with information (with objects and close attention to some aspect of the environment) and attaches this awareness to the construction (or discovery or creation) of a series of mental representations to engage the actor with the scene. The approaches of these teachers are first and foremost about engaging the organism—the actor—with the environment and facilitating a dynamic, active response to that environment, which is simultaneously both imaginary and real.

Viewed from a perspective emphasizing the psychophysical and environmental, the Method's basic principles, conditioned as they are by Euro-American cultural and historical contexts, are nonetheless grounded in basic human biology and sentience. While it is necessary to submit the Method to critique in the important project of probing how power works through narrative, mimesis, identity, the imaginary, and the real, too often the critiques have been generic and abstract, dismissing too easily what the Method's main principles may be getting at. We must closely reexamine what the Method actually proposes, reframing its dated language and taking into account its historical milieu appropriately in light of current developments in science. This will allow us to benefit from what is accurate and useful in the Method while eschewing its more culturally limited perspective. Recent developments in cognitive science, neurophysiology, and evolutionary biology provide a deep structure for indicating that Stanislavsky and his heirs were onto something fundamental not only about acting but also about the way humans work.

NOTES

1. For the purposes of this chapter, I use "Method" to include all the major American approaches to acting based in Stanislavsky's fundamental principles and strategies. Though this lacks subtlety, the term allows us to place these related approaches together and refers explicitly to two of the main forms, Stanislavsky's method of physical actions and Strasberg's Method.

2. See, for example, Richard Hornby, *The End of Acting: A Radical View* (New York: Applause, 1992); Colin Counsell, *Signs of Performance: An Introduction to Twentieth-Century Theatre* (London: Routledge, 1996); essays in *Acting (Re)Considered: Theories and Practices,* Phillip Zarrilli, ed. (London: Routledge, 1995) especially "Part I: Theories and Meditations on Acting" and Phillip Zarrilli's introductory essay; W. B. Worthen's "Actors and Objects," *Modern Drama and the Rhetoric of Theater* (Berkeley: University of California Press, 1992), 54–98; and Elin Diamond's critique of realism and mimesis, *Unmaking Mimesis: Essays on Feminism and Theater* (London: Routledge, 1997).

3. Steven Pinker, *How the Mind Works* (New York: Norton, 1997), 24.

4. Ibid., 25.

5. Among other differences, brains run in parallel, not serial, mode; brains are slower than computers; brains have more connections; and brains assemble themselves (see Ibid., 26–27).

6. Pinker, *How the Mind Works,* 42.

7. Or "A human being is simultaneously a machine and a sentient free agent, depending on the purpose of the discussion." Ibid., 56.

8. Ibid., 61.

9. Ibid., 61.

10. Ibid., 355.

11. Human thought is deeply, organically structured this way because of our primitive ancestors' need for dealing continually with hunting and being hunted; survival depended on knowing where they were in relation to other creatures and on knowing how their weapons would work. See Ibid., 355. In much the same way, many of us perceive and negotiate our ways around performance environments, academic institutions and conferences, and our most intimate relationships.

12.   Pinker, *How the Mind Works,* 76, 90–91.
13.   Ibid., 109, 140.
14.   Ibid., 136.
15.   Ibid., 79.
16.   Ibid., 285.
17.   Ibid., 364.
18.   Ibid., 373–74.
19.   Ibid., 413.
20.   Current work is being done to unlock the actor's access to emotion through focused manipulation of the body, based on neuropsychological research. See, for instance, Bloch et al., "Effector Patterns of Basic Emotions: A Psycho-Physiological Method for Training Actors," in *Acting (Re)Considered,* 197–218, and Chapter 16 by Pamela D. Chabora in this volume.
21.   Pinker, *How the Mind Works,* 405.

CHAPTER FIFTEEN

RANDOM ACTS

The Method and Nonrealistic Theatre

Paul S. Kassel

Hamlet splits with the ax the heads of Marx, Lenin, Mao. Snow. Ice Age.
—*Heinrich Müller*, Hamletmachine

In 1984, during my first year in New York City, I was cast in a very odd piece called *Chaturanga* (Sanskrit for "chess"). The plot was nonlinear, the characters mostly chess pieces, and the text vague and confusing—at least to me. I have particularly strong memories of using our bodies collectively to create an elephant. It was fun, interesting, audiences seemed to like it (whatever it was), and we received a decent notice in the *New York Times*.[1] But I was at sea—I didn't know what to do. Fresh out of graduate school, where the Meisner technique was taught and the theatre was classic rep, I was completely unprepared—or so I thought. The experience forced me to confront my training, to ask whether it would serve me as an artist in this kind of material. That is the question posed by this chapter: Can traditional actor training in the Method and/or its variants serve the contemporary theatre artist?

Actors must traverse performance genres and forms in a burgeoning variety of media, especially at educational institutions where productions attempt to fulfill educational, artistic, and cultural missions. The particular demands made on the performer by these varying media call into question the very foundations of what is called performance. Shall teachers of actors merely resort to a smorgasbord-style of training—a little Method, a little mask work, a dash of Grotowski or Suzuki? Or is it preferable to pick one specialized approach and stick with it?

There are as many acting techniques as there are actors. No single approach will serve all actors. However, *any* single approach may serve a single actor, no matter the genre or form. Certainly, an actor in the play *Hamletmachine* can utilize the Method, just as, for example, the Viewpoints technique can be used by an actor in *Take Her, She's Mine*.[2] While it can be argued whether one approach or another is *preferable* for working on *Hamletmachine* or *Take Her, She's Mine*, my goal is to demonstrate that training in the Method is acceptable preparation for work in a variety of genres and forms. But specifically, the Method is exceptionally good preparation for the actor working in so-called nonrealistic, experimental, avant-garde theatre.

Group Theatre founder and Method teacher Harold Clurman has said that the question as to the applicability of Stanislavsky's work to contemporary theatre "betrays a fundamental misunderstanding: the System wasn't conceived to produce a particular stylistic result. . . . It is a means whereby a particular artist or group of artists may most authentically and completely manifest whatever they wish in the theatre."[3] The two primary ways the Method prepares an actor for work in nonrealism are its emphasis on playing actions and creating characters. At first glance this may seem paradoxical, for much nonrealistic theatre lacks linear action and character. But underlying the work of playing actions and creating characters are fundamental building blocks, a "grammar" of acting that is generally applicable to all performance modes.

PREMISES

Action is eloquence.

—*Shakespeare*, Coriolanus *III.ii.*

At its foundation, acting is the application of energy to a task. To act is to act upon, to "do to." Regardless of the genre or form of a performance, actions in performance are by nature the same as actions in everyday life. Whether one is performing in the work of Robert Wilson, Kabuki, or a traditional well-made play, one is always doing, always acting.[4]

In looking for a more effective way to introduce and practice the playing of actions in my basic acting class, I adopted a step-by-step approach with verbs. Students practiced a "verb du jour," adding to their action vocabulary with each class. I started with two simple, basic verbs that engaged the body quickly: *push* and *pull*. I soon discovered that *push* and *pull* have two variants: *to* and *from*. That is, *push to* something, *push from* something, *pull to* something, or *pull from* something. It appeared to me that *all* verbs were variations of push and pull. I designed a simple diagram for students with push and pull occupying opposite ends of a continuum, with the *to* and *from* variants above and below the continuum axis. (See figure 15.1) My thinking was that *any* verb could be located on the continuum.

However, as I quickly learned, some verbs fall outside this continuum. There are critical moments in scenes, whether scripted or not, during which change is imminent.[5] Two more verbs are needed to augment push and pull. Logically, the next verb is found in the middle of two pushes or two pulls, for example. When two opposing forces meet, there is a moment when they are balanced, either in stasis (pull-pull) or continual motion (push-pull). Although energy is flowing, change has not yet occurred. *Hold* is the verb that aptly describes this moment. *Hold* has ambiguous connotations (without being physically vague), and it does not mean stop, end, or withdraw energy. The opposite of *hold* is *release*.[6] When asked to *release* in a moment, students always know what to do. The *to* and *from* variants apply to *hold* and *release* as well. Together, the four fundamental verbs and their variants make what I called a *Verb Mandela* on which all acting verbs can be located. (See figure 15.2)

Figure 15.1   Verb Continuum

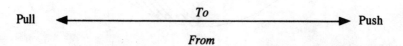

It is important to state that all verbs probably are not reducible to push/pull/hold/release; however, the idea is a unique way to help actors play clear, effective actions. In addition, the simplicity of the four-verb concept lends credence to its fundamental nature. Although not proof per se, a suggestion of the validity of the four verbs can be found in early childhood development. The initial *volitional* behaviors of infants are sucking (pull), eliminating (push), grasping (hold), and letting go (release). Although these volitional behaviors include only humans born without physiological, neurological, or genetic abnormalities, nevertheless, the approach is generally applicable to all performance and quite handy for students immersed in Western theatre who encounter other (cultural, structural) performance modes.[7] These actions achieve results in both realistic and nonrealistic environments. No matter the performance genre or form, action is required. Moreover, these four fundamental verbs—push, pull, hold, and release—are well within the capabilities of the actor properly trained in the Method.[8]

Figure 15.2   Verb Mandela

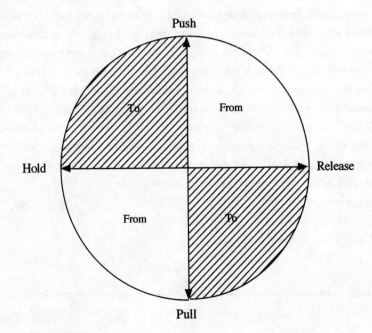

APPLICATION IN ACTION

A jar could be thrown out into an empty space, and a minute later a stick from offstage could push that jar one inch forward. That would function as theater.

—*Richard Foreman,* Unbalancing Acts

The question now is: How to apply an action-based pedagogy to performing in nonrealistic theatre? In many acting classes, action usually is described relative to the character—what the character wants and how he or she gets it. Character A has an objective, such as "I want X to leave me alone." The objective has an inherent obstacle in it that the character must overcome to achieve the objective. The manner by which the objective is achieved is called the action,[9] or what acting teacher Robert Cohen calls the "tactic."[10] Typically, the text, situation, and/or relationship suggest tactics the character employs to achieve the objective. In every acting book I have read and every class I have taken that is based on Stanislavsky, the practice has been to perform actions arising from character. *What* the actor does comes from *whom* the actor is supposed to represent.

Literary scholar Northrop Frye states in *Anatomy of Criticism* that in drama, "characterization depends on function; what a character is follows from what he has to do in the play." Dramatic function, Frye adds, "depends on the structure of the play; the character has certain things to do because the play has such and such a shape."[11] At its essence, Frye's analysis means that the actor performs a function within a structure. The particular function performed is perceived as character. The problem in playing actions in nonrealistic theatre arises from the fact that characters, objectives, or tactics are not present (or represented) in the text. The traditional approach to answering "How shall I do this"—motivation, character biography, the cause-and-effect sequence of the play—often is not only unnecessary but can be a hindrance to effective performing in nonrealism. Yet, performers in nonrealism are not merely performing mechanical behaviors—sitting, standing, and eating. These behaviors often require a *specific* energy and function. Someone performs actions in some sort of sequence. Although the linear arrangement may not be grounded in a cause and effect, these actions, as in realistic plays, are functional. However, these activities are not *necessarily* tied to subjectivity. The fictional

"I"—the play's character—often associated with an action is emphasized; instead an actor performing the action is the sole presence.

For example, observe the following directions from the prolog of Robert Wilson's *Deafman's Glance:* "In extreme slow motion, she pours milk, gives it to boy, returns to table, picks up knife, gently stabs boy, wipes knife clean."[12] In this task the actor must apply the necessary energy to fulfill the requirement. The actor performing the action must *intend* to accomplish the task. The actions in both realistic and nonrealistic theatre coincide through similar activities: purposeful accomplishment of specified goals. An action, whether arising out of character motivation or not, is in fact, intentional. The actor's job is to fulfill that function.[13] Using the four verbs, the actor can fill each behavior with a specific action without reliance on character to justify action. *Push the knife into the boy. Pull the knife out of the boy. Pull the blood off the knife.* The function appears to be a ritualistic murder of some kind, but as Sheryl Sutton (the actress who performed these actions) has said, "There are so many paradoxes, it's so hard to define or delineate what you see. That's what makes it rich."[14] Wilson's work in particular emphasizes spectacle, so judgments and implementation of the action are in the director's hands. The fundamental verb approach provides the actor (and the director) with useful options, which can be developed in rehearsal.

It is essential for an actor to understand function and structure relative to action. Method-trained actors already understand this and are prepared to fulfill the particular demands of nonrealistic theatre pieces. Playing actions freed from text and character can be accomplished by using the four fundamental verbs.[15] The verbs presuppose no subjectivity, avoiding character and motivation. However, they remain fundamental actions that are playable and aesthetically significant.

Often a director will communicate to an actor in images or other nonactive terms. The actor's job is to translate that image into action. The director may say, "I need that walk across stage to be incredibly slow, as if you're walking in honey." One approach might be to imagine walking through honey. But the actor also can translate the direction into one of the verbs. Walking through honey implies a great resistance to motion, so that it could be translated as a *pull from.* The advantage of using a verb is that it gives the actor a specific, repeatable thing to do. Imagining walking through honey, though possibly useful (and perhaps preferable for some actors), will be more ambiguous and variable than the verb *to pull from*. In either case, it is an additional tool for the actor, one more way to answer the question: How shall I perform this?

APPLICATION IN CHARACTER

I've been in this business for over fifty years, and I don't know what character is.

—*Joel Friedman, actor/teacher*

Creating a character is one of the more controversial aspects of the Method. The various schools—Strasberg, Meisner, and Adler—have significantly different takes on the matter. Theatre scholar Richard Schechner compares the character-building work of the Stanislavsky actor to the trance state of a Balinese dancer,[16] what Stanislavsky himself called "living the part" (*AP* 15). In *A Practical Handbook for the Actor*, one of the chapters is entitled "The Myth of Character," which denies the existence of character altogether.[17] As stated earlier, playing a *role* is performing functions—*what* is done. Playing *character* is the manner in which the functions are performed—*how* it is done. An actor's job is to apply specific energy in a specific manner. Physical and vocal choices of the actor, as well as adornments, defects, or other externals are essentially *pathways of energy* through the body/voice and *patterns of energy* manifest in action. Pathways and patterns of energy are made evident by the selection of verbs performed. All genres and forms require specific and appropriate choices regarding the pathways and patterns of energy. Although there are differences, realistic and nonrealistic acting share a common idea: Both embody specific pathways and patterns of energy.

The Method actor frequently asks the following questions when creating a character: Who am I? What has led me to this moment in the play? What do I want? For example, in portraying Willy Loman in *Death of a Salesman*, answers to the first question might include finding a walk evocative of age, creating a vocal pattern (dialect) evocative of New York in the 1940s, and developing an understanding of the traveling salesman's life. The answer to what has led Willy to this moment in the play (say, the beginning) might be found in creating a full biography culminating in his return home from an abortive sales trip. Willy may want to secure his sons' future, for example, as an answer to last question.

The Method actor must ask the same questions but in a form more applicable to nonrealism. What is my function? What is the nature of the energy in the moment? How does the energy play through me? In Theatre de Complicite's production of *The Three Lives of Lucie Cabrol* (New York, 1996), the company of actors played multiple characters and created animate objects as well as locations, sounds, and moods. At one point in the play, "Lucie" is climbing the mountains with her soon-to-be lover. The rest of the cast created the rise of the land on which Lucie was traveling by propping wooden planks on various cubes. They also created the mushrooms Lucie picked, hiding a finger and making a popping noise with their mouths as she plucked each mushroom, then rushing ahead to lay more planks and sprout more mushrooms. Later, during a lovemaking scene in a shack, the shack (created by the actors holding the planks) exploded, suggesting the violence and passion of the sex.

The mushrooms functioned to evoke the mountainside and create the illusion of the carefree activity in which Lucie and her lover were engaged. The actors had to be still, except for the movement of fingers being "plucked." Then they had to react quickly to the next level of planks once they were "picked." The plucking sound had to be short and could not interfere with the dialogue. The actors had to meet these specific requirements in order to fulfill their function. The nature of the energy at that moment was to capture the charm of the moment within the world of the play. The audience laughed at the noises and movements of the mushroom-actors. The action made a highly theatrical virtue out of the fact that the actors were creating the world of the play with only their voices, bodies, and actions. It is a common technique in children's theatre, but was used expertly in this adult play. The energy traveled through the actors based on the demands of their function. They had to crouch to hide most of their bodies, extend their fingers stiffly and withdraw them quickly. Then those choices had to be immediately discarded when the actors playing mushrooms next played the shack. But Method actors can apply their training just as ably to such work because it requires the same principles. Actors who are masters at embodying pathways and patterns of energy can effectively fulfill a variety of functions in various structures.

CONCLUSION

Stop Making Sense

—Album title, Talking Heads

Director Charles Marowitz questions whether the competing impulses of nonrealism (he uses the term "Performance Art") and traditional theatre will connect and whether the practices of each will integrate into the other. He asks if "the actor can be persuaded that 'acting' need not, in every case, involve the construction of three-dimensional characters within a realistic framework or be circumscribed by boundaries drawn by the playwright or dictated by the director, Performance Art offers a fertile field for genuine artistic expansion."[18] I believe the question, in fact, is being addressed, and not merely by the ideas just put forth. A number of actors and acting teachers are trying to traverse the broad venues of theatrical practices. But while on that journey, it is important not to abandon past practice entirely. Teachers and actors nurtured and raised on action-based pedagogy such as the Method more often than not prove highly effective when encountering the range of theatre forms. While we must continually adapt and transform the way we create and the way we teach, actors have always learned to play actions.

NOTES

Portions of this chapter, and the ideas presented herein, were first published in Paul Kassel, "The Four Fundamental Verbs: An Approach to Playing Actions," *Theatre Topics* 10.1 (Fall 1999): 181–96.

1. Mel Gussow, "Chaturanga," *New York Times*, April 28, 1984, C3.
2. Viewpoints is a technique for working on stage created by Mary Overlee and developed by Anne Bogart. Instead of action, the Viewpoints emphasize relationships—actor to actor, actor to environment, and so on. See *Anne Bogart: Viewpoints*, Michael Bigelow Dixon and Joel A. Smith, eds. (Lyme, NH: Smith and Kraus, 1995), for a fuller explanation.

3.   Harold Clurman, *On Directing* (New York: Collier, 1972), 147.

4.   The difference between performing and not performing is important but cannot be discussed in a short chapter. I refer the reader to Alice Raynor's, *To Act, to Do, to Perform* (Ann Arbor: University of Michigan Press, 1994); and Bert O. States, "The Actor's Presence," and Michael Kirby, "On Acting and Non-Acting," in *Acting (Re)considered: Theories and Practices*, Phillip Zarrilli, ed. (London: Routledge, 1995).

5.   In realistic theatre, these are the changes in beats or transitions from beat to beat; but change, in fact, occurs in *all* forms of performance.

6.   I considered *free*—seemingly more basic than *release*—but in my experience *free* is vague and causes confusion for actors.

7.   See Michael Cole and Shelia R. Cole, *The Development of Children* (New York: Scientific American Books, 1989), chap. 5, for suggestive evidence of this assertion.

8.   In many texts on acting approaches are action-oriented. But most books neither discuss fundamental actions from which all other actions might spring nor discuss actions that eschew subjectivity.

9.   *A Practical Handbook for the Actor* (Bruder, Cohn, et al. [New York: Random House, 1986], 13), presents an excellent list of what comprises a "good" or playable action.

10. Robert Cohen, *Acting Power* (Palo Alto, CA: Mayfield Publishing, 1978), 68.

11. Northrop Frye, *Anatomy of Criticism* (Princeton, NJ: Princeton University Press, 1957), 171.

12. Arthur Holmberg, *The Theatre of Robert Wilson* (Cambridge: Cambridge University Press, 1996), 13.

13. It may be argued that intention is not always present, but I believe it is *a priori* to all action. For example, an actor sleeping on the floor could be said to have no intention. However, prior to sleep, the actor came to the space *intending* to sleep. Improvisation could be seen as unintentional, but rather it is accidental. The intention in improvisation still exists, namely, to improvise.

14. Laurence Shyer, *Robert Wilson and His Collaborators* (New York: Theatre Communications Group, 1989), 7.

15. See Kassel, "The Four Fundamental Verbs."

16. Richard Schechner, *Performance Theory* (New York: Routledge, 1988), 175.

17. Bruden, *Practical Handbook*, 74.

18. Charles Marowitz, *The Other Way: An Alternative Approach to Acting and Directing* (New York: Applause, 1999), 174.

CHAPTER SIXTEEN

EMOTION TRAINING AND THE MIND/BODY CONNECTION

Alba Emoting and the Method

Pamela D. Chabora

A large part of every impersonation is, and must be, as mechanical as the putting on of a wig or the painting of crow's feet under the eyes. But comparatively few dramatic characters consist of manners alone. It is passion that interests and moves us; therefore the reproduction of passion is the actor's highest and most essential task. By what methods, then, can this reproduction be most fitly accomplished?

—William Archer, *"Mask or Faces?"*

Do actors really need to experience true emotion on stage? According to Alba specialist Roxanne Rix, assisting "student actors safely and effectively to expand their emotional range and expressiveness is an issue which concerns instructors at all levels of training."[1] The controversy between those who favor emotion training and those opposed remains an important issue. Most significant in this debate is Lee Strasberg's Method acting techniques. This discussion focuses on the affective or emotional memory and personalization techniques of Lee Strasberg, and on *Alba Emoting,* a "psychophysiological technique to help actors create and control real emotions" developed by neuropsychologist Susana Bloch.[2]

Having trained and successfully utilized both Method and Alba techniques separately and together, I hope to demonstrate the values inherent in their combined usage. The reference "Mind/Body" in the title is related to neuropsychology, which suggests the synergistic dialogue occurring between the body and the brain. Strasberg's personalization and emotional memory techniques can be deemed a mind-to-body approach, whereas Alba Emoting starts first with physiological patterning (body), which in turn affects the emotional state (mind). In combining the Method and Alba, actors can develop a rich reservoir of tools that can be utilized in numerous instances. In this chapter, I first supply a detailed description and examination of the aforementioned emotion training tools and then consider implications for the future of emotion training.

STRASBERG'S EMOTIONAL MEMORY

Stanislavsky's pioneering efforts in emotion training, incorporating the scientific discoveries of Ivan Pavlov and Théodule Ribot, set the agenda, but it is Lee Strasberg who really forged a tradition of emotion training in the United States. By the 1960s, Strasberg had adapted and established his own emotion training techniques utilizing affective memory, personalization, and substitution. His work in emotion training heightened the controversy between those who believe in emotionalism in actor training and those who do not. In the late 1970s, emotion training received scientific support through the work of emotion scientist Paul Eckman and neuropsychologist Susana Bloch.[3] Beginning in the early 1990s, emotion training in the United States was encouraged by the introduction of Bloch's Alba Emoting, a psychophysiological method for inducing basic (pure) emotion.[4] Bloch's research introduced the application of neuroscience to performance pedagogy. Advancements in neuropsychology have come a long way in clarifying the mind/body connection. Emotion scientists such as Bloch have capitalized on Strasberg's affective (or emotional) memory techniques and personalization work to advance the research in this area.

Strasberg emphasizes emotion as the basic tool in actor training. Psychologist Michael Schulman, in Loraine Hull's book *Strasberg's Method*, says that emotional memory, "involves the response to imaginary stimuli." The actor, he notes, "tries to reexperience the specific stimuli of the past event instead of simply recalling the event or remembering the emotion. The actor uses affective memory to evoke the most powerful emotions, and frequently, this exercise leads him to recall forgotten incidents with great intensity."[5] In his work with affective memory, Strasberg discovers that the most potent and useful emotional memories are lodged deep in the actor's past, distilled and purified by time. The further one goes back, he says, "the stronger the emotional memory."[6] He also discovers that a person could not tap the emotional memory by directly thinking of the emotion itself. Rather, the actor must focus on the specific sensory details of that memory, such as smell, sound, taste, touch, and sight of each specific object in the actors' memory. Within the sensory details would be what master acting teacher Uta Hagen describes as the "release trigger" that would evoke an emotion.[7] Sense memory is, thus, a major tool for tapping the body's associative memory processes.

In 1978, I worked with Lee Strasberg at the Strasberg Institute in Hollywood in an effort to learn his technique. At the core of this first-hand experience with the Method was a deep physical preparation via relaxation exercises prior to any sensory or emotional memory work. Each day began with at least an hour of relaxation in a chair to *open the vessel*. As students identified tensions, they were asked to *make a sound* in order to connect the release of tension to the sound. In accordance with conditioning techniques developed by Pavlov and later by B. F. Skinner, eventually they would be able to repeat the specific sound and release the tension that inhibited full expression and emotional vulnerability onstage. In addition to the hour of relaxation, students spent at least another hour and a half working on a series of sensory exercises that often entailed a miming of, or a re-creation of, one or another specific sensory experience. Students progressed from re-creating the coffee cup (or morning drink), to good smell/bad smell, to the mirror, to the shower, and finally into the famous "private moment" exercise.[8] As each sensory assignment was explored, a repertoire of *emotional memories* was developed and stored for future use. At times in the training, we would take *emotional memory walks.* Either out loud (guided by the instructor) or silently, we would narrate with vivid sensory detail a specific emotional experience. Strasberg or one of his associates would guide student actors through the emotional memory walk, assisting in specificity and focus on sensory details versus the emotion itself. As the memory incited a reexperiencing of the emotion, the actor would release any obstructing tension and note the sensory detail that triggered the emotion. Experiences of *remembered emotions* were then collected into the repertoire of emotional memories to be used in later roles.

Since my firsthand experience in the 1970s with Strasberg's emotional memory work, several neuroscientific studies have been conducted that confirm the effectiveness of affective memory techniques for professional actors. In the early 1990s, researchers discovered that emotional states have a powerful impact on the immune system. In a 1993 airing of Bill Moyer's *Healing and the Mind* on PBS, a segment was shown on how emotion can affect the immune system. This segment cited the joint efforts of Arizona State University's Institute of the Arts and of neuroscientist Nicholas Hall, along with his colleagues in the area of theatre at University of South Florida.[9] Most significant is that Strasberg's emotional memory techniques were the tools that they used for scientific research on emotion to induce pure emotion in test subjects. In a controlled environment, researchers used trained Method actors to explore the impact of extreme sadness or extreme happiness on the immune system. Electrocardiogram readings, diagnostic tests on blood chemistry, and data on vital signs revealed that emotion has a profound effect on the immune system. The application of such data has affected not only the health profession, validating previously scorned homeopathic approaches to healing, but also our sensitivity as actor training specialists to the impact of intense emotional experiences on student performers.

Ironically, this recent neuropsychological data on the power and impact of emotional memory techniques has served merely to widen the division between emotion training and those opposed to it. Many contemporary critics claim that the Method actor's energy and concentration is misplaced. Rather than focusing on another actor, the actor utilizing affective memory techniques often can turn inward, evoking a consuming, almost exploitative, wallowing in true emotion (a subjective and visceral arousal of the emotional system) instead of concentrating on actions or situation. Acting teacher Lawrence Parke observes: "[T]he actor simply isn't there in the right place or even in the person of the character to note [the other actors] and to respond truthfully to them."[10] Actors using affective memory techniques to evoke emotion are often accused of being inconsistent or generalized in their expression with no shifts in intensity, no *in the moment* variation of expression. Even Strasberg recognized the dangers of affective memory work. In his training, he carefully monitored those who trained and those who did not based on their psychiatric history. He said: "What an overwhelming obligation this places squarely on the shoulders of any coach teaching its use—the determining with any accuracy which members had need of psychiatric treatment and, after exposing them to this 'how to do it' procedure, also assuming the responsibility of making sure that they wouldn't do it privately at home."[11] Parke confirms Strasberg's concerns, noting that "there are teachers and coaches who find this exercise a handy time-killer and confidence destroyer in acting classes who would be happy to explore the affective memory with any [actor] over a long period if asked and paid to do so."[12]

Strasberg defended his work, cautioning against trying to recapture emotion directly.[13] He maintained: "[E]motion is not directly controllable." He acknowledged the possibility of counterconditioning where an emotional memory that may have worked once has lost some of its emotional force; moreover, he said, "[T]he emotional value of the experience might even have changed substantially." But with such counterconditioning or "wired in association," Strasberg claimed that the actor could build a storehouse or repertoire of emotional memories and could pull from a variety of memories when necessary: "It does not matter what an actor remembers, so long as it is the proper degree of belief and the proper stimulus to make him behave as he would under the conditions in the play—the actor ultimately fuses his recall with the lines of the play."[14]

In response to the question of how it is possible to be in a play and think of emotion, Strasberg argued: "[T]he actor works on various levels of his being simultaneously. He remembers his cues, and if he sees something happening, he corrects it and so forth. All of this is part of the actor's reality."[15] Strasberg contends that affective memory work is linked to *personalization*. Serving a similar function as emotional memory, personalization is utilized to help the actor make a personal and specific connection to the character's given circumstances and needs. According to Method teacher Dwight Edward Easty, personalization is described as "finding a common ground with our own life desires, relationships, and involvements. The actor will find a greater affinity for the circumstances within the role by a direct association of that circumstance which is real to him because it stems from his own life and the one present in the script."[16] By finding a similar incident, a familiar desire, or a similar relationship that correlates with the action and central theme of the play, the actor mentally replaces the author's situation with his or her own situation. The idea is that if the fictional circumstances of the script fail to stimulate the actor, personalization helps to stir the actor's imagination. Personalization, Hull asserts, "can be utilized to replace a co-actor, a model the actor is talking or thinking about, or an imaginary person offstage." However, "the most important thing is to use the other actor."[17]

ALBA EMOTING

According to Susan Bloch, Alba Emoting "helps an actor summon and control emotion at will and is based on psychophysiological data obtained in laboratory conditions." The findings, she says, show "that the precise *objective* management and monitoring of the respiratory and expressive components of emotion contribute to an actor's *subjective* experience of emotion" (emphasis added).[18] Bloch claims that the emergence of Alba Emoting might present a new approach to the emotion debate. Of all the theories and approaches on emotion training that I have experienced, none has been more controversial and had a more profound effect on me than Alba Emoting, a psychophysiological approach to emotion training for actors developed by Bloch. It exemplifies the potential benefits of intercommunication between neuropsychology and actor training.

Bloch's history underscores her knowledge of the subject. She served as a senior neuropsychologist with the *Institut de Neuroscience* at the *Université de Pierre* and *Marie Curie* in Paris. As an experimental psychologist and neuroscientist, she was concerned primarily with human brain function, animal learning, and visual perception. For the past twenty years, her research has been focused on the psychophysiological study of human emotions. She developed "a method that can help actors enter into emotions and control emotional states," which she has dubbed Alba Emoting.[19] Bloch's work parallels and capitalizes on many of the current research on emotion and brain function. She states: "Cognitive scientists are now referring to emotion as 'hot cognition.'" Current neuroscientific data on the synergic relationship between the brain and the body have led to a holistic recognition of emotion. In addition, researchers are beginning to understand that emotions *have a profound impact on memory, motivation, judgment, learning, health, and self-use* in general. In fact, all of our cognitive processes are influenced by our emotions. Bloch perceives emotion as a "functional state of the entire organism—intuitively holistic."[20]

Bloch has divided the study of emotion into three levels: *physiological,* dealing with the visceral, endocrine, chemical, molecular, and autonomic respiratory reactions; *expressive,* concerning somatic, muscles, posture, gestures, facial, vocal, and controlled respiratory movements; and *subjective,* stressing internal, affective, personal, and "what we call feeling."[21] These three levels of emotion are always interacting and reacting to each other. Bloch is careful to note that emotion and feeling are not one and the same; rather feeling is a *product* of emotion. In addition, a human being is always experiencing an emotion and thus is always feeling.

In her efforts to arrive at a more innovative way of teaching psychology to actors, Bloch decided to design an interdisciplinary research study, a workshop on emotions using the actors as participants. With her neuropsychologist colleague Guy Santibanez-H and with one of the rising directors in Chile, Pedro Orthous, Bloch created a series of projects dealing with basic emotion and acting.[22] They attempted to measure what happens when someone is really experiencing a basic *pure* emotion. For two years, they measured heart rate, blood pressure, temperature, breathing, facial, and bodily postures of professional actors and students of psychology using emotional memory techniques and deep hypnosis. In analyzing the data, they recognized specific repeated patterns of breathing, facial expression, body tension, and postural behavior. They also noted that measurable patterns were repeatable. In other words, one could initiate and control the contraction of the muscles at will. By returning to these controllable *emotor effector* patterns and by physically reproducing them in a relatively mechanical manner, one started to feel actual emotion. This is called an *emotional induction.* Most significant was the discovery that just as the emotor effector patterns could trigger the induction of a pure, basic emotion, a different effector pattern could neutralize the emotional experience, allowing the subject to "step out" of the emotion. This allowed the subject to "cool down" from the intensity of the emotional induction. Bloch and her colleagues isolated the emotor effector patterns for six basic emotions: anger, love/tender, love/erotic, fear, joy, and sadness. They contend: "[I]t is the performance of the respiratory/postural/facial patterns of an emotion that evokes the corresponding subjective activation or feeling in the performer as well as in the observer."[23] The facial, postural, and respiratory patterns of the six basic emotions are categorized by facial tension especially around the eyes and mouth, by postural tonus and direction, and by composed versus saccadic (or staccato) breathing patterns.

Of all the controllable effector patterns that induce the six basic emotions, the breathing pattern is the key stimulus in the Alba Emoting method. Three of these six basic emotions (anger, eroticism, and tenderness) are all made up of a composed breathing pattern. Composed breathing is characterized by a single, main cycle of breath that follows a regular rhythm and tempo. But the frequency and volume of the composed breathing pattern is very different for each of these three basic emotions. For anger, the breathing is at a high tempo and a high amplitude, and is done primarily through the nose because the facial muscles are tense. The lips are pressed tightly together and the eyes are semiclosed. The torso, which is prepared to attack, exhibits a high level of muscular tonus, or tension. Although eroticism also uses the composed respiratory cycle, the frequency and amplitude increases with the "intensity of emotional engagement."[24] Contrary to the postural and facial patterns for anger, the muscles of the face and torso are relatively relaxed. The mouth is open, the eyes are closed or semiclosed, and the head tilts backward, exposing the neck. Tenderness shares certain characteristics with eroticism, in that the facial and postural muscles are in a relaxed posture of approach. The mouth is slightly open and the head is slightly tilted to the side, but the breathing cycle is at a low frequency and maintains an even, regular rhythm.

The emotions of joy, sadness, and fear all exhibit a more saccadic type of respiratory pattern. Saccadic breathing involves an uneven series of short staccato inspirations or expirations. The respiratory pattern for joy is characterized by an abrupt and full intake of air followed by a series of saccadic expirations until all of the air is expelled. The posture is relaxed with a strong loss of tonus in the anti-gravitational muscle group (the muscles that hold one upright, such as thighs, back, and internal muscles in the chest and abdomen). The eyes are relaxed and semiclosed, the mouth is open with the upper teeth exposed. Sadness is characterized by the exact opposite breathing pattern of joy. The saccadic pattern occurs on the inspiration and sometimes even continues into the long expiration. Like joy, the posture is relaxed with a tendency to give in to the gravitational pull. The eyes are semiclosed or even tensely closed with eyebrows contracted together to create a frown. The rest of the face is relaxed, literally drooping. Of all the basic emotions, fear has the most complex breathing, postural, and facial patterns. "The respiratory pattern consists of a period of inspiratory hyponeic movements followed by passive incomplete exhalations, and sometimes an expiratory-inspiratory 'sigh-like' phase."[25] The posture and facial expression is characterized by extreme tension, with protective avoidance gestures, eyes wide to increase peripheral vision, and the mouth open wide.

After students are trained in the use of these emotor effector patterns, they are then taught how to control the level of pure emotion. They then mix different levels of the separate pure emotions to evoke *mixed* or *blended* emotions such as irony, jealousy, or ambition. For example, jealousy consists of anger, fear, and eroticism. The actor was told to contract the body while breathing with the anger pattern and at the same time to open the eyes so as to give part of the facial pattern of fear. Along with the experimental application of these effector patterns of pure emotions, Bloch discovered a technique for stepping out of the emotional experience. The development of the simple procedure was motivated by the observation that subjects had a tendency to stay with, almost luxuriate, in the induced emotion. By producing at least three "slow, regular, and full breathing cycles" and by altering the facial/postural positions, subjects can bring themselves to a neutral state, freeing them from "emotional hangover."[26] For the psychological and physiological health of the student, the step-out is now an integral part of Alba Emoting.

Bloch's experience with the student actors in her original study revealed that several preliminary steps were needed before they actually could apply these emotor effector patterns to characterization and scene work. She noted that most actors were not able to show a pure, basic emotion and that they were often incorrect in labeling what they really felt. "They don't know what they are talking about in emotional terms."[27] Because of the sensitivity and physiological danger of manipulating breath, students are guided through a series of self-use exercises. For example, warm-ups are primarily Alexander-based exercises (dealing with centering, posture, and the work of F. M. Alexander). In longer intensive training programs for Alba Emoting, actors undergo extensive self-use training, developing perfect control of their breathing. They must be able to modulate it with different rhythms and intensities. They also must learn to control their body musculature with correct, localizing tensing/relaxing modulations of different muscle groups in order to accurately adopt the facial/postural effector patterns.

Actors are frequently unaware of their body-expressive possibilities. For example, at the beginning of the general training, actors would very often contract both arms when specifically asked to contract only one shoulder. The capacity to dissociate different groups and to combine such postural modifications with different breathing rhythms is very important as a preparation for the work with mixed emotions. The newly acquired skills therefore complement the physical training normally imparted in theatre schools.[28] Once the student has arrived at an acceptable level of ideal self-use, the Alba Emoting techniques are introduced and synthesized with continued self-use training and other acting requirements. To Bloch, training in Alba Emoting provides actors with a tool for identifying the specific emotions at the moment they need them. The technique, she adds, "allows actors to control at will the expression and communication of their emotions in an objective and unambiguous way."[29]

In response to accusations of robotic or even "puppet-like" behavior that these manipulations of emotional response can create, Bloch emphasized the freedom that such control of emotions provides to the actor. According to Bloch, actors who have trained in Alba Emoting have expressed great freedom, confident that emotions that they will need in a role are readily available. "It's like the arpeggios. . . . If I am a pianist . . . you have to have the technique to be free." Bloch's psychophysiological approach liberates the actor from relying solely on the emotional memory techniques. "You don't have to worry about feeling or remembering your mother's death so that you are sad enough or whatever—you have to have [emotional] freedom in the same way that your body knows exactly how to move."[30] She views Alba Emoting as a synthesis of the objective and subjective experience of emotion, neurologically stimulating true emotion while safeguarding the actor against psychological trauma.

Still, some critics have suggested that Alba Emoting treads dangerously near an external, almost robotic, behavior. They fear that such analysis and practice of emotor effector patterns can result in a stifled imagination and muted creativity, nurturing clichés and stereotypes by reducing complex subtextual coloration down to a few *pure* emotions. Acting instructor Ramon Delgado, for example, states that there is a "big danger of totally externalizing." He adds: "Actors are not bio-mechanical robots, but complex human beings responding to the real or imagined stimulus in the play, their partners, and themselves."[31] Some acting teachers go so far as to regard the emotion notation system as a bypassing of *in-the-moment* responses in service to a preprogrammed "emotional melody." Bloch insists, however, that training in Alba Emoting will not hamper the performance any more than preplanned blocking of movement does. The emotor effector patterns do not inhibit responses *in the moment*. They do not negate the need for careful characterization analysis or commitment to the inner life of a role. Rather, this system is to be used as a tool to assist in emotional honesty, specifically for emotional highpoints in a role. With this system actors are aware of one more aspect of themselves. Alba Emoting provides an additional tool, a physiological and organic one, for creating genuine feeling onstage. Knowing how to express a specific emotion and which emotion it is brings actors one step closer to ideal self-use with an informed response to expressive use. Actors have a firmer grasp on the outcome of a role instead of having to depend on the director's guidance and/or the caprice of their feelings. Bloch explains:

> One must not forget that here I am talking of technical support for the actor that in no way affects his creativity and imagination. Quite the contrary, the technique acts as a trigger by activating an emotional network that elicits corresponding images and subjective feelings, sustaining them in a controlled way for longer periods of time than can be achieved by other means.

Whatever the actor's choice, it cannot but be of help to know that a slight change in the aperture of the eyes, for instance, will modify his facial expression, or that in a state of anger the body is in preparation for attack, or that it is impossible to feel joy or tenderness without being very relaxed.[32]

To those who believe this technique runs counter to the objectives of the Method, Bloch refers to her interaction with Sonia Moore and other eminent disciples of the Stanislavsky system. They have assured her that what she is doing is not going against Stanislavsky. Robert Barton asserts that Bloch's work is suited to Stanislavsky's method. He also argues that Alba Emoting is "a direct answer to the request of Artaud, that an actor become an emotional athlete and that breath is an enormous sense of power for the actor."[33]

When I was first introduced to Alba Emoting in a workshop with Bloch in 1992, I was struck by the power of this body-to-mind approach. I found her emotion-training tools liberating. As I began to trust the patterns, induction of genuine emotion was inevitable. After several summer intensive training sessions in Alba Emoting, I have incorporated this emotion tool in my performance, teaching, and production work.[34] In performance, Alba Emoting has proven to be a valuable addition to the basic Method work on which that I have always relied. The emotor effector patterns do not impede or negate the Strasberg Method; rather Alba seems to mesh well with personalization and emotional memory work. In fact, a "souvenir" (as Bloch calls an emotional memory) is inevitable once the emotion has been triggered in the actor.

The combination of personalization, emotional memory, and Alba Emoting are complementary and powerful. Personalization provides an internal focus and stimulation; Alba Emoting pattern provides for the appropriate basic emotion. Together they evoke powerful emotional commitment, genuine feeling that can be shaped and controlled at the moment. For example, as an actress for a day-long Ohio Medical Conference on Ethics to play the role of a mother who had just given birth to a premature infant (only twenty-two weeks), I was asked to face a hypothetical ethics committee and plead for my child's life. The role demanded that I portray high-pitched emotions for the entire day, facing a number of hypothetical ethics committees in this crisis situation. Had I relied solely on my Method training (i.e., emotional memory and personalization), I probably would have collapsed halfway through the day. However, because I was able to utilize the Alba Emoting patterns for fear, anger, and sadness, I was able to sustain genuine emotional commitment for the duration of the performance and suffer no emotional hangover.

In actor training, Alba has proven highly useful for enhancing self-awareness. As a teacher, I have incorporated a brief exploration in Alba Emoting into voice/movement courses and advanced acting courses. The isolation of universal emotor patterns provides an opportunity for student actors to identify chronic or tonic levels of certain emotions within themselves. The step-out pattern has become a regular vehicle in classes and productions for cooling down and neutralizing the student actor. In addition, Alba Emoting can be an incredible diagnostic tool for teachers well versed in the patterns, helping them to recognize or foresee emotional crises and assisting in fostering a safe and healthful environment.

The strongest evidence of the power of Alba Emoting has been revealed most profoundly in production work. As a director, I have found many instances where a struggling actor was supplied with a specific emotor effector pattern to connect to a challenging moment in the script. For example, in a production of Steinbeck's *Of Mice and Men,* a relatively inexperienced actor was cast in the role of Lenny. He was a football player who had a lot of instinct (but no training), and he struggled at times, especially when Lenny is supposed to burst into tears like a child over the loss of his mouse or over the death of the puppy. It was here that the emotor effector pattern for sadness assisted the actor in acquiring full emotional commitment during key moments in performance.

While the controversy between the emotionalists and anti-emotionalists continues, many specialists in actor training recognize that there is no singular art of acting. If we close off Method or Alba Emoting as indulgent and outdated, then we run the risk of eliminating proven options.

NOTES

1. Roxanne Rix, unpublished paper, Panel Chair, "Emotion Training and the American Acting Student," Association for Theatre in Higher Education (ATHE), New York, 1996.

2. Susana Bloch, "Alba Emoting: A Psycho-physiological Technique to Help Actors Create and Control Real Emotions," *Theatre Topics* 3 (Sept. 1993): 121–37.

3. See, Paul Eckman and Lauren Friesen, *Unmasking the Face* (New York: Prentice-Hall, 1975).

4. For a discussion on "pure" emotion, see Susana Bloch, Pedro Orthous, and Guy Santibanez-H, "Effector Patterns of Basic Emotions: A Psycho-physiological Method for Training Actors," *Journal of Social and Biological Structures* 10 (1987): 4.

5. Loraine Hull, *Strasberg's Method* (Woodbridge, CT: Oxbow, 1984), 83.

6. Ibid., 107.

7. Uta Hagen, *Respect for Acting* (New York: Macmillan, 1991), 48.

8. Dwight Edward Easty, *On Method Acting* (Florence, AL: Allograph Press, 1966), 33–50.

9. For a discussion on this, see Pamela D. Chabora, "A Descriptive Study of the Application of Research in Neuropsychology to Self-Use Training for Actors," Ph.D. diss., Michigan State University, 1994, 49–141.

10. Lawrence Parke, *The Method as a System for Today's Actor* (Hollywood: Acting World Books, 1985), 163.

11. Quoted in Ibid., 162.

12. Ibid., 163.

13. Richard Schechner, "Image, Movement, and the Actor," *TDR* 10.3 (1966): 50–59.

14. Quoted In Hull, *Strasberg's Method*, 84.

15. Quoted in Ibid., 97.

16. Easty, *On Method Acting*, 124. This was the manual that Strasberg used in his classes.

17. Hull, *Strasberg's Method*, 156.

18. Susana Bloch, "Alba Emoting," 121.

19. Personal Interview with Block, August 2–4, 1992.

20. Ibid.

21. Ibid.

22. See Susana Bloch and G. Santibanez-H, "Commentaries on Effector Patterns of Basic Emotions," *Journal of Social Biological Structure* 11 (1998): 201–11.

23. Ibid., 202.

24. Bloch et al., "Effector Patterns," 5.

25. Ibid., 6.

26. Bloch, "Alba Emoting," 8.

27. Bloch, personal interview.

28. Bloch et al., "Effector Patterns," 14.

29. Bloch, "Alba Emoting," 11.

30. Bloch, personal interview.

31.   Ramon Delgado, personal interview, November 23, 1992. Delgado is the author of *Acting With Both Sides of Your Brain* (New York: Holt, Rinehart, and Winston, 1986).

32.   Bloch, "Alba Emoting," 12.

33.   Robert Barton, address, "New Emotional Freedom for Actors: Discoveries for Helping Actors Summon and Control Feelings," ATHE, Atlanta, August 4, 1992.

34.   Since 1996, standards have been developed for official certification of Alba Emoting, along with a trademark and incorporation in Chile (Alba Emoting, Inc.) and the United States (Alba Emoting in North America, Inc.).

CHAPTER SEVENTEEN

METHOD(ICAL) HYBRIDITY

Stanislavsky Meets Suzuki: An Interview with Steve Pearson and Robyn Hunt

Terry Donovan Smith

> *On stage you do it.*
> *On TV you do it less.*
> *On film you just think it.*
> *But "it" never changes.*
>
> *—Anonymous*

American approaches to Stanislavsky's System of actor training and rehearsal techniques are varied and often contradictory. Actors have cordoned themselves in opposing schools, self-identifying with Meisner, Strasberg, Adler, et al., developing what amounts to theoretical "lines of business." The focus of contention is often how each approach delimits the relationship between the internal condition of the actor/character and its external manifestation. No approach denies the need to express action visually. Some teachers want the expression to be spontaneous; others attempt to *fill* preplanned gestures. However physicality is expressed, encoded in the vocabulary of even the most ardently psychological approaches is the body as metaphor: Character and narrative are defined through a *spine* that is manifest through *action*. The spine is the superstructure of meaning.

However contentious and mutually exclusive each version of the Method may be, all are clustered at one end of a continuum that places "theatrical" approaches at the opposing end. This polemic begins in Enlightenment philosophy that focused the discourse of social relations on the expressions of individual will. At least since Denis Diderot's *Paradoxe sur le Comédien*, written in the mid eighteenth century, the theatre has been making a progressively manifest distinction that, as performance approaches "reality," it recedes from the theatrical, even the sublime. Given the fundamentally ideological structure of the United States and its aggressive focus on what has been called the "cult of individualism," it is easy to understand how the Method gained such a pedagogical hold here. But it is also easy to see how it has been misinterpreted. Arguments *against* the Method always have centered on its inability to transcend crass and facile responses to complex social issues, which is not a result that Stanislavsky or other Method teachers would have preferred.

Nonetheless, when theatre practitioners set out to express something "beyond psychology," they often feel the need to reject the Method and are thus compelled to undermine its theoretical and aesthetic processes and assumptions. One notable exception to this model is the Professional Actor Training Program (PATP) of the University of Washington's School of Drama. The core faculty has developed, and continues to explore, the relationship between the physical and the psychological, the internal and the external. They continue to work on "truth" that is theatrical and realistic.

Steven Pearson and Robyn Hunt direct the PATP. They have created what they call a "new American system" that combines the expressive discipline of Suzuki Tadashi and the psychological verity of the Method. I interviewed Pearson and Hunt (and others) over several days in March 1999, to understand how they have hybridized two training philosophies that at first glance seem mutually exclusive. However, working with Actors Studio member Mark Jenkins, Linkater voice teacher Judith Shawn, and Alexander trainer Kathy Madden, they have created a uniquely American admixture. In this form, action is the primary consideration; moment-to-moment work is given a physical treatment; improvisation is enhanced; anticipation is dealt with; and techniques of personalization and the *magic if* are blended with slow-motion walking and *image rehabilitation.*

Like Stanislavsky's and the Method's own development, Pearson and Hunt continue to change and work through issues and problems unique to the American stage. But as Pearson points out, like Stanislavsky's system, "Suzuki training was developed to make plays better. It was developed by a director, for actors." He also insists that if they could meet, "Suzuki and Stanislavsky would be friends."

THE INTERVIEW

Smith: *Talk about the program. How is it that you are attempting to bring Suzuki training and the Method together?*

Pearson: What we're trying to do is to help people integrate some physical conviction with an internal conviction in their acting and to bring those things into alignment, into synchronicity, into harmony, whatever you want to call it. It seems like with great actors that will happen. Their body means what they say. And whether or not that comes from intensive physical training or comes from intensive training on internal conviction, based on maybe what Stanislavsky was after—in great actors it comes together. If you have very skillful theatrical presentation without any heart (for want of a better word), any sense of a reason why that drives one from the inside (and those are dodgy terms)—then you have less than good acting. By the same token, if you have inner conviction about what is going on but the body is not involved as an available vessel, then you have less than good acting. In other words, there's no pathway for one's ideas.

What conveys information to the audience is the body—breathing and making sounds. And, yes, those sounds are then formed into words sometimes and those successions of words mean things, of course, but a lot of what goes on is nonverbal communication. It has to do with empathy—physical empathy—between people. We tend, if we wait long enough, to breathe in a similar pattern, if we are focused on a similar thing. We tend to understand physically within our own bodies when watching other people. That is, we have a physiological empathy, a muscular empathy with things that we see.

For instance, you watch somebody do a beautiful jump shot in basketball. The reason that we describe it as beautiful is because it's effective. Your body memory will help you to copy that form more easily, and of course, form follows function follows form. So if you copy the form, if you mimic a very good jump shot, there is a higher percentage that you'll be successful in the *content* which here is to get the ball in the net, because that form was developed for a reason. It developed because it's practically effective.

[At the University of Washington] we start with nonrealistic work in the first year, some kind of nonrealistic work to get at action. Then we do two [academic] quarters of Shakespeare—so we're working on direct action and nonrealistic material. Then we do another quarter of nonrealistic work. In the winter quarter of their second year, we get to the beginnings of realism with Chekhov or Ibsen. But by then they've had a year and a quarter of adjusting their ideas about what constitutes acting—and that Realism is another style which is probably more difficult: It's not behaviorally based, necessarily. It's not scratching and should be easier because it looks more like what we do every day. But actually the opposite is true. It's more difficult because it looks like what we do every day. We have to have a great level of selection and sophistication in what we choose to do and control over it to make it *appear* real, while having it be clear, while having it respond to the selective realism in Chekhov. [It's the juxtaposition of moments] that gives us the sensation of watching something real. But as an actor, you can't mistake that for behavior. One of the problems—and this is just my bias—that you see in so-called traditional productions of Chekhov is that there is a lot of sitting around stewing in the psychology of the piece and *being* as opposed to *doing things*. Chekhov's plays are full action all the time; you just have to find it.

After a year and a half of doing *direct* action in Shakespeare— no subtext: you say what you do, you do what you say—then they get to Chekhov, who's the master of indirect action. By the time they get there, they're beginning to understand that this requires the same level of physical decision that doing a Feydeau farce does.

Hunt: I'm now more an *action man* than I've ever been. You figure out the action is to *blank*, right? So what does that mean with a body/head unity? How is that expressed so that the audience gets no cognitive dissonance? "Oh right, I get that she's supposed to be doing that, but what I'm seeing is the opposite." So what is the clearest transmission that could be made physically? Everything unifies in terms of that action.

Smith: *I don't think that most people see Suzuki as an action man.*

Pearson: If you look at what Stanislavsky is after and what Suzuki is after they really are the same thing. They are just going at it from different directions. How Stanislavsky is explained is that if you get the inner thing going, the body will naturally reflect it. And if you just look around you'll see that's not necessarily true because the actual expressive possibilities of the body are decreasing.

Our history and palette are decreasing. As a result, our ability to imagine is decreasing. You can see it now. You ask people in the television age to imagine something and they imagine something about the size of a screen. You say: "imagine a tree" and they imagine a little tree out there. [Pearson points to his computer monitor.] And they can be very concentrated on that tree, great concentration. But they don't see scale and they don't see past the limitations of that. That also has to do with the three-dimensional experience with the body.

So what Suzuki is also talking about is the primacy of the actor and the actor's body. What is *the thing*? The thing is living, breathing in the same time and space. What does that really mean? In the same time and place we experience technology—watch a mediated thing—that's a very different thing than the actor actually being there.

Smith: *Is the actor's body focused on physicalizing an internal state?*

Hunt: That's right. We are really passionate about not working on something exclusively physical without figuring out the psychological inner state. And we also think that the outward, strong, physical, gestural, particularly presentational form of Suzuki is not the thing that's going to help people do Chekhov, but that it is rather the articulateness of this inner sensibility. That is to say, the body's vocabulary begins to come up with the sophistication of the mind's analytical articulateness. That's what we're working on. We have in America this incredible analytical possibility and this way of talking—I mean, Freud is a household word and we don't even say his name when we talk about motivation, and then connecting that with Strasberg's Stanislavsky. What is fear? What is disappointment? If that doesn't register in the body, then you just have a talking head and the audience is not going to buy it. That's one aspect.

This thing that Suzuki works on, this inner sensibility, is where conviction comes from. It's not just centering but it's breath and it's functioning with this [the pelvis] as a center instead of the head. The gesticulation and the pursuance of objectives do not happen from up here but in fact come from down here. You start to get at what I think is real conviction. But it is so close to what real conviction feels like that something is fooled enough and anyway the audience is going to buy it.

Smith: *Do you see a relationship between fooling yourself in Suzuki and in the Method?*

Hunt: I think that's what all actors do in a way. And if you do it entirely it's schizophrenia, so it's not devoutly to be wished. But with a more physical approach you have a replication of some of the symptoms of fear, joy, etcetera. So you don't have to crank anymore to make them happen, they actually result. What did Clurman say? "We need a body that is relaxed. We need the relaxation that will allow the free flow of emotions." Again, first the relaxation and then the emotions—not going after the emotions.

Smith: *Was there a moment that you recognized that Suzuki would work for you in American theatre?*

Hunt: Yes. I was three years into this intensive work with Suzuki so it was three months with him and then we were coming back to the United states and Steve and I were running a theatre at that time in downtown San Diego. We were working on *Angel Street*, where the lead woman thinks she is being driven crazy. She starts at a level right at the top of the play where she's going nuts. She's afraid of this kind of horrible incarceration like her mother had and it escalates. It starts high and it just goes [up]. And all of a sudden here I was three years into learning this training of Suzuki's and I had years and years of Method stuff and I was sort of bifurcated somehow. I thought, "Oh, I can only use the Method stuff because I have to produce tears at this point and so on and so on." And that's were I had an epiphany and started to see how I could use the training to achieve what I had thought was heretofore just a Method thing.

So I made abrupt turn (I had done the bio work) and figured out what the anatomy of fear was, based on the development of my inner sensibility that I had begun to tap into with Suzuki. So what is the real body unity of fear that this woman is going through? What does it mean physically that she's on laudanum? How is her breath different from mine? Where is her fear center? I shortened her stride and changed her breathing and worked on some physical stuff that, granted, I could have done with an Alexander person with me. So that's where it started, where I started to see how practically that I couldn't work in a Method way alone any more.

Smith: *Did you discard the Method at that point?*

Hunt: Absolutely not. We couldn't do without it. Who is her mother? What is the fear of what happened to her mother? What is the relationship between the two of them? How is it good? How did she fall in love? All that stuff has to be tracked.

Now, jump cut to several years later. I've got this gig playing Lady Capulet and the play is about the parents—[that director Jon Jory] has rewritten it, and it's all this grieving stuff "Oh Prince, oh, oh, oh, oh, oh!" Jory says, "And when you find out about the possibility of Juliet's body at the end of the play, I want an inhuman animal sound as you come across from left" (in this big barn room theatre). "Can you do that?"

In rehearsal that day, he was staging all these green apprentices into the crowd scene where I wasn't the problem and I must have done it twenty times. I was completely influenced by Suzuki's Kyoko Shirushi: how every rehearsal I saw her, she changed what she was doing. Every time, she was exploring something else. She was never on autopilot and she was working at 200 percent every time.

So we've got to get a body/mind integration of Lady Capulet—she's grieving in her head and she's grieving in her body. And we've got to find out what is the action—is it *true?* Suzuki's thing is that you never know. Since you're not performing for the audience anyway, you're performing to please the gods who are watching, therefore pandering is not possible and stopping is not possible. Instead you're shooting so high that the audience then witnesses that attempt. So here I am in rehearsal and I'm giving it 200 percent and Jon [Jory] loves it but he keeps saying "Take care of your voice because I'm just staging this." And I'm thinking: "No, I'm rehearsing." I learned to rehearse in Japan.

Smith: *This sounds like moment-to-moment work.*

Pearson: Take, for example, the principles of aikido, which is developed so that the body can respond in an extremely efficient and calm way to aggression and attack. Well, if you extrapolate from that, if you have a similar sense of preparedness, readiness, or potential energy, or reserve, then it's not too far a step to say, if I'm ready for aggression, I'm also ready to respond to all kinds of stimuli: from another actor, and then from a sense of my own imagined world outside of me. Getting to that sense, first of all, where that center is and how it allows you to breathe, it allows you to move quickly, it allows you to be on balance, it allows you to move with power, it allows you to point. When you point—if you point from your center and are relaxed—that point continues on beyond you rather than [being] merely a gesture. So that all gesture begins from there, from the core of you. We also read that as conviction. Now, it may or may not *be* conviction, but certainly we read it as conviction. I think actually it is connected to true conviction; because if the breath comes from very low and I'm on balance and my body is focused with a sense of potential energy on what I want to accomplish, I know that I have conviction then about what I'm going to do.

     We've also been working on this idea of walking: what it means to walk across the stage with intent. Suzuki was working a lot with slow-motion walking, what that meant to be able to do that with control and intent. And then he began increasing it and changing tempo and so on until I got to the point where I wanted to do Peter Handke's play *The Hour We Knew Nothing of Each Other,* which is all about walking and what happens when people encounter each other. Robyn started working on this and we both continued, where people just move slowly across the stage and then turn and move slowly back, attempting to make fictional time. Well if you add, then, contact [with another actor] at some point, it becomes extremely powerful if I'm turning and I see you—it's going to be new every time. And what we're working on is actually seeing, rather than "oh, it's another actor" or "oh, it's my overlay of what I think the other actor's supposed to look at."

Smith: *Are you referring to your slow-motion walking exercise using* Hamlet?

Hunt: We have to credit Eric Hill with the Hamlet/Ophelia slow walking. Eric was directing *Hamlet* at the Togah festival and was using an Enya song. We adapted this to Suzuki's "slow ten teka ten," which is not a word but the sound of the drums. *Slow ten* is a thing that Suzuki created which was just to work on slow motion in which there needs to be perfect continuous energy, particularly with the feet so that ultimately it should look like the actor is standing still and the scenery is moving. That's extremely difficult to do. People think it's the easiest thing because it looks like what we do in daily life, which is walking, and it turns out that it's almost the most elusive thing in the entire training: to get at that thing of floating.

So we took that and said: What if we could set up a condition which several of the problems of acting manifest—that is, anticipation, going for the emotion, having a set a priori idea about how it's supposed to go? What is love and what is the absence of sentimentality? How could we set up a condition to be surprised? And we put it into the form of the training; which is, we need continuous energy: so that's the play, that's the "iambic pentameter" of the piece, since we are not speaking text that they have to be true to. Can we set up a context in which people share the scenario without the need to do any homework? Everybody knows *Hamlet* and we've just set it that she's dead already and he's doing without her. She has a chance to revisit in order to teach him something.

[In this exercise, two lines of actors face each other from across the studio. To the sound of Enya's "On Your Shore," and with a neutral face, the actors move in incredibly slow motion toward each other. One group of actors are Hamlets, the other are Ophelias. Each pair of Hamlet and Ophelia approach and pass each

other, finding a physical action to play. After they pass, they each look back and "see" the other. From this, they "respond" physically to the other character, continuing to the other side of the studio. Afterward, they talk about the exercise. Hunt says there is, at first, a tendency to sentimentalize the experience, but after some months, the actors begin to understand the phenomenology experience of being innocent of the future.]

The other thing is: What is the action? Given that meeting and that discovery with surprises without anticipation, what then is the action? Since you don't have text they think, "Well then, what is the physical action?" And then that starts to be the whole action and then you have some possibility of being real.

Pearson: We do a fair amount in slow motion to get at this basic acting problem of being innocent of the future. It's the real paradox of rehearsing for the present, rehearsing for innocence. Suzuki got at it a different way: He had people do statues and he hit a stick.

[In "statue" the actors respond to the hits of a stick by creating individual "tableaus." They oscillate from statue to a relaxed position, usually on their backs using their backsides as the fulcrum for the statue. The exercise is physically taxing and requires very well trained abdominal muscles.]

So not only do you have to be innocent of *when* you're going to be required to do something—you don't have that choice, so your habitual rhythm is taken away from you—you have to be innocent of *what* is going to happen and then be surprised and fully involved with it physically. This is the exact same story as from *An Actor Prepares* where he sends the girl up to find the broach—as she goes around *pretending* to find the broach. Then he actually hides it and she actually looks for it. We're working on that in slow motion so that people can begin to contact each other. Suzuki would say: "Walk, but walk with these conditions—that you don't go up and down and you move at the same pace. Do that and be on the stage." This means have an image, have an idea, have a thought, and have an *action*.

Hunt: That's the brilliance of Suzuki's System. He set up conditions where repeating was not OK. In "statues" the whole point was to see what your habits are. "Ah, I see, I continually keep making that gesture." And if I have that habit, what do I have to do to change that? We're asking "What is transformation?" If you're going to be an actor, you have to transform from role to role, so you better bloody well figure out how to do that. And your Hamlet better not look like your Lady Bracknel. So how do you do that? Well, the fastest way I know is physical transformation because it affects the psychological so much more quickly and yet it is so much more profound. The audience can read the transformation so much better.

In everything that Suzuki does there is a built-in obstacle. Nothing can be done easily. And that's the gift. It's not that I have to master this training so that I can replicate it, it's that if I solve that obstacle, that stands for being able to change in any circumstance. And if I as an actor look at a form and am asked to replicate it right away, then I can read a director who gives me the sense of "this moment wants to be like that." Then I can instantly read all the signs and symbols of what is going on and then that moment can be more profoundly expressed and replicated.

Smith: *There is a common critique of Suzuki's work that there seems to be a great deal of tension involved.*

Hunt: Steve and I continue to be performers and we continue to try to figure out what's necessary to cry on cue, and tension doesn't get you there. We think that working on this strong, rigorous formal training, and finding out how to do it without tension, replicates exactly what you need to do in a play. It's formal. It has staging. It has rules. You're trying to be in one world. You have to be crisp. You have to drive it. You can't have pauses that trucks can go through. And how do you do that without tension? That's exactly what we're trying to do.

Pearson: I think that Suzuki's intention was never to have tension but to have power, to be able to move extremely strongly, to be able to do very difficult physical tasks and remain relaxed in your upper body. Well, when you first attack that and if you're not really looking at the content of the training, but looking at the form, the first impression is that it takes a lot of upper body energy and holding to try to make that happen. But that's not what it is. The "it" of it is to be able to move with incredible quickness and power, but having a relaxed upper body, so that you can speak with power for long periods of time. Even Laurence Olivier says the best actors are the ones with the strongest thighs. And when you have good strong thigh muscles in connection with your center as a basis from which to speak and then have a relaxed upper body, you can go on for a long period of time in moments of high passion. And then, in moments of great delicacy, you still have a base from which to move with incredible alacrity and responsiveness. So tension, any kind of tension, is the great robber of that. And if you watch the best people train—the difference between Suzuki's apprentices and the most senior actors—was the amount of extra energy that was being expended to make something happen. Almost in an inverse way, the amount of actual power, which was conveyed, is the opposite. The more energy the actor uses, the less he or she is truly strong. On the stage if you use too much energy, there is a sense that you are proving something—you're not doing it, you're proving that you're doing it, which is a totally different thing.

Smith: *I noted in your work on* Cherry Orchard *yesterday, you came back to helping the actors personalize the material.*

Pearson: We work from both ends. Stanislavsky was really good at the internal conviction. He came from a tradition where people were trained in highly theatrical, highly stylized playing. So they already knew all that external stuff. They knew how to walk through doors— he was trying to give some internal truth to that.

Hunt: When you work only psychologically, you move around in basically Freudian circles as you try to figure out what the motivation is and why people are the way they are. When you start developing and exploring character physically simultaneously, and you begin to understand how you can use your instrument but then how you can alter parts of it or shift orientation, change the parts that lead or dominate or how you stride or where the question are physically answered, where you physically receive anger. That stuff necessarily means that the actors have to get past habitual responses.

　　　　　It's like insurance in a way. If you set up a condition in the body in which these things might happen and you have the *magic if* going in terms of the circumstances, you are less vulnerable to inspiration failing you. The head is really fickle, and unless you've been trained as a Zen monk, you can't do a perfect Bergman storyboard in your head when you're working on images. But if you can be working simultaneously physically and are setting up conditions in which someone might be fearful, the chances of the audience reading and getting what it needs to despite of your lack of inspiration are much greater. I'm sure of it.

Smith: *Can you describe some conscious ways that you've adapted Suzuki's work for the American actor?*

Pearson: In terms of teaching it, we don't teach in the Japanese way. The Japanese way is a lot of repetition, and rote, and then questions, and then the odd comment after someone has tried it seventy-five times. Our students in the United States—and we ourselves—are used to this idea that unless we're getting something new every other second then we're not learning. So one has to adapt to that. One has to talk a bit more about what the thing means, trying to bring people to some experience of practice, in the Eastern sense. We do this while at the same time not letting them intellectually become stagnant because they're not getting new information. And the way to do that is to give their analytical mind lots of interesting stuff to do. And that, of course, is what any actor does—have a rich image all the time. And it gets richer and richer and more fully imagined.

Smith: *How can your work help where a traditional "method" background can't?*

Pearson: I think we're trying to get some way of treating that which not only has to do with psychology and experience and so on, but has to do with the body. You can't use a psychological model or even an experiential model to get to truth about doing Medea, for example. I don't even think you can with Shakespeare. The technical demands of doing Shakespeare are too vast to use one's own personal everyday experience either of your history or your physical experience. Most people now don't have the lexicon, the physical grammar, to play a queen. We don't even have physical paraphrases for it. And not only is the grammar not there, but the actual phonemes are getting less and less and less. Nowadays, this [typing at a keyboard] is probably the extent of a fair bit of what people do everyday—that movement, back and forth, in front of the screen, hours every day. And in the television age, the physical passivity—television is based on passivity because that's the state in which people can actually accept things like "ring around the collar"—there's no physical paraphrase. So one needs a practice, a training, which expands the sense of being in the world. What is it like to move? It means to move with strength, and to relate to things outside of you.

Suzuki training happens to address a lot of things from Japanese theatrical practice which are extremely useful for Americans: a very relaxed upper body, a very powerful sense of where the center of gravity is, the natural harmony between mind and body relative to the core of where all movement is, which is at the center of gravity or slightly below the navel—in Japanese they call it *kee*, in Chinese, *chi*.

We're looking always at balancing what is dramatic and what is theatrical. I think the core of drama has to do with this connection between the humanness of the actor and the humanness of the audience and the shared understanding of some kind of struggle. Suzuki talks about how you get at a physical struggle—what a physical struggle means. Sometimes he even laughingly calls his theatre a theatre of pain. So you give yourself a very strong physical struggle—you begin to really understand what the dramatic, intellectual struggle is. Suzuki was figuring out ways to challenge the body so it requires a high level of concentration to accomplish something. And the higher the level of concentration, the more complete, total commitment one is involved with. It doesn't really matter how much the actor was involved in the thing himself—and I think that's a problem. It's really a problem with this idea of "truth" because we sense that the marker of truth is emotional availability. And if the actor cries tears or hyperventilates or gets really angry and throws things around, that somehow equates with truth; it must be true because one has real tears. But I can tell people that I've seen who can cry real tears and it means nothing. And the audience is weeping, saying, "It was so true." There are all kinds of ways at this idea of truth and connection with characters, and the results are some kind of emotion: because emotions are always results and always site specific and event specific.

This is all emotional talk we're talking about—and thought talk. This is not Suzuki-exotic. These things interconnect and Suzuki addresses them, but not from thinking yourself into a place where you can get at an emotional state. Now it's possible that if you actually convince yourself that you were in some kind of emotional state that your breathing would respond. But if your body doesn't have, habitually, the everyday experience of changing that way very much, then the amount that you can actually change physically is small. Your actual experience brings about a small result and as a result the emotional experience or the intellectual experience that you have on stage is small. If you can do training which causes you to breathe really deeply and with a great sense of control and power, then you can actually deliver those things like a thought in Shakespeare which is sometimes four, five, six lines long. If you can deliver that and have the wherewithal to do it, not only can we understand it as an audience but also you can have the experience of being King Richard II. That's what Suzuki training is intended to do.

SOME FINAL THOUGHTS

This interview, edited from three days of interviews, was gathered from eight hours of tapes of classes, rehearsals, and discussions, conducted March 3–5, 1999, at the School of Drama studios and offices on the University of Washington campus. The present format cannot detail all the ways Pearson and Hunt have created an effective, hybrid form of actor training. Actors Studio member Mark Jenkins thinks of himself not as "the Method man" but as a "teacher of acting." However, imbedded in his (and the program's) philosophy is Jenkins's acknowledgment that *the principles of Stanislavsky are undeniably useful for the actor.* These principles form the foundation of the work in the PATP and inform the ways in which Suzuki's training techniques are adapted for the American actor. The Method has always been a living technique, less about specific "methods" and more about principles of mimesis. The American Method continued to adopt ideas for changing social conditions. Following in this tradition, the PATP continues to work on ways to help actors express, for a new generation, some form of "truth" for the human condition.

CHAPTER EIGHTEEN

THE PARADOX OF THE METHOD ACTOR

Rethinking the Stanislavsky Legacy

Dennis C. Beck

The founders of the American Method articulate an ambivalent attitude to the teachings of Constantin Stanislavsky. Lee Strasberg calls
them "directly responsible not only for my own development, but for the
creation of the Group Theatre" (*DP* 40). Yet when Stella Adler staged her
historic confrontation in the Group Theatre after studying with
Stanislavsky in 1934, Method teacher and director Robert Lewis recalls
that Strasberg announced that "he taught the Strasberg Method, not the
Stanislavsky System."[1] Adler and Sanford Meisner similarly recognize
that their approaches are based in the Russian's ideas but include their
own additions (*TA* 6; *MA* 183). Because, however, Stanislavsky's ideas
form their point of departure, the American Method(s) share with the
Russian teacher's "System" essential qualities not necessarily related to the
Realist style.[2] Stanislavsky's core concept of the performer's dual consciousness, in fact, reasserts the humanity and agency of the
individual/actor while also providing, like poststructuralist approaches

beholden to Bertolt Brecht, a framework within which identities and their formative influences can be questioned and critiqued. In a century of totalitarian and technological forces that threaten the status of the individual, methods of performance that challenge authoritarianism represent a subversive opposition.

Distortions of Stanislavsky's thought on both sides of the former Iron Curtain foster the misperception that Stanislavskian and Method concepts cannot accommodate the late-twentieth- and early-twenty-first-century playfulness and questioning of identity formation that poststructuralist approaches claim. Such misperceptions, resulting from unintentional mistranslations of his meanings, have conceived two of a trio of "Stanislavskys" from the East and West. Proponents of socialist-derived realism in the former communist bloc typecast the first, while in the West a second version represents a similar distortion of Stanislavsky's ideas as the antithesis of everything Brechtian. A third Stanislavsky, however, grew out of his thought on the dual consciousness of the actor, which concerns me here. The second version formed west of the Iron Curtain, where Brecht's criticism—rather than praise—of Stanislavsky's ideas has been adopted and extended by thinkers such as theatre scholar Elin Diamond, who argues that Stanislavsky's concepts conform "to stable representations of identity." Theatre historian Lauren Love adds to this, perceiving Stanislavsky as "embedded in dominant ideology."[3] East of the Iron Curtain, Polish critic Edward Csató notes that modernization of Polish theatre after 1956 occurred "against Stanislavsky—in truth, against the fiction that ruled the previous period, but a fiction that was identified with Stanislavsky himself."[4] Thus, two Stanislavskys were implicated in opposing dominant ideologies and acting aesthetics.

Perceptions, however, differ. While, ironically, many American critics rehearse realism's conflation of signifier with signified—blaming Stanislavsky's ideas[5]—Soviet bloc critics take care to fault, instead, realism's conflation. The distinction is as crucial as it is critical, for in the West, and the United States in particular, it has meant Stanislavskian and Method ideas are moribund. Brecht carries the mantle of transgressive acting, while Stanislavsky forms a hegemonic monolith. Lost in this rush to judgment are Stanislavsky's teachings regarding the dual consciousness of the actor, which, while inherited as the basic structure of the American

Method, remain unacknowledged and unexamined by many critics and teachers. Consequently, American actors and theorists exploit only a portion of the Method's potential. In Eastern Europe, however, longer-standing political skepticism spurred a continuing search to elucidate Stanislavsky's key theories in contemporary contexts. The artistic and "spiritual" stigma of socialist realism provoked conscientious theatre artists to disentangle his ideas from the realist form. The third Stanislavsky they unearthed inspired the development of acting styles founded on the paradoxical relationship between actor and role. In contrast to the "Stanislavsky" acting style that conflates actor and role, making them complicit with ideologies scripted from authorities, actors opposing the status quo translated the third-Stanislavskian ideas into sociopolitical efficacy won through popular trust. This subversion of the dominant ideology allowed actors to play a significant role in the revolutions of 1989.[6] In Poland, Russia, Hungary, but most dramatically in the former Czechoslovakia, the ideas of an allegedly politically ignorant Stanislavsky formed the theoretical barricades from which oppositional theatre artists steadily attacked, rather than affirmed, the status quo.[7] This actor-role relationship used to criticize authority similarly informs the American Method. Unraveling these performances from formal associations reveals concepts and potentials obscured by reading the Method exclusively through the lens of realism.

Ironically, the Stanislavskian theories that formed an ideological and aesthetic "velvet prison" of socialist realism simultaneously provided the means to escape it. Hungarian dissident Miklós Haraszti uses the phrase "velvet prison" as shorthand for the sophisticated network of factors in "pacified post-Stalinist neocolon[ies]" that kept artists in the thrall of state ideology.[8] Breaking free of a similar Western conceptual prison requires the recognition that reading Stanislavsky's work as inevitably "conforming to stable representations of identity" is to perceive him incorrectly. To read Stanislavsky as a slavish adherent of realism is to understand him solely through the *effects* of those who have co-opted and forcibly unified his theories in much the same way that socialist realist theorists and the editor Elizabeth Reynolds Hapgood did.[9] In the East, Stanislavsky's evolving process was requisitioned as an officially fixed "system of laws" for stage production and acting by communist authorities wishing to save

Stanislavsky the person from political oblivion or to capitalize on his international celebrity.[10] A commission vetted his books to bring them in line with dialectical materialism, and his experiments beyond realism were, as Stanislavsky scholar Sharon Carnicke notes, "conveniently forgotten."[11] Realist appropriation imposed closure on the productive and unresolved tension that characterized his thinking.

That tension found its fulcrum in the paradox of acting defined by Enlightenment philosopher Denis Diderot in the eighteenth century. Within the confines of realism's verisimilitude, the paradox might be stated as *one performs without appearing to perform*. Expressed so that it applies to diverse theatrical modes, the paradox questions how an actor can be harpsichordist and harpsichord, subject and object, self and creation of the self, simultaneously. Diderot pondered: "If he is himself while he is playing, how is he to stop being himself? If he wants to stop being himself, how is he to catch just the point where he is to stay his hand?"[12] Subsequent debate centered on what relationship between these two "persons" of the actor (character or self) might best be emphasized.[13] In his early writings, Diderot favored the actor of "sensibility" who follows nature's course and "loses" (or discovers) the self in the character and raptures of emotion. With *The Paradox of Acting*, however, he came to champion the actor of sense, of conscious artistic choice who guides the creation while remaining "unmoved" and "imitating" emotion. Actors, he observes, "impress the public not when they are furious, but when they play fury well."[14] Still beholden to the Enlightenment penchant for binaries, Diderot sets the terms of the discussion as irreconcilable polarities.

After the rise of romantically influenced melodramatic acting and the collapse of the apprentice system of training in the nineteenth century, the debate took on new urgency. In 1906 Stanislavsky retreated to Finland in a crisis over his own approach to acting and began to search for a process of creation that might resist designer and theorist Gordon Craig's reduction of the actor to puppetry. He took with him Diderot's essay.[15] How, he asked, might the actor step beyond Diderot's polarities? How might he live or experience the role and simultaneously shape the creation? How might the paradox of the actor, (re)solved by Diderot and Craig by giving dominance to the role over the self, remain a living and usable paradox? How might acting throw off the puppet and once again become dynamic?

Although Stanislavsky's idea of "truth," or authenticity, is often perceived as abiding in emotional honesty or use of the actor's self, it resides most fundamentally at a deeper level, in the reactivation of acting's inherent paradox.[16] If the actor as human being always coexists with the performed persona/character creation, then only a theory that accommodates both aspects (human being *and* character) can be true to the actor's experience. In this sense, Stanislavsky's ideas are realistic, since they seek to account for and utilize phenomena, the experienced world. Such realism, however, oversteps the confines of surface verisimilitude or psychology. Like linguist Roman Jakobson in "On Realism in Art" and Bertolt Brecht in "The Extent and Diversity of Literary Realism," Stanislavsky understands realism as a process measurable only through its experience and effect, and consequently he stresses the need for formal transformation to prevent calcification into a single (realist) form.[17] His creation of the studios attests to this continuing exploration of reality ("truth") unhitched to the realist form. Moreover, the nonrealist productions characteristic of self-proclaimed successors like Euvgeny Vakhtangov, Michael Chekhov, Jerzy Grotowski, and Yuri Lyubimov testify to the application of Stanislavsky's ideas beyond realism's bounds. In the United States, however, the third Stanislavsky remains obscured within the realist style so closely associated with the Method. Pulling aside the Iron Curtain throws light on the Method's *possibility*.

Two orienting points repel and attract each other in Stanislavsky's theory: the character and the actor. These points represent, if not prefigure, two inescapable and perhaps primary poles repeatedly rearranged in twentieth- and early-twenty-first-century theatre: the fictional versus the documentary, the transcendent versus the material, the illusionary versus the real, the signifier versus the signified, the text versus the body. Stanislavsky mapped the shifting terrain and defined the paradoxes of modern acting (character and persona), which theatre historian William Worthen expounds as the "theatrical versus the real, acting versus being, public versus private, the theater versus the actor."[18] By actively involving the actor's unique person in the creation of the role, Stanislavsky was "the first to suggest that the actor was an integral part of the theatrical artwork, not just its transmitter,"[19] according to Timothy Wiles. Stanislavsky thus introduced the implication that the person of the actor constituted a theatrical reality onstage as significant as the dramatic reality of the character. "Always act in your own person," Stanislavsky advised. "The moment you lose yourself on the stage marks the departure from truly living your part and the beginning of exaggerated, false, acting."[20] Despite this dialectical process of the actor struggling with the differing melodic lines of self and character, the final product played for the audience was to be univocal, two voices singing as one in indistinguishable unison. Paradoxically, Stanislavsky makes the revolutionary move to bring the actual onto the stage, but fences it in fiction. "The difference between my art and that [practiced by others] is the difference between 'seeming' and 'being,'"[21] he claimed, but here the contradictions proliferate, for while the actor was to be, the audience was to see a character who would *seem* to be. Seeming has lived on, but behind it lies the subversive potential of the actor living/experiencing the role. Within the realm of performer, Stanislavsky liberates actors to speak in their own voice, rejects a naturalistic determination by environment, and empowers them as artists making artistic and inherently political choices, oriented on their own sense of truth. Actors can exercise this freedom, however, only within the walls of a unified illusion. When considering the character, in contrast, Stanislavsky subscribed, as philosophy and cultural critic Raymond Williams remarks, to the naturalistic and deterministic emphasis on "the *production* of character or action by a powerful natural or social environment" (emphasis in original).[22] Thus, Stanislavsky posited character and actor on two distinct and often-conflicting views of reality. The character's dramatic reality lay in the realm of nineteenth-century realism, which culminated four hundred years of developing notions of how life looks (verisimilitude), while the actor's theatrical reality resided in how life is experienced, the same relativistic view of "reality" that gave rise to surrealism and expressionism, to name two related theories.[23]

More than any other aspect of his "system," Sharon Carnicke asserts, Stanislavsky stresses the "experiencing" of the role *(perezhivanie)* and uses it to capture the precarious balance between theory and practice.[24] With it he sets his type of acting apart from two others: craftsmanship *(remeslo)*, which relies on external effects or clichés, and representation (in current terms, "presentation"), which overemphasizes the person of the actors, abandoning their active experiencing in rehearsal for the objectified imitation of their passive and preplanned images in performance.[25] Stanislavsky's theatre, in contrast, activates two types of the actors' experiencing, related to his revised understanding of the actor-character "paradox." Experiments in the First Studio to overcome the paradox of the actor on the one hand and the character on the other through affective memory and attempts to fuse the actor with the character had failed. As Russian scholar Pavel Markov, in a translation done for the Group Theatre, observed, the actor, attempting to fully accommodate the character, "had to dissemble inwardly. Or he had to put the content of his own daily life in place of . . . the experience of the character."[26] Later articulated in *An Actor Works on Himself, Part II* (the Russian and less-edited version of *Building a Character*), Stanislavsky adapts Diderot's dual consciousness (being self and not-self) as a split in the performer's sense of self (*samochuvstvie*), which Carnicke calls the notion of "two equally important perspectives—being on stage and being within the role." Actors no longer negotiate between two selves—one of which they can never "be"—but between two types of experience, both oriented in themselves. Stanislavsky reflected this alternating consciousness by terminologically yoking, as Carnicke notes, "human being/self" with "actor" (*chelovek-akter*) and "actor" with "character" (*artisto-rol*).[27] With the "magic if," which asks *what would I do if I found myself in this circumstance?* actors begin to use imagined or remembered personal experience to create/enter the character's behavior and experience as shaped by circumstance. The actor as artist mediates the experience of the self and character. The paradox of acting's two irreconcilable personalities continues to exist for spectators, but for performers the obstructions of a paradox disappear in the links created through experiencing.

Actors no longer dutifully render the playwright's character but cocreate it, coauthor it. The actors become authorial. In this act arises actors' second and more influential type of experiencing, for they do not, like sentient tape-recorders, simply play back the playwright's character or their own ideal model (as Diderot would have it) but embody the ephemeral creative act itself in performance by presenting each actors' active imagining to the audience directly. Such performance "is itself a genuine, conscious process," an active creative negotiation between self and role in the process of performance.[28] Stanislavsky shifts additional attention to actors in the process of creation by equating "to experience" (*perezhivat'*) with "to create" (*tvorit'*). In so doing, notes Carnicke, actors further identify "time on stage with real time, hence life experience."[29] Thus, Stanislavsky looks forward into the late twentieth century, for he was, as Wiles observes, "the first to sense (although not specify) that what is essentially 'real' about theatrical realism lies as much in the reality of the performance itself as in the true-to-life quality of the play's details."[30] He had, in fact, reoriented the idea of "truth" so that "On stage truth is whatever you believe and in life truth is what actually is."[31] Viewing truth as relative to the imaginative world of the actor and the play anticipates developments in modernism that no longer rely, like realism, on external "objective" sources of the real. Yet unlike Albert Einstein, who perceived the basic ramifications of his contemporaneous discovery of relativity, Stanislavsky continued to use *his* new theory often to serve an objectivist worldview, that of the character produced by a natural and social environment. This vestige of nineteenth-century vision would keep him, as Wiles notes, unable to recognize that an actor as an actor upon the stage "is a more primary reality than his attempt to live the part he plays."[32] Although the ramifications of setting actor and character as dual realities on stage eluded him, Stanislavsky nonetheless established the poles between which actors would perform throughout the century.

Socialist realism clung to the character pole and Stanislavsky's most objectivist, deterministic ideas. By purging the "system" of realities that might be discovered in an actor's personal emotions, experience, perceptions, and presence, socialist realism and its later softened forms not only portrayed a singular, "official" reality but created what critic Alexander Gershkovich recalled in 1986 as the "lifeless Moscow Art Theatre of the last thirty or forty years."[33] Actors, deprived of subjective paths into characters that were no longer individuals but types, found themselves, ironically in a Marxist context, alienated from the product of their labor. By the 1950s, new interpretations of Stanislavsky's thought were emerging east of the Berlin Wall. Polish director Jerzy Grotowski, and Yuri Lyubimov, director of Moscow's oppositionist Taganka Theatre from 1964 to

1981, both claimed Stanislavsky as their role model, rejected the idea of a "system," and incorporated the person of the actor into performance as a philosophical and political choice. Exploring the body and person of the individual became a battle tactic in keeping clear the interplay of being (creating, experiencing) and seeming (transmitting, representing), which communist governments and media had an interest in conflating. In Czechoslovakia, where the Soviets had helped install a particularly hard-line government after their 1968 invasion and where the dissident move-ment took on particular force, this interplay was keen. The felt need to concretize and relearn the truth of *being* in an environment of seeming in-spired a whole subset of alternative theatres in communist Czechoslova-kia fittingly dubbed *autorské divadla* (theatres of authors). As the most public component of a larger Czechoslovak dissident community, they fulfilled the task of bringing countless people into an expanding opposi-tional movement.

In the same year that playwright and future political leader Václav Havel scored his first absurdist success at the Theatre on the Balustrade (*Divadlo na zabradlí*) in 1963, the earliest of the authorial theatres emerged. Studio Ypsilon's method of juxtaposing character with actor would be more overt and less somber than Grotowski's or Lyubimov's. Play, in fact, forms the company's major theoretical orientation. To ground themselves in being or "authenticity" rather than seeming, direc-tor Jan Schmid notes that when working with texts, themes, or charac-ters, Ypsilon's actors do not simply play them (*"hrát"* = to play) but play *with* them (*"hrát si"* = to play with).[34] The actor in Ypsilon makes the space between the actor and role the primary domain of his or her cre-ative activity, which is a montage of attempts to take on the character in different ways. Actors present the role in different styles or from a suc-cession of perspectives. The person of the actor might move into the character, identifying with it, "disappearing" or "fusing" in a tragic mode, then reemerge momentarily as the actor, resubmerge to retry a few of the lines as comedy, or continue the performance in a farcical or romantic mode, as joyous rather than nervous, and so on. Actors, like workers in the middle of a task, often toss in moments of *oblique* direct address. Be-tween attempts to enter the role, they may launch into long speeches or dialogues with the audience outside character or actor persona, but with the kind of familiar, unmediated personality that years of communication with the same spectators fosters. Topics range from allusions to current affairs to personal complaints, comments on the play, or observations of life. As actors and audience members question each other and introduce the actual, conditions outside the theatre walls and in individual lives become the text or transparent subtext of the exchange. Yet the dramatic action does not stop as much as suspend—for the other actors do not exit the dramatic world but continue in character or in the reactive space between character and actor, activating other layers of subtext and associations. Then, in a split second, the actor jumps back "into" character and the action moves on without a beat lost.

The audience sees the actor move fluidly and rapidly between the modes of character, actor-persona, and individual, the three orienting points in Stanislavsky's self/actor *(chelovek-akter)* and actor/character *(artisto-rol)*. Spectators watch the actor work, brought into the process almost like the actor's superego, while the actor rehearses the role in a number of ways. Rather than an attempt to create complete and seamless characters, Ypsilon acting is, according to critic Vladimír Just, "a struggle over the role, which is filled with deviations, adjuncts, comments, unfitting associations and mistakes."[35] The focus of performance shifts from an attempt to present what might be thought aesthetically or politically correct (in order to create a perfect illusion) to what is possible and most provocative in the free space of interpretation/authorship. The shift therefore engages the audience in considerations of effectiveness, potential, and choice, rather than rectitude. As a result, critic and dramaturg Zdeněk Hořínek observes of Ypsilon that "the unifying element in performance does not become the ideal dramatic character, but that which is most real in the play: the actor's personality."[36] Jana Synková, a veteran of the company, underscores this point physically: Whether playing Lady Macbeth or the Devil, she wears the large, round, thick-lensed glasses that the audience associates with her irascible, mischievous personality.

The Ypsilon actor becomes the pivotal figure in the dual dialogues between role and actor, actor and spectator. A sense of becoming rather than accomplishment, future possibility rather than past product, listening and responding rather than being deaf to and denying others decisive force characterizes performances. Such performances constitute, in the context of totalitarianism, an exercise in democracy, a dialogue among a citizenry audience, actor representatives, and the sociopolitical roles they must, or choose, to play. As such, their purpose is not unlike that of radical director Augusto Boal, whose inspiration, Paulo Freire, wrote, "Cultural action for freedom is characterized by dialogue, and its preeminent purpose is to conscientize the people. . . . [It is opposed by] cultural action for domination [which] . . . serves to domesticate the people." The subjects of Ypsilon's performances provided spectators with points of reflection if not education about current conditions, while its method revealed ways to subvert the scriptedness of scripted roles, thus maintaining the actor's integrity. It also gave spectators a voice, a public forum in which to respond in political conditions that would not have allowed the kind of overt, interventionist, and participatory theatre Boal practices. In this way Ypsilon participated in what Freire calls the "conscientization" of the oppressed, "the process in which men, not as recipients, but as knowing subjects, achieve a deepening awareness both of the sociocultural reality which shapes their lives and of the capacity to transform that reality."[37] Adapting Stanislavsky's ideas, Ypsilon's artists helped audience members discover ways in which spectators might be actors making current choices rather than characters in a political drama scripted by absent authors.

A second Czech authorial theatre configured the actor-role relationship differently, expressing another aspect of a similar politics. Whereas an Ypsilon actor moves through three points of orientation—self, actor-persona, and character—*sequentially,* the actor in HaDivadlo (HaTheatre, or HaDi, a shortened form of Hanácké Divadlo, or Theatre of the Haná region) activates three levels—self, role, and type—*simultaneously,* corresponding to the personal, political, and mythic levels of their text. HaDi types, however, rather than prescribed to fit a predetermined form that actors in turn are forced to conform to, as with socialist realism, are customized for the actors based on their personalities. Such types activate what psychological researcher Ignacio Matte Blanco calls "emotional thinking," in which, he posits, we tend to "idealize" situations and persons into a "maximization of magnitude" that contains all the attributes of "the type" so that we "carry to their extreme and utmost potentialities the characteristics of a given situation or person."[38] A HaDi actor's type, then, although based in his self, looms behind him, in the audience's view, as a maximized shadow filled with potentialities cast on the social wall. The set of qualities associated with an actor's type might shift in priority or emphasis, depending on the role, but the basic outlines of the "son," the "mother," the "outcast," and so on, continue from role to role. In this framework, type accords most with a mythic level. The nature of the role, however, influences the function of the myth and the relationship of the actor to the type. For example, actor Miloslav Maršálek, a large man capable of tenderness and volcanic fury from one moment to the next, often represents a father figure of common sense, reasonableness, and authority who can be alternately gentle and understanding or severe, fanatic, and manipulative. As the Job character, Mendel Singer, in *Job: An Oratorio for Actors*, Maršálek's type became a symbol for the suffering, loss, and dislocation endured not only by Jews in Eastern Europe but by Czechs as a whole under the influence of more powerful forces and nations. An actor's type, depending on the role, can conversely represent negative potential, as in *Mirroring*, a montage of works by twenty Russian writers. Here Maršálek played an unnamed official who, as writers, composers, painters, and actresses introduced themselves and their professions to him, responded, "You mean shit to me," whereupon the artists fell promptly to the floor dead.

To distinguish themselves from the maximized image of their types, HaDi actors adopt what theatre scholar Eva Šormová calls *personality acting*, in which the individual qualities and personal themes of each actor are included in the meaning of the performance. This began with what scholar and dramaturg Vlasta Gallerová calls HaDi's "working clothes," which consist of recurring basic pieces on the same actor from role to role and others that are part of the actor's own daily wardrobe. They form, proposes Gallerová, part of the actor's signature in the same way as does the voice. To these working clothes, other pieces are added as appropriate. Actor Ján Sedal, for example, always wears garments that fail to fit but accord with his particular quality, which suggests "the fumbling movement of a wanderer pondering the sense of his journey."[39] Such an apparent breakdown of the traditional divisions between performing personality and performed role serves, paradoxically, to distinguish actors from their roles. Actors walk onstage with a bodily sense of the continuation of their offstage selves, reflecting a playing method that expresses

Stanislavsky's admonition that "an actor cannot be merely someone, somewhere, at some time or other. He must be I, here, today."[40] Although HaDi actors use direct address, the sense of intimacy, authenticity, self-revelation, and perhaps even confession—recalling Grotowski—for which they are noted emanates from their basic approach to the stage as an extension, as it were, of their living rooms. The person that the audience has learned the actor to be might stand in jarring contrast to the role, even though the role fits the actor's type, as with Maršálek's official. The actor, as an individual, stands in living relief to the rigid maximalization of type and scriptedness of the role. Actors show possible ways to be, ways in which they, or people like them, can react, can either follow the beliefs they as persons hold, or depart from them. Outside the theatre spectators may create illusions of verisimilitude with a public role that demands the appearance of support for a system and lies no one believes in, and thus publicly betray the private self they are with trusted friends and family. Critical actors, in contrast, dare not only to present the private self publicly but also to assert it as empowered to choose and to confess its relationship to an externally imposed role. Not disappearing into the character thus became one political act that began in the theatre and extended beyond it. Refusing to distance characters completely from themselves, however, represents actors' recognition of responsibility for the character's at least partial presence in them and how they had come to acquiesce to the character's power. Stanislavsky's belief that acting was ultimately about ethics and the denial of artifice found new depths and implications in HaDi.

Nonetheless, as in realism, type and character at some moments seem to fuse with the actor. HaDi's playing style, however, repeatedly peels them apart by rejecting simple mimesis and identification, as when Mendel Singer's daughter, Mirjam, loses her virginity and part of her identity to a Russian soldier. Four soldiers stamp an accelerating rhythm at each corner of the stage as the actor Mariana Chmelařová writhes, driven by their tempo, alone atop a table and beneath a hanging light she has set swinging, which expressionistically elongates and foreshortens her shadow. The actor expresses the character's experience, and perhaps her own ecstasy and anguish, but despite the visceral and emotional impact of the segment, the context induces a sense of the partial extrication of actor from character, but one more subtle than Brecht's. Such moments do not divorce character from actor so much as make the audience subtly aware of the actor performing an activity that *symbolizes* the character's activity/experience. The actor steps discreetly into the realm of metaphor rather than mimesis. In contrast to a Brechtian method's appeal to clear reason through breaks and stoppage in the action, the emotional power of such moments remains uninterrupted yet bifurcates as the spectator witnesses simultaneously the character's experience and the actor's art, in which, in turn, an ongoing sense of confession seems to express the *actor's* experience. The HaDi actor thus avoids the self-betrayal of first and second Stanislavsky actors by standing beside the character as metonym, able in a single action to split perception between the dramatic and theatrical levels, to symbolize the role on one level and to confess the self on the other. Symbolizing the role and experience of the character, rather than laminating the self to the character through identification, allows the actor to remain the orientation point of the performance. It allows actors to remain true to themselves and to be perceived as true to themselves, rather than being true to an imposed idea, ideal, or ideology. Such liberation, effected by developing Stanislavsky's dual focus on character and actor, expressed an emerging philosophy that became the ideational hammer used to chip the Berlin Wall down.

The motto of this philosophic tactic became known as "living in truth," a phrase first used by dissident Václav Havel. Havel proposed a personal strategy of quietly refusing to misrepresent oneself in the hundred small ways that fear induced, thus living in truth and healing the "crisis in human identity" and morality experienced in radically opposed private and public selves of life in the Eastern Bloc.[41] Public roles must be played, authorial actors seem to say subtextually, but how they are played, what relationship one will take to them, and which of their signs will be rejected or altered can be chosen to a significant degree. The belief in character/actor as object, which Boal notes characterizes Brecht's conception,[42] had become in the Soviet Bloc the very dogma that kept an unjust system in place by preaching individual disempowerment. Practicing a convincing agency depended on undermining enslavement to the role, on orienting action in the person acting, on living in truth. People are able, argued Havel and other subversive theatre artists, to move themselves from being objects of a system to subjects making daily, albeit often small, choices about their relationship to it. In this way, theatres and individuals become, in theatre critic Baz Kershaw's formulation, efficacious, by making "the immediate effects of performance influence, however minutely, the general historical evolution of wider social and political realities."[43] In the streets of Prague and Brno in November 1989, Czechs embodied the fruition of an approach to acting suggested by the bourgeois individualist Stanislavsky before the Soviets took power. As they cheered "Long live the actors!" in the mass demonstrations during that revolutionary November,[44] they were perhaps only subconsciously aware that, as much as for the men and women onstage who had demonstrated to them a method of living in truth, they cheered for themselves.

In the United States, meanwhile, less overt political threats to identity transformed individuals into objects, and, in response the actor's liberation, agency and antideterminism emerged. In theatres with ethnic, feminist, queer, or postcolonial consciousnesses, Brecht became the theorist of choice, though how an outlook that posits the character/individual as an object of economic and historical forces translates into actor agency without inherent contradiction is rarely addressed. Although theatre historian Janelle Reinelt, in "Rethinking Brecht," observes that the "Brechtian actor portrays character in such a way as to draw attention to the possibilities for alternative behavior in concrete historical moments," she must posit an implicit theory "of the subject in process" to locate a human subject in Brecht. To introduce that subject in performance, however, Reinelt notes that feminists have found it "necessary to combine two styles of acting," Brecht's and the Method/Stanislavsky.[45] Critics willingly expound the political significance of Brecht's ideas to their projects but seem unwilling to rethink Stanislavsky and the Method, though they nonetheless appropriate these approaches to express their philosophies performatively. The reason may lie in the form—and political associations—that also obscured the third Stanislavsky "behind" the Iron Curtain: realism.

Dominant aesthetic and political conditions in the United States have confused how the Method employs Stanislavsky's dual consciousness. With artists' work disguised as "natural" reality in the most prevalent style, realism, Method acting's two poles appear collapsed into one. Spectators tend to see only the character or, in an apparent contradiction that makes sense in light of realism's rhetorical power, only the actor. However, Method acting, Strasberg asserts, is not so simplistic. "What I believe is important is Stanislavsky's recognition of the dual nature of the actor's experience. Many people have assumed that Stanislavsky's emphasis on the actor's need to experience truly is predicated on the assumption that the actor is not aware of the imaginary nature of the performance. . . . Obviously that is impossible" (*DP* 52). The Method actor's experience encompasses both the dramatic/character and theatrical/actor poles, while the mode of realism produces the uncontradictory entity condemned as a stable representation of identity. Practitioners like Lauren Love who adopt a "hybrid Brechtian/Method technique" to (rightfully) challenge aesthetic and political structures confound the conflation by forswearing their Method training as implicitly Realist and imagining that they have stepped beyond it rather than further realizing its potentials outside the bounds of realism. Love's dream of "a more complete feminist performance technique [that] could clearly reveal the state of tension created between the actor's and character's identities" more closely reflects the developments of Stanislavsky's ideas in East-Central Europe than it does the depersonalized methods of Brecht.[46]

Meisner's approach, Adler's technique, and the craft of acting that Strasberg created activate three essential types of awareness in the actor that correspond to Ypsilon's, HaDi's, and Stanislavsky's three orienting terms in the actor's dual consciousness. The first type, represented by Strasberg's private moment and emotional memory exercises, Meisner's "actor's self," or Adler's source of justification, engages the actor as him- or herself (*DP* 145; *MA* 162; *TA* 48). "Only in theatre do we have the emotions, soul, spirit, mind, and muscles of the artist as the material of art," observes Strasberg, while Meisner notes "when it comes down to it, it's always *you*" (*SS* 81; *MA* 159). The second, character-related type emerges in Meisner's pressure to move beyond spontaneity or "merely the truth," Adler's character-directed exercises, or Strasberg's animal exercise, which "trains the actor by forcing him to deal with the character's behavior rather than relying on his own feelings" (*MA* 161; *TA* 210; *DP* 147). The third type, implicit in Adler's discussion of "working on the stage" and "the actor's contribution" or Meisner's stress on choice and explicit in Strasberg's song-and dance-exercise, develops the relationship between these poles. It activates the actor as actor/artist (*TA* 58–65, 115–17; *MA* 188; *DP* 151–59). By requiring actors to perform the "song-and-dance exercise" that Strasberg developed in the late 1950s in order to break out of learned rhythms or repeated rhythms and movements they established on their own, he achieved that *connection between impulse and expression* that characterizes the actors' alternation between self and presented image/character.

In that alternation, the Method actor activates Stanislavsky's two types of experiencing. "The use of the soul of the actor as material for his work," which Strasberg cites as Stanislavsky's most significant idea (*DP* 62), suggests the dynamic relationship within the Method's "self/actor" pole. The Method gives that self a position Stanislavsky suggested when considering the actor but then limited by demanding the actor create a character objectively produced by natural and social environment. In a move that Ypsilon and HaDi actors make implicitly, the Method explicitly reformulates Stanislavsky's "magic if." Rather than actors having to leap into the unknown of characters' circumstances (and run the risk of answering that they would *not* act in them as do the characters, but nevertheless having to conform to the written text), the Method adopts Vakhtangov's modification. The new question—*what would motivate me, the actor, to behave in the way the character does?* (*DP* 85) orients actors toward the creative use of their self/experience. Such a formulation does not demand, as Stanislavsky's does, that plays be "close to the contemporary and psychological experience of the actor" (*DP* 85) but allows for the intensity, magnitude, and nonlinearity of classical and non-Realist works. Additionally, it maintains a continuous sense of the real/authentic, the refusal of "self-betrayal" that East-Central European actors used in opposition to official mendacity and that Americans have made, as Americanist Miles Orvell details in *The Real Thing*, part of their self-understanding.[47]

Like HaDi's actors, who juxtapose their experience with their "types," or Ypsilon's, who play with the fit and unfittingness of roles, Method actors negotiate between the individual reality of their experience and the typical and stereotypical aspects of the scripted character. It is Marlon Brando's Stanley, not Tennessee Williams's character, who hesitates for a moment as if unsure how to act, as if hurt and lost, before exploding in a rage that clears the table at which he sits with Stella and Blanche. Rather than the impulsive, unthinking animal Blanche would make of him and readers of Williams might assume, Brando reveals a sensitive man searching for honest and effective ways to act in a threatening situation. Utilizing the same procedure, though with more overt reference to her own experience set against the stereotypes of a (performance) text, Peggy Shaw of Split Britches plays (with) Brando's Stanley, yet makes it her own in the performance that became *Belle Reprieve*. In doing so she departs from and critiques the stereotyping in/of Brando's performance. The Method approach thus avoids the self-betrayal that a slavish attitude to text would require and allows actors to break out of and subvert the scriptedness of roles. Like Czech actors opposing the erasures of socialist realism, Method actors refuse to play a cog in either a creative or social machine. They assume an authorial position.

Like the Czech approach, however, Method acting's structure avoids the reduction of performance to the personality of the actor, though self-indulgence is one of the Method's greatest traps. The actor's self is not an "objective" observer or referent outside the process, but as part of it, it is open to question, as is the scripted character. This process is contained in Strasberg's song and dance, a "simple exercise of will" (*DP* 153) in which actors' control is developed and their agency as artist is engaged in the mediation between the self and character poles. Yet more is latent in it. By going "against the grain of [their] training and habit" (*DP* 154) actors are forced to confront their habits of self. Though some habits are unique, others constitute the "scripts" of gender, class, and culture that feminist scholar Judith Butler proposes individuals unthinkingly incorporate.[48] Revealing the scriptedness of social and ideological behaviors and perspectives introduces the potential, through this new sight, of playing with them and, in this playfulness, going beyond them, authoring through choice, at least in part, the "scripts" of one's words and body. Here is the playfulness of the Ypsilon actor or the layering of self, myth, and character by the HaDi performer. Like the Ypsilon or HaDi approaches, the Method potentially allows for the critique of identity formation and yet rejects deconstruction's infinitely dispersed subject as part of a project that, like the one that gave rise to socialist realism, would create a world of human objects, deny agency, and subject individuals to what Havel calls a "general automatism."[49] Through non-Brechtian means, Method actors thus present a "subject in process."

In this lies the paradox of Method actors. While they ground their conviction, inspiration, and experiencing in their sense of self, and through that sense open means to act and react spontaneously to theatrical and dramatic given circumstances ("becoming" the character), they also act as artists making choices, utilizing their selves in relationship to the scripted characters, and express their own conceptions of the performance and the roles. In this assertion of creative agency lies, according to Strasberg, "the strong, intense, ideological base on which [the Method] rests" (DP 198). That base asserts that rejecting the determinism of a "kind of knowledge" that would persuade people to feel and function "as mere cogs in an enormous wheel in which human will, desire and feeling are irrelevant" is a necessary step in reclaiming human identity and the ability to act (DP 200). Václav Havel, who articulated the beliefs underlying Czech political and theatrical opposition, states the position more assertively. He says that grounding expression rigorously in one's own beliefs and self, or living "within the truth, as humanity's revolt against an enforced position, is, on the contrary, an attempt to regain control over one's own sense of responsibility. In other words, it is clearly a moral act." Such meanings do not disappear in democratic environments. It was in large part because he identified the political crisis of Eastern Europe as a "planetary challenge" that Havel was awarded the 1986 Erasmus Prize in recognition for his outstanding contributions to international understanding. Writing from the perspective of the Soviet Bloc in 1978, Havel observed that "[i]t may even be said that the more room there is in the Western democracies (compared to our world) for the genuine aims of life, the better the crisis is hidden from people and the more deeply do they become immersed in it."[50] The Method, paradoxically, illuminates the determining power of forces within which we are immersed in the process of rejecting their determinism.

NOTES

1. Robert Lewis, *Slings and Arrows: Theatre in My Life* (New York: Stein and Day, 1984), 71.

2. Sharon Carnicke, *Stanislavsky in Focus* (Australia: Harwood Academic Publishers, 1998), 6. By "Method(s)" I acknowledged that differing interpretations have developed in the United States of an approach to

acting that still retains a coherent foundation of understandings. Hereafter the singular "Method" will express this variegation.

3. See, Bertolt Brecht, "The Street Scene," *Brecht on Theatre*, John Willet, ed. and tr. (New York: Hill and Wang, 1957), 125; Elin Diamond, "Brechtian Theory/Feminist Theory: Toward a Gestic Feminist Criticism," *The Drama Review* (Spring 1988): 86; and Lauren Love, "Resisting the Organic: A Feminist Actor's Approach," *Acting (Re)Considered: Theories and Practices*, Phillip Zarrilli, ed. (London: Routledge, 1995), 276.

4. Quoted in Juliusz Tyszka, "Stanislavsky in Poland: Ethics and Politics of the Method," *New Theatre Quarterly* 5 (November 1989): 368.

5. Love admits she received her Stanislavsky through Method classes ("Resisting the Organic," 340, n. 1).

6. About the role of Czech theatre people in the 1989 revolution, see Petr Oslzly, "On Stage with the Velvet Revolution," *TDR* 34 (Fall 1990): 97–108; and my "Divadlo Husa na Provázku and the 'Absence' of Czech Community," *Theatre Journal* 48.4 (December 1996): 419–41.

7. See Carnicke, *Stanislavsky in Focus*, 72–82, for the sophistication with which Stanislavsky "side-stepped the censor[s]" of his work.

8. Miklós Haraszti, *The Velvet Prison: Artists Under State Socialism*, Katalin and Landesmann, trs. (1983; New York: Farrar, Straus and Giroux, 1989), 161.

9. Carnicke deals in detail with the issues of translation, publication, politics, and miscomprehension that distorted Stanislavsky's thought in both political blocs.

10. Peter Hercombe, director and scriptwriter, *The Stanislavsky Century*, videocassette, 3 parts, System TV: The Union of Russian Theatre/La Sept, 1993. Part III.

11. Sharon Carnicke, *Stanislavsky in Focus*, 80, 33.

12. Denis Diderot, "The Paradox of Acting," *The Paradox of Acting and Masks or Faces*, Walter Herries Pollock, tr. (New York: Hill and Wang, 1957), 15.

13. William Worthen, *The Idea of the Actor* (Princeton, NJ: Princeton University Press, 1984), 133.

14. Diderot, *Paradox of Acting*, 71.

15. See Carnicke, *Stanislavsky in Focus*, 115. David Magarshack sets Stanislavsky's encounter with Diderot in 1914 (*Stanislavsky: A Life* [New York: Chanticleer Press, 1951], 335–37).

16. Joseph Roach notes that Stanislavsky did not express the idea that sincerity was necessary to good acting: "[T]he reader will search Stanislavski's trilogy in vain for any such fatuity." Roach, *The Player's Passion: Studies in the Science of Acting* (Ann Arbor: University of Michigan Press, 1993), 216.

17. By 1923, Stanislavsky had "moved beyond realism and established a System which he did not associate with any particular style" (Carnicke,

Stanislavsky in Focus, 28). Also, "Stanislavsky fought against artistic stagnation" by exploring formal innovations, while "Nemirovich-Danchenko [cofounder of the Moscow Art Theatre], not Stanislavsky as is generally assumed, became the true champion of Realism" (30). See Roman Jakobson, "On Realism in Art," *Readings in Russian Poetics: Formalist and Structuralist Views,* L. Matejka and K. Pomorska, eds. (Cambridge, MA: MIT Press, 1971), 38–46; and Bertolt Brecht, "Weite und Vielfalt der realistischen Schreibweise," *Der kaukasische Kreiderkreis* (Berlin: Aufbau-Verlag, 1958), vol. 13, 97–107.

18. Worthen, *Idea of the Actor,* 154.

19. Timothy J. Wiles, *The Theater Event: Modern Theories of Performance* (Chicago: University of Chicago Press, 1980), 14.

20. Constantin Stanislavski, *An Actor's Handbook,* Elizabeth Reynolds Hapgood, ed. (New York: Theatre Arts Books, 1963), 91.

21. Ibid., 91.

22. Raymond Williams, "Social Environment and Theatrical Environment: The Case of English Naturalism," *English Drama: Forms and Development,* Marie Axton and Raymond Williams, eds. (Cambridge: Cambridge University Press, 1977), 205.

23. See Jakobson, "On Realism in Art," 39–41.

24. Carnicke, *Stanislavsky in Focus,* 107.

25. Constantine Stanislavsky, Bancroft Library early draft of *An Actor Prepares,* typescript (Bancroft Library, University of California, Berkeley), 134. Stanislavsky notes Sarah Bernhardt and Constant Coquelin as typical (re)presentational actors.

26. Pavel Markov, "The First Studio," typescript, Mark Schmidt, tr., 1934, The Group Theatre, The New York Public Library for the Performing Arts, New York, 57–58.

27. Carnicke, *Stanislavsky in Focus,* 119.

28. Stanislavsky, Bancroft typescript, 116.

29. Carnicke, *Stanislavsky in Focus,* 120.

30. Wiles, *Theatre Events,* 14.

31. Qtd. in Carnicke, *Stanislavsky in Focus,* 120–21.

32. Wiles, *Theatre Events,* 36.

33. Alexander Gershkovich, *The Theater of Yuri Lyubimov: Art and Politics at the Taganka Theatre in Moscow,* Michael Yurieff, tr. (New York: Paragon House, 1989), 179.

34. Jan Schmid, personal interview, February 12, 1997; Jan Schmid, *Způsob myšlení a přemyšlení,* Jan Kolář, ed. (Prague: Svaz českych dramatickych umělců, 1984), 2. All translations from Czech are my own.

35. Vladimír Just, "Jednota v mnohosti," program to *Outsider aneb životopis slavného muže* by Jan Schmid (Prague: Studio Ypsilon, December 2, 1981).

36. Quoted in Jan Schmid, "O dílně Studia Y zevnitř," in the playbill to *Krokodyl* (Prague: Studio Ypsilon, April 9, 1986).

37. Eugène van Erven, *Radical People's Theatre* (Bloomington: Indiana University Press, 1988), 22.

38. Ignacio Matte Blanco, *The Unconscious of Infinite Sets: An Essay in Bilogic* (London: Duckworth, 1975), 243–45.

39. Vlasta Gallerová, "Několik poznámek ke scénografii Hanáckého divadla," *Pokus o zachycení specifiky tvorby*, Vlasta Gallerová, ed. (Prague: Svaz českych dramatickych umělců, 1985), 100, 101.

40. Stanislavski, *Stanislavski's Legacy*, Elizabeth Reynolds Hapgood, ed. and tr. (New York: Theatre Arts Books, 1968), 20.

41. The major essay in which Havel did so, and one that articulated the political and philosophical beliefs underlying the emerging underground movements throughout the Soviet Bloc, was "The Power of the Powerless" (1978), in *Václav Havel or Living in Truth*, Jan Vladislav, ed. (London: Faber and Faber, 1987), 62.

42. Augusto Boal, *The Theatre of the Oppressed* (New York: TCG, 1985), 92–95.

43. Baz Kershaw, *The Politics of Performance: Radical Theatre as Cultural Intervention* (London: Routledge, 1992), 1.

44. Timothy Garton Ash, *The Magic Lantern: The Revolution of '89 Witnessed in Warsaw, Budapest, Berlin and Prague* (New York: Random House, 1990), 121.

45. Janelle Reinelt, "Rethinking Brecht: Deconstruction, Feminism, and the Politics of Form," *The Brecht Yearbook/Das Brecht-Jahrbuch* 15, Marc Silberman, ed. (Madison, WI: International Brecht Society, 1990), 103–4, 105.

46. Love, "Resisting the Organic," 279, 288.

47. See Miles Orvell, *The Real Thing: Imitation and Authenticity in American Culture, 1880–1940* (Chapel Hill: University of North Carolina Press, 1989).

48. Judith Butler, "Performative Acts and Gender Constitution: An Essay in Phenomenology and Feminist Theatre," *Performing Feminisms*, Sue-Ellen Case, ed. (Baltimore, MD: John Hopkins University Press, 1990), 270–82.

49. Havel, "Power of the Powerless," 52.

50. Ibid., 62, 115–16.

PART IV

METHOD SCHOOLS

CHAPTER NINETEEN

THE ACTORS STUDIO

Doug Moston

D irectors Elia Kazan and Robert Lewis and producer Cheryl Crawford founded the Actors Studio in New York City in 1947. In 1949 Lee Strasberg was asked to serve as its artistic director, which he did until his death in 1982. Ellen Burstyn and Al Pacino were co-artistic directors the following year. Ms. Burstyn then served as artistic director until 1988. Frank Corsaro served as artistic director from April 1988 through June 1995. The current artistic director, as of this writing, is Estelle Parsons. The president of the Actors Studio Board of Directors is Arthur Penn. Vice presidents are Estelle Parsons, Lee Grant, Norman Mailer, James Lipton, and Mark Rydell. There is also an Actors Studio West, in Los Angeles. Its three directors are Sydney Pollack, Mark Rydell, and Martin Landau.

The Actors Studio is a theatre workshop for professional actors, a place to work. It was created to be a place where actors of all ages could work together between jobs or during long runs to continue to develop their craft and to experiment with new forms in creative theatre work. (It is not a beginning drama school, nor should it be confused with the Lee Strasberg Theatre Institute.)

The Actors Studio is a nonprofit organization dedicated to the development of actors, playwrights, and directors. The work of the Studio is made possible in part by contributions from Studio patrons. There are currently 800 members of the Actors Studio, some invited at the Studio's inception by Elia Kazan, Robert Lewis, Cheryl Crawford, and Martin Ritt. But most have become members through auditioning. The Studio is a continuing active membership group, not a school with "alumni" or "graduates." Any professional actor over eighteen years of age is eligible for an audition. This consists of a five-minute scene (no monologues ever). Actors are advised to choose contemporary material close to themselves in age and experience. Auditions are presided over by the members of the Audition Committee.

Once admitted to the membership (if an actor is accepted it is for life at no cost ever), an actor is free to use Studio facilities. An extensive library of theatre books and manuscripts and rehearsal space are available for a member's projects. On this stage members have seen actors such as Marlon Brando, Shelley Winters, Karl Malden, Al Pacino, Ellen Burstyn, Robert De Niro, Dustin Hoffman, Harvey Keitel, Marilyn Monroe, Eli Wallach, Anne Jackson, Paul Newman, Sally Field, Faye Dunaway, Christopher Walken, and many more explore their art, challenge themselves creatively, and break through to new areas of creative expression.

The Actors Studio began the original Playwrights Unit in 1952, started by Clifford Odets and Molly Kazan. Lee Strasberg started the first Directors Unit in 1960. William Inge started the Writers Unit at the Studio West, and Jack Garfein formed the Directors Unit there. Arthur Penn and Frank Corsaro have led the Playwrights/Directors Unit in New York, currently in abeyance. It involved projects recommended to them. In the past Elisa Kazan and Joseph L. Mankiewicz have led the Unit. Lyle Kessler supervises Studio West Playwrights and Directors Unit.

The basic work of The Actors Studio happens on Tuesdays and Fridays, from 11 AM to 1 PM at the Acting Unit or the acting sessions, as they are called. Here members may work on any material they choose. It can be from a play, a novel, a short story, contemporary, classical, opera, ballet, teleplay, screenplay, song, poem—anything. Actors can also write their own material. They are free to choose their own partner and no longer wait to be cast by others. The work may be presented rehearsed or unrehearsed, directed or undirected, staged or not. The members present then comment upon the work at the session with guidance given by the moderator. Moderators have included Ellen Burstyn, Frank Corsaro,

Arthur Penn, Elia Kazan, Lee Grant, Carlin Glynn, Harvey Keitel, Stephen Lang, Martin Landau, Estelle Parsons, Sydney Pollack, Vivian Nathan, Mark Rydell, Gene Saks, Christopher Walken, Eli Wallach, and Shelley Winters.

Arthur Penn started the newest program at the Actors Studio in 1997, The Actors Studio Free Theatre. Here is a theatre where great plays such as Clifford Odets's *Awake and Sing* can play with stars like Anne Jackson and a stellar cast of established professionals who come together to offer patrons a theatre that is free to all. At the bottom of the Actors Studio brochure it says, "For nearly fifty years The Actors Studio has lived a very rich artistic existence and will endure as long as talent needs a home."

THE ACTORS STUDIO DRAMA SCHOOL

In the fall of 1994, The Actors Studio, in association with the New School University in New York City, engaged for the first time in its history in offering a Master of Fine Arts degree program in Theatre Arts (Acting, Directing, and Playwriting) with James Lipton as program chair and Dean. This three-year, full-time postgraduate degree program has since evolved into a full-fledged college in its own right, the School of Dramatic Arts, a completely autonomous division of the New School University with the Actors Studio Drama School as its core curriculum.

The three principal books describing the Stanislavsky System, *An Actor Prepares, Building a Character,* and *Creating a Role* form the template for the three years of this program. In the first year of the program all three subjects—acting, writing, and directing—are studied side by side, all of them studying the actor's craft. While the playwrights and directors are mastering this new theatrical vocabulary, they are also being trained in their own crafts. These first-year directing and playwriting classes enable them to fulfill the demands that will be made on them in the Playwrights and Directors Unit, which begins with the first session of the second year.

In the second year of the program, the year of highly specialized training, all three disciplines move onto parallel tracks. In the third year, the three tracks reconverge in a Repertory Season at the historic Circle in the Square Theatre on Bleeker Street united by a common language and craft they have learned in their three years together.

Some of the unique features of the Actors Studio Drama School include a series of Craft Seminars, fourteen per year, where the Studio's most distinguished members, and their colleagues in all the creative and performing disciplines, come to share their most intimate craft secrets with the students—who become their students as each seminar is followed by an intensive classroom session with the MFA candidates.

In the first four years, these seminars have introduced the students to Al Pacino, Alec Baldwin, Paul Newman, Stephen Sondheim, Sidney Lumet, Shelley Winters, Sally Field, Dennis Hopper, Arthur Penn, Estelle Parsons, Neil Simon, Sydney Pollack, Mary Stuart Masterson, Lee Grant, Faye Dunaway, Glenn Close, Holly Hunter, Ellen Burstyn, Jessica Lange, Carol Burnett, Christopher Walken, Gene Wilder, Gene Hackman, Martin Landau, Mark Rydell, Nathan Lane, Christopher Reeve, Mike Nichols, Julia Roberts, Meg Ryan, Anthony Quinn, Harvey Keitel, Shirley MacLaine, Eli Wallach, Anne Jackson, Lauren Bacall, Anthony Hopkins, Danny Glover, Whoopi Goldberg, Jack Lemon, Kathy Bates, Meryl Streep, Stephen Spielberg, Susan Sarandon, and Robert De Niro among others.

These Craft Seminars have given birth to the award-winning television series *Inside the Actors Studio* with host James Lipton, Dean of the Actors Studio Drama School. This series appears weekly in more than 40 million homes in the United States, in all of Canada and Latin America, and in many European and Asian countries. These vast national and international audiences in the classroom segment of the program see the Studio's MFA students regularly, which have been praised as an exciting and often moving element of the series.

The Friday Workshops are another Actors Studio Drama School feature unique to the program. Many of the Studio's most distinguished artists have committed themselves to teaching these workshops in rotation. Studio President Arthur Penn and Studio members Ellen Burstyn, Estelle Parsons, Lee Grant, Carlin Glynn, Shelley Winters, Anne Jackson, William Greaves, and others, bring their unique interpretation of the Studio's "process" to the MFA candidates in this intensive workshop environment.

The movement training at The Actors Studio Drama School has been placed in the hands of the Alvin Ailey American Dance Center at Lincoln Center. Students train in the modern dance techniques of the Ailey Company three days per week. The mandate of the Ailey teachers is to deliver to the Actors Studio Drama School strong, healthy, supple instruments/bodies that will serve the students all their working lives. The voice program is under the direction of the Center for the Professional Care of the Voice, created by the renowned otolaryngologist Dr. Wilbur James Gould and his associate, Dr. Gwen Korovin, who have been responsible for the care and training of the world's outstanding operatic, popular-music, and acting voices.

MFA students are also granted observer privileges to attend closed-door "sessions" at the Actors Studio. The program contains academic courses, such as a thorough study of theatre history from the plays of ancient Greece to the most advanced contemporary theories and techniques, and intensive training in Shakespeare, the classics, and style.

CHAPTER TWENTY

THE NEIGHBORHOOD PLAYHOUSE

C. C. Courtney

Although Sanford Meisner was associated with it for fifty-five years, the Neighborhood Playhouse was not a Meisner creation. It was founded in 1915 as an off-Broadway theatre and acquired an august reputation as the home of nonrealistic, experimental plays. The theatre ceased production in 1927, becoming the Neighborhood Playhouse School of the Theatre on the same Lower East Side premises in 1928. The more famous graduates, such as Dylan McDermott, Tony Randall, Robert Duvall, Joanne Woodward, Eli Wallach, Diane Keaton, Gregory Peck, Christopher Lloyd, Steve McQueen, David Mamet, Mary Steenburgen, Sydney Pollack, Jeff Goldblum, and others, do not begin to reveal the huge number of Neighborhood Playhouse graduates.

Sanford Meisner joined the faculty of the Playhouse in 1935 and proceeded over the years to develop his technique, which stressed truthful, believable behavior above all. This does not mean, however, the abandonment of nonrealistic theatre. Meisner asserted: "In no sense is the Stanislavsky trained actor limited to naturalism."[1] Meisner spent much of the second year of his two-year course on exercises using scenes from nonrealistic plays and, though not most of the time, he often chose nonrealistic plays for the final productions, stating over and over that one of the actor's greatest challenges is to be believable in unbelievable circumstances.

These practices are still part and parcel of The Neighborhood Playhouse effort to turn out well-rounded actors.

The dominant Meisner exercise is the repetition exercise. The complete repetition exercise cannot be taught in a few classes or even in a semester. At the Neighborhood Playhouse the basic repetition alone is the only exercise in acting class three hours a day, five days a week, for the first several months. It is also deceptively simple. Initially, two actors sit facing each other and comment on what they observe. Whoever feels impelled to do so speaks first; the other must repeat the exact words. The initial dialogue is kept to the minimum. The purpose of the exercise is to learn to read behavior and to respond truthfully. The repetition exercise removes the pressure to be clever, interesting, exciting in what one has to say. The focus isn't on the self but on the partner.

Through the remainder of the first year additional elements are added with scenes dispersed throughout to allow some practice in the application of each element. One of the elements of the repetition exercise deals with emotion. Meisner did not care how the actor achieved the needed emotion: It could be from a memory, a piece of music, or a picture. However, he felt that emotional preparation could best be achieved through the imagination. He did not discount the power of emotional memory; he merely felt that the imagination was more dependable. If you listen to a piece of music repeatedly, it will sooner or later lose its power. It is the same with a memory. No matter how traumatic, a memory will lose its effectiveness after numerous performances. However, if the actor can learn to create with the imagination scenarios that trigger intended emotions, this is a bottomless well.

The full Meisner exercise is rounded out toward the end of the first year with work on relationship. If the playwright fails to supply clear relationships and circumstances, the actor must create them from imagination. Once again Meisner, while demanding truthful, in-the-moment responses to other actors, focused much of his class time on creating with the imagination. In fact, Meisner defined talent as *the ability to create freely what the imagination dictates*. The critical dictum lodged in that effort is to be specific.

In addition to acting classes, first-year students receive voice training everyday in both speech and singing classes. The singing classes under J. Ronald Shetler concentrate on the requirements of the actor, including relaxation, preparation, musical voice production, and introduction to interpretation of songs. The work on the body is centered on both ballet and modern dance classes. Even those students who cannot dance are made stronger and more flexible. It is constantly rewarding to see how many graduates gain work and the opportunity to show what great actors they are because of what they learned in dance class.

At the end of the first year, each section has a day to demonstrate the results of their efforts to the other sections, the second year, and the staff. Then begins the process for admission to the second year at the Neighborhood Playhouse, which is by invitation only and is based on unanimous vote of the faculty. Usually about one-third of the first-year students are asked back. This extreme selectivity is certainly part of why such a high percentage of Playhouse graduates go on to work as actors and are able to support themselves throughout a long and productive life in the field.

The second year is even more crammed than the first. All of the acting classes, with the exception of Acting for the Camera, which is taught by C. C. Courtney, are personally administered by Richard Pinter, Director of the acting program. It is here that character work comes to the fore, with considerable work on impediments and dialects. The scripts turn to more complex texts with deeper emotional problems. Script analysis is intensified and styles are introduced, including work on Shakespeare and other classics.

The second year adds jazz movement to the dance schedule. Alexander technique and fencing round out the training of the body. Performance techniques and advanced speech/voice techniques support these investigations. The Director of the school, Hal Baldridge, works on script and style and teaches classes outside the acting curriculum. These include an investigation of the history of theatre, providing the actor with examples of practical solutions to style and character problems.

The repetition exercise, a more complex, "full exercise," provides the basics of the Meisner technique. Throughout the training, when trouble arises the actor is told to revert to the basic repetition. Even in the second year during the character work, text work, and scene analysis, actors are directed toward a constant return to the basic repetition exercise.

All of the Neighborhood Playhouse acting teachers studied with Meisner when he was at his peak. For example, Richard Pinter and Ron Stetson were in the classroom on the teacher side of the desk with him more than fifteen years each, and I spent the same number of years teaching around the country under his tutelage.

The program at the Playhouse has remained faithful to the Meisner technique. There are additions to the program, such as acting classes focusing on work for the camera and an Alexander class in the dance department. The school now participates in the Federal Aid program, making it possible for students to receive financial aid in the two-year certificate program.

The applications for enrollment at The Neighborhood Playhouse decreased some in the 1980s, when Meisner's retirement approached. However, in the 1990s, the Neighborhood Playhouse remained strongly committed to his technique. The strong staff in acting as well as singing, speech, and dance has helped the enrollment requests climb to new heights.

Besides the two-year certificate program, the Neighborhood Playhouse offers three other sessions. The Professional Actor Training Summer Workshop is six weeks of full-time work, including ninety hours of acting, forty-five hours of voice/speech, and forty-five hours of jazz movement. The Teacher Training Summer Workshop allows teachers to observe the summer sessions and then meet with Mr. Pinter and other faculty to discuss methods and to practice-teach in special training sessions with advanced students. Students in this workshop must have previous practical background in teaching. The British Classic Theatre Workshop is seventy hours over two weeks offering work on acting Shakespeare and the other classic playwrights. The small classes are conducted under the London Theatre Exchange.

In the future, the Neighborhood Playhouse will remain the premier Meisner School. Some changes inevitably will occur in the format of the class structure. When Sanford Meisner began to develop his technique, many of his students had never seen a professional play, some had seen only a few movies, and none had seen television. Most of the work they had experienced was of an old way of acting, stylized and "stagey." Today our students cannot remember when TV was unavailable. They have watched thousands of hours of simple, realistic, believable acting. Of course, they have spent even more hours watching bad acting, which helps them learn to distinguish the good from the bad. As a result, we can now focus on craft quicker. We can institute and foster strong work habits (in those truly dedicated) and arrive at creative freedom sooner than in the past. Doing so enables us at the Neighborhood Playhouse to change our class structure format, but we will not change what we teach—the Meisner Technique. Like learning scales in music, there will always be just a few simple notes.

NOTES

1.   Sanford Meisner, "The Reality of Doing," *TDR* 9.1 (Fall 1964): 155.

CHAPTER TWENTY-ONE

THE STELLA ADLER
CONSERVATORY

Mark Hammer

The tendency among acting teachers is too often toward deification of a particular process as an end in itself, rather than as a means toward an end. Stella Adler was, however, an actress first, a teacher second, and a theorist a far distant third. She was a discipline of Stanislavsky who made little claim of being a master. (Perhaps the same may be said of Lee Strasberg and Sanford Meisner, on whose behalf claims of mastery are often staked by their disciples and adherents.) Stella's approach to curriculum was eclectic, drawing teachers from a range of theoretical backgrounds. Some of her most trusted and influential colleagues were not former students but people who learned much of their craft elsewhere. In the classroom she was apparently not given to looking for only those symptoms that could be treated with predetermined remedies but those that could and would improvise brilliant solutions, addressing whatever problems might arise. If she contradicted herself, it was because she was an actress and therefore "contained multitudes." In fact, most attempts to get a clearly defined picture of either her teaching technique or her ideas of discipline and process are met with a frustrated surrender to the idea that "you really had to be there." This fact doesn't imply that she didn't have definite ideas about process and discipline, but the impression remains that the abundance of such ideas was presented more by example than by precept.

After her death, the Stella Adler Conservatory inevitably inherited a somewhat custodial role. The institution, however, is not merely a monument to Stella but a living continuation of her mission. It is also a living, changing, and progressing continuation of her sense of mission. Protecting the legacy of influential personalities from damage at the hands of their advocates and adherents (often more than of their detractors) has always been a subplot of the history of learning. Stella's legacy is no exception.

Where, then, does an institution that has made a serious commitment to perpetuating the artistic influence of a dominant and charismatic presence go when that presence is absent? The Stella Adler Conservatory has taken two paths: a memorial and a continuation. The physical setting has always had a museum-like atmosphere, decorated with inspiring artifacts of both the Yiddish theatre of Stella's earliest artistic home (founded by her father, Jacob Adler) and the Group Theatre, cofounded by Harold Clurman. Across from the reception desk is a bust of Stanislavsky.

Since 1995, however, when Stella's grandson, Tom Oppenheim, assumed the artistic directorship, the emphasis has shifted in favor of revamping the curriculum and staff. The curriculum at the Adler Conservatory (which is now part of the New York University Bachelor of Fine Arts Program) is a fixed sequence (with evening and summer programs offering an à la carte menu). A course called "Adler Technique" is required in the first year. It consists mostly of exercises that explore importance of the circumstance of being on a stage yet seeming not to be. Oppenheim has enlarged and extended the school's connection with humanistic studies and communal responsibility. These are attributes of art organic to the Adler's heritage in the Yiddish theatre, explicit in Clurman's critical writing, manifest in the work of the Group Theatre, and implicit in Stella's approach to "text analysis." The actor's instrument is the self, but if actors are to avoid shrinking into self-referential, self-enclosed, and isolated people, then the "self" the actor calls upon must be the self that includes the world. As part of what is arguably America's best-integrated program of combined undergraduate liberal arts education and serious actor training, the combined Adler and NYU-Tisch BFA

Program is designed to help the professionally committed young actor to maintain a connection with the idea of drama as a humanistic discipline.

Affiliations have been sought throughout the city of New York that have set up channels for students to do volunteer work in various venues. In addition, the Harold Clurman Lecture Series includes guest speakers from other arts and now include concerts and readings as well. Speakers are chosen for their reputations for engagement with the world outside of theatre and are encouraged to share a sense of their reasons for having pursued a life in art. Classes are focused on not only learning how to act but also on discovering what to act based on why to act. The extracurricular atmosphere is scrupulously devoted to reinforcing the idea that artistic identity emerges through the connection to the social world. Still, any school is primarily defined by what happens in the classroom. Here, beyond taking pains to ensure that her exercises are accurately and effectively taught, the perpetuation of Stella's influence has been largely a matter of seeking ways of applying principles derived from both her thoughts and her feelings about art, drama, acting, and Stanislavsky.

Moreover, if Stella Adler's legacy is to have a shot at perpetual usefulness, it must shake off the stigma of being considered inextricably bound to realism. Adler's teachings were consistently categorized as a product and promoter of the realistic movement. This is understandable in light of the fact that her exercises in the exploration of place, for example, presume the use of realistic sets and props. In addition, her examinations of the circumstances that drive dramatic texts indeed emphasize the impact of the everyday life being lived off- and onstage in the particular society being represented. But to treat such evidence as definitive realism fails to take into account other sources behind her work. She was not inclined to equate truth with mere accuracy. Her father, Jacob Adler, the great actor of the Yiddish stage, was of a tradition that thought of art more as transformation than as duplication. He brought to America a culture built on the idea that liberation of the spirit was often the only available response to bondage of the flesh. His art was influenced as much by artist Marc Chagall's playful surrealism and the fantastic as it was by fellow artist Ben Shahn's social realism. His daughter had high regard for observation as an instrument of creativity, but she also placed great faith in imagination.

Adler's quarrel with her contemporaries' emphasis on emotional recall was more than a claim for shared regard between imagination and memory; she was skeptical of the actor's goal to locate the fullest range of motivating sources merely through experience. For her, doing so implied settling for mundane actuality when richer possibilities beckoned. Her skepticism regarding "emotion memory" was not focused solely on the "memory" part. She objected to the limited scope imposed by too-exclusive reliance on memory as a source of connection between the actor and the role. She felt it devalued the imagination. But she also questioned the "emotion" part, the implication that emotion is the actor's principal connection with the role. Adler appreciated passion and the need for it as a motive force, and she was impatient with tendencies to equate the work with mere intellectualization. Still, she was emphatically convinced that by its nature drama dealt with doing, not feeling, and that feeling was a by-product of doing. This fierce commitment to the importance of action informs her views on all aspects of drama.

During Adler's tenure as head of the school and in the years immediately following, acting Shakespeare was taught as either a discrete performance style or as a character-driven narrative with the similarity of intent with the texts of other plays. It was fundamentally a Stanislavskian approach to Shakespeare. Kristen Linklater and Cicely Barry, both of whom emphasize the humanity of the actor's voice over any preconceived Shakespearean sound, influence voice technique at the school. Diction is evaluated more on the basis of the vividness of a thought or image than on an externally imposed standard of "good speech." Consistent with both Adler's and Stanislavsky's essential beliefs, speech on stage must be treated as an instrument of action, not as a mere medium of information or as a self-contained aesthetic commodity bearing no relation to character or circumstance. The approach to movement is similarly organic and focused on efficiency and economy rather than a standard of grace for its own sake. Alexander, ideokinesis, LeCoq (through use of the neutral mask), and various approaches to character silhouette heavily influence the approach to movement in the present curriculum. While Adler's approach to text is deeply respectful of the playwright, her work aimed at empowering the actor. A text, once its author has surrendered it to the actor, has come to be seen as an object with its own life. "The play is not in the words," Adler was often heard to shout: "It's in you!" Adler honors the playwright by honoring the play in its fullest range of possibilities.

She was also influenced by Paul Sills's work in improvisation. The Sills/Spolin–based improvisation classes have become an important part of the curriculum. Adler's most successful former students have offered varied accounts of her impact on their lives and work, but one common theme appears: Her work ethic, which derived from the spirit of Stanislavsky. "Appreciating the art in yourself, not yourself in your art," was a continual refrain. That and Stanislavsky's stricture against "bringing muddy feet into the theatre" permeate the atmosphere of Adler's school. In the spirit of Stanislavsky, she reserved her truly enthusiastic approval for those who extended their natural gifts with ferocious determination, hard-earned craft, and relentlessly persistent artistic conscience.

Current teacher Jimmy Tripp has been quoted as saying "If one life is enough for you, you have no need to be an actor." As long as life becomes livable for our audiences, one life will never be enough. Thus by daring to contemplate the idea of perpetuity, those currently serving and being served by the Stella Adler Conservatory intend to perpetuate her spirit and her influence.

CONTRIBUTORS

RHONDA BLAIR is Professor in the Division of Theatre, Southern Methodist University. She is an actor, director, and solo performer who has received grants from the National Endowment for the Arts, the National Endowment for the Humanities, and the Massachusetts Council on the Arts and Humanities. Her essays appear in *Upstaging Big Daddy: Directing Theater as if Race and Gender Matter; Tennessee Williams: A Casebook; Women & Performance: A Journal of Feminist Theory; Theatre Topics,* and *Theatre Journal.*

DENNIS C. BECK, Assistant Professor of Theatre at Bradley University, is also an actor, director, and lighting designer. He received a Fulbright Fellowship for research on Czechoslovakian dramaturgy and history of alternative theatres. His work has appeared in *Theatre Journal, TheatreForum, Slavic and East European Performance,* and *Theatre InSight.*

MARLA CARLSON is a Ph.D. candidate in Theatre Studies at the City University of New York Graduate School. She has published articles and reviews in *Theatre Journal, Text and Performance Quarterly, The Early Drama, Art and Music Review,* and *Western European Stages.* In addition to acting and directing, she has produced her own dance/theatre works in San Francisco.

PAMELA D. CHABORA is an Assistant Professor of Theatre at Susquehanna University in Selinsgrove, PA. She has also maintained a parallel career in the professional theatre as an actress and choreographer. She is a founding member of Alba Emoting of North America (AENA) and has served as a chief officer for the Acting Program Focus Group of the Association Theatre in Higher Education (ATHE) and as editor for *THE BEAT.*

C. C. COURTNEY left his native New Orleans to study with Sanford Meisner at The Neighborhood Playhouse. After a successful career as an actor, he pursued a career as a playwright, where his plays were produced on Broadway, Off-Broadway, and in regional theatre. He has earned two MFA degrees and is currently a full-time teacher of acting at The Neighborhood Playhouse.

JEAN DOBIE GIEBEL teaches beginning through advanced acting technique at Hofstra University. Formerly an Associate Director of both the Mint Theater and Riverside Shakespeare Company in New York City, she appeared Off-Broadway with Riverside Shakespeare, as well as in Off-Off Broadway and regional theatre productions. She resides in Long Island with her husband, fight choreographer Tim Giebel, and daughter, Amelia Louise.

MARC GORDON is an Assistant Professor of Drama at Saginaw Valley State University in Michigan. He has worked professionally as an actor, director, and producer in both New York and Los Angeles, and is currently completing his dissertation, *The Impact of Stanislavsky in America*, at Tufts University.

MARK HAMMER spent sixteen seasons as a resident actor at Arena Stage, Washington, D.C., where he played such roles as Sheridan Whiteside, Bottom, Capt. Shotover, and DA Norman in Emily Mann's *Execution of Justice* and was twice nominated for the Helen Hayes Award. His Broadway performances include appearances as Creon opposite Diana Rigg in *Medea* and as Leonato with Sam Waterston in *Much Ado About Nothing*, and films include *Being There*, *Kiss of Death*, and *Year of the Dragon*. He has performed continuing roles on *Law and Order* and *One Life to Live*. He teaches improvisatory acting at the Stella Adler Conservatory and does private coaching.

PAUL S. KASSEL is Assistant Professor of Acting and Directing in the Department of Theatre Arts, SUNY Stony Brook. A professional actor (AEA, SAG), director, and writer, he has worked on, Off, and Off-Off Broadway, in regional theater, and as a guest artist. His scholarly work includes several articles/paper presentations on acting and performance theory, an article in *Theatre Topics*, and book reviews.

DAVID KRASNER is Director of Undergraduate Theatre at Yale University. His book, *Resistance, Parody, and Double Consciousness in African American Theatre, 1895–1910* (St. Martin's Press, 1997), received the 1998 Errol Hill Award from the American Society for Theatre Research. He is coeditor with Harry Elam of *African American Performance and Theater History: A Critical Reader* (New York: Oxford University Press, 2000).

PETER LOBDELL is a Senior Resident Artist and Chair of the Department of Theater and Dance at Amherst College. He directed movement for the Broadway companies of *Equus* and *The Elephant Man* and has created and performed more than fifty works of movement theatre. He has taught at the National Shakespeare Conservatory, the Eugene O'Neill Theater Center's National Theater Institute, the Institute for Professional Puppetry Arts, the Stella Adler Conservatory, and the Michael Howard Studio in New York.

JAMES LUSE is a Master Teacher of Acting and Directing at Yale and Wesleyan universities. He has taught, directed, and acted for the Long Wharf Theatre, the Berkshire Theatre Festival, the Circle Repertory Company, the Virginia Shakespeare Festival, New York University, the College of William and Mary, the American Academy of Dramatic Arts, Hampton University, and Northern Michigan University.

DEB MARGOLIN is a playwright, performance artist, and founding member of the Split Britches Theater Company. *Of All the Nerve* (Cassell/Continuum Press, 1999) is a book of her plays and performance pieces. She is the recipient of the 2000 OBIE Award for Sustained Excellence of Performance and currently teaches Performance and Playwriting at Yale University.

DOUG MOSTON has acted in stage, film, and television for over twenty-five years. He has directed many plays and has taught at The Actors Studio Drama School, NYU Tisch School of the Arts, Yale University, and privately. He is the author of *Coming to Terms with Acting* (Drama Publishers, 1993), and the newest facsimile of Shakespeare's First Folio, *Mr. William Shakespeare's Comedies, Histories, and Tragedies* (Routledge, 1998).

BRANT L. POPE is the Director of the FSU/Asolo Conservatory for Actor Training and Associate Artistic Director of the Asolo Theatre Company, Sarasota, Florida. A member of Actor's Equity and the Society of Stage Directors and Choreographers, his numerous credits include acting and directing in theatre, film, and television. He is the coauthor of the book, *The Theatrical Imagination* (Harcourt Brace, 1997) now in its second edition.

DAVID Z. SALTZ, Ph. D., Stanford University, is Assistant Professor of Performance Theory and Interactive Media at the University of Georgia, Athens. He has published in journals including *Theatre Research International, The Journal of*

Aesthetic and Art Criticism, and *TheatreForum,* and is also an active director and installation artist.

TERRY DONOVAN SMITH is an actor and director. He received his Ph.D. from the University of Washington's School of Drama and is currently Assistant Professor of Dramaturgy and Critical Studies at the University of South Carolina.

LOUISE M. STINESPRING studied acting for two years with Sanford Meisner at The Neighborhood Playhouse School of the Theatre in Manhattan. During her years as a professional actress under the name Louise Turner, she worked in commercials and performed in Equity productions in and outside New York. She is a Visiting Assistant Professor in the Department of Theatre and Dance at Texas Tech University.

ELIZABETH C. STROPPEL is an Assistant Professor of Theatre at William Paterson University in Wayne, New Jersey. Prior to receiving her Ph.D. from the University of Texas at Austin, she taught at the Sonia Moore Studio in New York as well as acted and directed. She is currently researching the contribution of Stanislavsky's sister, Zinaida, to his Moscow Art Studio and acting technique and continues to pursue feminist perspectives in acting.

DAVID WILES is an Associate Professor in the Department of Theatre, Speech, and Dance at the University of South Carolina, where he teaches graduate and undergraduate acting. He has performed with the Yale Repertory Theatre, the Cincinnati Playhouse in the Park, The Aquila Theatre Company, and the Actor's Theatre of South Carolina. He received his MFA from Yale and has trained as an actor and teacher at Shakespeare & Co. in Massachusetts.

INDEX